THE
WOMAN'S
ADVANTAGE
DIET

THE WOMAN'S ADVANTAGE DIET

by
Dr. Henry Mallek

POCKET BOOKS

New York   London   Toronto   Sydney   Tokyo

Another *Original* publication of POCKET BOOKS

POCKET BOOKS, a division of Simon & Schuster Inc.
1230 Avenue of the Americas, New York, NY 10020

ISBN: 0-671-67675-X

First Pocket Books Hardcover printing May 1989

10 9 8 7 6 5 4 3 2 1

CONTENTS

INTRODUCTION

If you're going to follow my advice on how to lose weight and how to keep it off, you're entitled to know something about me. As an undergraduate, I was originally interested in dentistry. While I was pursuing the medical aspects of my degree in that field (I hold two graduate degrees from Tufts University), I became fascinated by questions of nutrition and health. This led to my changing the emphasis of my studies. I earned my doctoral degree in nutritional biochemistry from the Massachusetts Institute of Technology, and I have worked in nutrition ever since.

Currently I'm a professor at Georgetown University Medical Center in Washington, D.C., and I teach nutrition. I've conducted many research studies on eating disorders, some in conjunction with the National Institutes of Health on a grant. I also have a private practice in clinical nutrition in Washington, D.C., and lecture nation-wide to health professionals on diet and nutrition. My new system of weight loss is based both on what I've learned—and what I teach— in university classrooms, and on the practical experience I've gained from working with my patients in a clinical setting.

The majority of my patients come to me because they are overweight. Some want to lose five pounds, others want to lose twenty or thirty pounds, and a few need to shed more than a hundred pounds. But no matter how much weight they want to take off, all of them face the same problem: *Losing weight is very hard to do.* I never tell people who come to see me that they're not trying hard enough or that they lack discipline. Instead, I offer them my support and help in facing this difficult challenge.

The Woman's Advantage Diet was born not long after I opened my clinical practice, when I first noticed that many of my women patients complained that their menstrual cycles sabotaged their weight loss efforts. Whether it was because they retained water, gave in to food cravings, or tried to soothe their PMS (premenstrual syndrome) with food, they found themselves gaining instead of losing in the midst of following even the best diets. The phenomenon suggested an exciting possibility to me: Perhaps a woman's menstrual cycle played such a powerful role in affecting her overall weight that it could be used in conjunction with a special diet to help her *lose* weight.

I began my investigation of this idea five years ago, combining my clinical observations of women's eating patterns with research into the newest studies on the role of nutrition in modulating hormonal activity. I noted precisely when in their menstrual cycles my women patients reported fluctuations in their weight, appetite and food cravings. I soon saw a correlation between those fluctuations and the natural changes in the levels of different hormones in their systems caused by their menstrual cycles.

I also researched the role of progesterone in eating, appetite and weight gain. The level of this hormone increases during the luteal (or premenstrual) phase of a woman's cycle, and it appears to stimulate appetite. Many studies indicated that progesterone selectively metabolizes (or very efficiently burns) the protein that a woman eats.

Next, I needed to find out what effect protein, high fiber carbohydrates and low fiber carbohydrates had on the hormones of the menstrual cycle. Studies show that the dietary ratios of these foods can actually affect the levels and actions of the hormones of the menstrual cycle. At this point in my research, I saw clearly that staying on a high protein diet, or a high fiber diet, *all* of the time was wrong for women. The key to successful dieting for a woman is to time carefully at which point during her cycle she eats protein, high fiber carbohydrates and low fiber carbohydrates. (Those of you who are interested will find the research I used to develop the theoretical basis of the Woman's Advantage Diet in the bibliography).

Over the last two years, I have developed and refined the Woman's Advantage Diet in a clinical setting. Once I had established which foods most effectively contribute to weight loss at particular times of the cycle, I concentrated on designing an eating program that would be nutritionally balanced. And then I watched as my woman patients began to lose weight more safely and easily than they ever had before.

I named this weight loss program the Woman's Advantage Diet because it can be used by (premenopausal) women only. Let me show you some of the specific advantages this diet has to offer:

- You may lose as much as ten to fourteen pounds a month on the Woman's Advantage Diet, and you can continue to lose that much weight each month you stay on the diet.
- The Woman's Advantage Diet is based on the scientific fact that *what* (or how much) you eat is not as important as *when* during your menstrual cycle you eat certain foods. Carefully scheduled foods can interact with your hormones and metabolism in such a way as to make you gain or lose weight.
- No matter how many other diets you may have tried without success, the Woman's Advantage Diet can work for you because it works in conjunction with your body's natural mechanisms. The Woman's Advantage Diet is safe.
- The Woman's Advantage Diet is easy to follow because it emphasizes eating different foods at different times during your monthly cycle; you'll never get bored.
- The Woman's Advantage Diet helps you to lose weight at a steady, continuing rate.
- The Woman's Advantage Diet can rid you of the pains and mental anguish of PMS.
- The Woman's Advantage Diet produces fantastic appetite control.
- The Woman's Advantage Diet will show you how to make any exercise you do much more effective.

These are just some of the advantages my patients have experienced on the Woman's Advantage Diet. I have used the diet with almost 200 women over the last three years, and have had success with every single one of them. Some of you may wish that the diet had been tested by a larger population, but I felt my findings were too exciting to wait the years such clinical research would require. So I offer the diet to you now in this book. Rest assured it is safe, and there is nothing risky or extreme about it. It is a nutritionally balanced eating program that works naturally with your body's hormonal fluctuations to achieve maximum weight loss. Of course, you should use this diet—or any diet—only in consultation with your personal physician, especially if you have special health concerns. But I think you will find, as all my patients have, that the Woman's Advantage Diet is the best diet you've ever tried, and the last one you'll ever need.

1 WHY IT'S CALLED THE WOMAN'S ADVANTAGE DIET

The Woman's Advantage Diet is based on your menstrual cycle. It's a new idea, because until now no one thought to create a diet based on the hormonal changes a woman naturally goes through every month due to her menstrual cycle.

I'm sure that you're aware that on some days of the month you're more energetic than on other days. You may be more alert, ready to go, eager to tackle any project. Other days you may be tired or depressed, unable to face even the smallest jobs. Perhaps some days you're so hungry you can eat anything, while other days nothing seems appealing and all you want to do is pick at food. And then there are those awful times when you crave a succession of chocolate bars or bags of salt-laden potato chips and pretzels.

Why do you feel this way? Your body is simply going through natural hormonal changes that affect how you feel, how much you eat, what you want to eat, and how your body metabolizes the food you take in.

Before the Woman's Advantage Diet, not enough attention was paid to the influence that these hormones have on eating patterns and weight. This diet recognizes important scientific facts: Hormones can make you want to eat certain foods; they can send messages throughout your body urging you to eat more; and what you eat can actually regulate the effect of hormones on you.

1

For Women Only

Only women go through the menstrual cycle, so only women can take advantage of the natural hormonal fluctuations of the cycle to lose weight. That's why I've called this weight loss program the Woman's Advantage Diet. On this diet you can safely and easily lose as much as ten to fourteen pounds a month. Your menstrual cycle is repeated every month, which helps you set realistic goals and reminds you to stay on the diet month after month, until you've reached your ideal, healthy weight.

"What Do I Have to Do?"

This is the question all my new patients ask whenever I get to this point in describing the Woman's Advantage Diet. I tell them what I now tell you: You have to understand your body, and move along in sympathy with what is happening within you. Appreciate the menstrual cycle as a wonderful advantage. Learn to use the Woman's Advantage Diet with the elements of that cycle and you will lose weight.

"But No Diet Has Ever Worked for Me"

When I sit in my office with a new patient, I hear one fear more often than any other: "I've tried a million different diets, but no diet has ever worked for me for long-term weight loss."

When I assure these women that the Woman's Advantage Diet has worked in the long term for my patients, more than one of them look at me skeptically. But after they have tried the diet, they have all come back to tell me that I was right. The Woman's Advantage Diet was the first diet that worked for them. On the average, my patients lose as much as two to four pounds in one week. Some patients who have come to me with severe weight problems—needing to lose more than one hundred pounds—have even achieved as much as eighteen pounds of weight loss in one month. But most of you will realize an average weight loss of ten to fourteen pounds a month. And with the easy-to-follow maintenance plan, you'll keep it off.

Other Advantages of the Woman's Advantage Diet

The first thing that you want from a diet is to lose weight. The Woman's Advantage Diet will do that for you; you can lose up to ten to fourteen pounds every month. In addition:

• *You will lose weight continually, month after month, for as long as you stay on the diet.* You won't suffer the usual up-and-down weight gain and loss associated with your menstrual cycle that you experience with other diets. If water retention, food cravings, mood swings or weight plateaus have sabotaged your best weight loss efforts in the past, the Woman's Advantage Diet will—finally—free you of these handicaps. The graph on page 4 illustrates just how much more weight you can lose—steadily—on the Woman's Advantage Diet than you can on a simple calorie reduced diet.

• *Your appetite will be controlled.* Many women complain that weight loss diets never work for them because they always end up feeling hungry; they're either always feeling deprived and miserable, or they just give in to their hunger and end up breaking the "rules" of their diet. For many women, this is especially a problem during the premenstrual phase of their cycle, when they feel extra hungry. In fact, studies have shown that women *are* hungrier just before their periods than at any other time of the month.[1] One study found women tend to eat about 500 more calories each day during the premenstrual phase of their cycle, after ovulation.[2]

My own clinical studies have shown the Woman's Advantage Diet to be very effective in appetite control throughout the cycle. The graph on page 5 shows you the result of one study I conducted with 22 women over a thirty-one-day period. I asked half these women to follow the Woman's Advantage Diet eating program, and asked the other half to follow a simple, calorie reduced diet. The Woman's Advantage Diet group varied the ratios of high fiber carbohydrates, low fiber carbohydrates, protein, and fat they consumed according to the principles of my program. The other, "control" group did not, and instead ate balanced ratios of these foods each day. The participants in this study were asked to rate their appetites at 10 A.M. and 4 P.M. each day, according to a 1-to-10 scale (10 being "most severe hunger," and 1 being "no appetite"). I then plotted the averaged results of these records on a graph.

This experiment dramatically illustrates how very effective the Woman's Advantage Diet is in controlling your appetite. When you

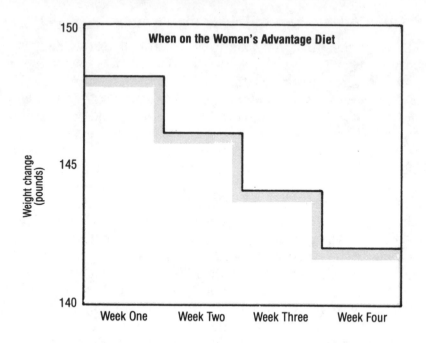

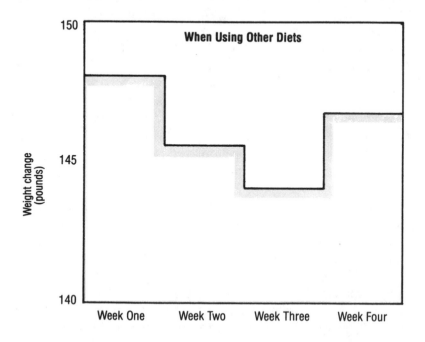

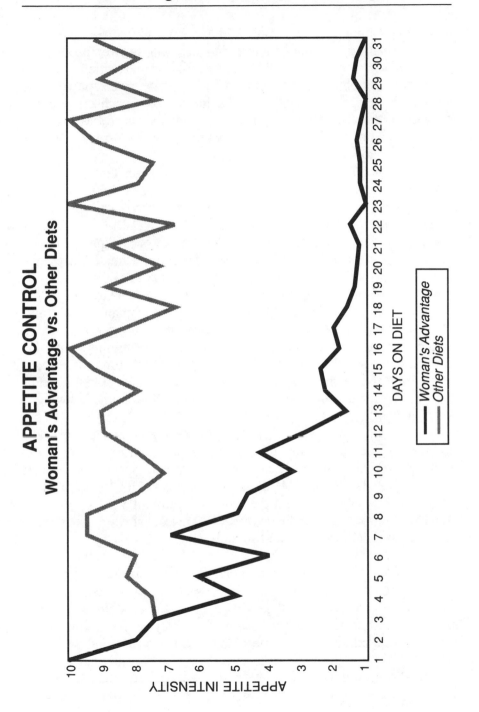

APPETITE CONTROL
Woman's Advantage vs. Other Diets

APPETITE INTENSITY

DAYS ON DIET

Woman's Advantage
Other Diets

follow this eating program, you'll find losing weight is easy, because you won't suffer from the hunger pangs other diets often produce.

• *You will overcome PMS.* The majority of my patients report relief from the physical symptoms of PMS. Some have reported that their PMS related headaches, backaches and stomach cramps are relieved. Others have told me that they no longer have PMS related aches or pains, and that the bloated feeling of PMS related water retention is gone.

• *You will feel better.* Hormones not only affect how much you eat, what you want to eat, and how your body uses the food you've eaten; hormones also affect your moods, your temper, your emotional highs and lows. The Woman's Advantage Diet will lessen anxiety and do away with those sudden bursts of nonspecific anger or depression, just as it will help you overcome other PMS symptoms. Once you've lost the weight, you will feel better about yourself, and that will also give you a great emotional lift.

• *You will free yourself of food cravings.* The Woman's Advantage Diet will help you control those powerful cravings for chocolate, sugar, salt and starchy foods. It does this as part of both its appetite control and its reduction of PMS symptoms. And, for those times when even the Woman's Advantage Diet isn't enough, I've provided a program of substitute foods that my patients have found helps fight even the worst cravings.

• *You can count on steady weight loss each month.* Do you want to lose five pounds? Ten pounds? Thirty pounds? After the very first month of the diet, you will see how much weight you can lose each month. You will then be able to set realistic goals for the amount of weight you want to lose and the amount of time it will take to lose it. The Woman's Advantage Diet will give you the consistent, monthly weight loss you need to reach your goal.

• *You'll never be bored by the same old food or a strict eating regime on the Woman's Advantage Diet.* Because this diet emphasizes not *what* (or how much) you eat, but *when* you eat certain kinds of food, the Woman's Advantage Diet is really four different eating programs in one. During one phase of your cycle you'll emphasize pasta, during another grains, vegetables, fruits or fish and meat. All in all, the program has the variety to make it easy and enjoyable for you to stay on the diet.

"But Is the Woman's Advantage Diet Safe?"

My patients, most of whom have tried many other diets, are often concerned about the health quality of the Woman's Advantage Diet. I am able to assure them, and you, that the Woman's Advantage Diet is a nutritionally balanced eating program that contains all the essential nutrients: vitamins, minerals, fiber, carbohydrates, protein and even some fat. The foods on this diet are varied—an important point in safe and healthy dieting—so that by the end of a given monthly cycle, all major food groups and their nutrients have been included.

"Is the Woman's Advantage Diet Difficult to Follow?"

Because the Woman's Advantage Diet involves a new concept in dieting, you will have to learn to think of yourself and your menstrual cycle in a new way. But once you understand the theory behind the diet, you'll find it the easiest, most pleasant diet you have ever tried. There's no calorie counting, no measuring of foods on diet scales, no requirements involving strangely cooked or difficult to find foods, and no need to cook one meal for yourself and another for family or friends. Those of you who go to restaurants and travel a lot will find the Woman's Advantage Diet easy to follow wherever you may be.

If You're on the Pill

The contraceptive pill works by providing synthetic estrogen and progesterone, which leads to a decrease in the levels of these (and other) hormones that a woman's body naturally produces. As a result, a woman on the pill doesn't ovulate—although her body is "tricked" into believing that she does so that she goes through a complete menstrual cycle.

If you're on the pill, you might be concerned that the Woman's Advantage Diet won't work for you. In my clinical practice, I have not found this to be a problem. My patients who use the pill find the Woman's Advantage Diet just as effective as my other patients do. I believe this is because the synthetic hormones the pill provides do not completely eradicate your natural hormones; residual levels do remain. I think the estrogen and progesterone remaining are enough for the diet to work with, but this explanation is only theoretical and others may be more accurate. In any case, you should be assured that the diet is completely safe for you if you are on the pill and, in my experience, completely effective.

"What If My Menstrual Cycle Is Irregular?"

The Woman's Advantage Diet is for premenopausal women of all ages. I find that many of my women patients assume that their menstrual cycle isn't "normal." They believe their menstrual period is longer or shorter than most women's or they believe the amount of time between periods is longer or shorter than it is for most women. Menstrual periods and menstrual cycles vary so widely that there's simply no such thing as an "average." Consider the following statistics for premenopausal women:[3]

19.1 percent menstruate for 1 to 3 days.
50.4 percent menstruate for 4 to 5 days.
27.2 percent menstruate for 6 to 7 days.
 3.3 percent over 7 days.

 5.3 percent have menstrual cycles that range from 31 to 41 days.
69.4 percent have menstrual cycles that range from 26 to 30 days.
23.0 percent have menstrual cycles that range from 21 to 25 days.
 1.4 percent have menstrual cycles that range from 14 to 20 days.

More than 90 percent of you will find you can use the Woman's Advantage Diet easily, according to the basic instructions in Chapter 2. Even those of you who have irregular cycles—meaning that the lengths of your periods and/or your overall cycles vary monthly— will find you can use the diet. Only those of you who have very special cycles (over 41 days) will find you need special help in order to use the diet. Chapter 2 will explain the details to you.

The Importance of Being You

I recommend to all my patients—and to each of you—that it's best before starting a diet to spend a little time getting in touch with your real motives for wanting to lose weight. I recommend weight goals dictated by health, not by fashion, concerns. And I do suggest that before you start this or any diet you consult with your doctor.

The Woman's Advantage Diet recognizes and appreciates the wonderful, mystical experience of being a woman, and I hope that every woman who follows this diet will recognize it as well. Don't look back at the diets you may have started and abandoned; don't spend time thinking about the months or years you have given to diets that didn't work for you. Instead, examine your own reasons for wanting to lose weight right now. Once you know *why* you want to lose weight, the *how* of losing it is easy. Your self-awareness combined with the Woman's Advantage Diet will result in the weight loss you have always hoped for. Read on, follow the program, and you'll soon see how easy it can be.

---

1. See Bibliography reference 14 (Cohen, Sherwin and Fleming 1987).
2. See Bibliography reference 16 (Dalvit 1981).
3. See Bibliography reference 62 (Wood, Larson and Williams 1979).

2 HOW THE WOMAN'S ADVANTAGE DIET WORKS

The Woman's Advantage Diet is based on the relationship of nutrition to hormones. As I studied this relationship, I began to understand that the hormonal changes that premenopausal women experience every month actually affects what they eat, how much they eat, and how much weight they gain or lose.

I developed a four part diet, each part of which is based on one of the four phases of a woman's menstrual cycle and the special advantage a woman gains from eating certain foods during each phase. The Woman's Advantage Diet is a natural diet. There are no pills, no special diet powders or liquids. There are no foods that you will never be able to eat again, and you won't have to live on any one food from now on. All that is employed here to lose weight is your own natural hormonal fluctuations.

The diet works according to the four phases of your menstrual cycle: menstruation, postmenstruation, ovulation and premenstruation. During ovulation, your body is secreting a large amount of estrogen; during the premenstrual phase, you are secreting progesterone as well as estrogen. The menstrual and postmenstrual phases of your monthly cycle are comparatively quiet times for these hormones.

Phase of cycle	Hormone
Ovulatory	Estrogen (high)
Premenstrual	Progesterone and estrogen (high)
Menstrual	Estrogen and progesterone (low)
Postmenstrual	Estrogen and progesterone (low)

Both estrogen and progesterone play important roles in the reproduction process. But scientists point out that these hormones also have far reaching effects on other body functions. The way hormone levels change during a typical menstrual cycle is illustrated by the following graph.

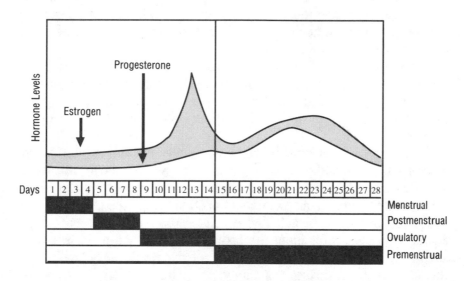

Progesterone and Your Metabolism

Progesterone is a hormone that can act to store body fat and increase appetite.[1] Eating protein during the premenstrual phase, when progesterone levels are high, counteracts this problem.

Let me take a minute to explain why this is true. Progesterone is a hormone that selectively metabolizes protein.[2] In other words, if you were giving a buffet dinner and invited progesterone, it would arrive hungry for chicken salad and cold roast beef. If the level of progesterone were as high at your dinner party as it is in your body in the premenstrual time, you would soon find all the protein gobbled up. As a result of progesterone's metabolic appetite, your body is left with low levels of the amino acids that are the building blocks of protein.[3] You end up feeling hungry, just as the progesterone at your dinner party would complain of being hungry even with plenty of coleslaw and potato salad available. The answer isn't to load up on more of these leftovers. Instead, you should plan your buffet menu with your guests' preferences in mind. Eat plenty of protein in the premenstrual phase and you'll keep blood amino acid levels high in your system and counteract the appetite increasing effects of progesterone.

There's a fringe benefit to satisfying progesterone's craving for protein in this way. Not only does progesterone prefer protein, but it also is very efficient in metabolizing it. In fact, it's so good at it that during your premenstrual phase your body can burn up protein 10 percent more efficiently than it can other foods.[4] It's as if 10 percent of your protein during this phase of your cycle were calorie free! Of course, that doesn't mean you can pig out on hamburgers. But it does mean that, in addition to being more satisfying to your appetite, foods high in protein will be less fattening to you during this phase of your cycle than the equivalent amount of the other nutrients.[5]

Unfortunately, progesterone is also quite efficient at storing fat in your fat cells—and protein, especially the meat and dairy forms of it, often comes with a lot of fat attached. While progesterone reduces the weight gaining effects of protein during the premenstrual phase of your cycle, it actually increases the harm your eating fat can do.[6] So be careful about the protein you eat, and make sure it's as low in fat as possible. By keeping your dietary fat very low during the premenstrual phase, you deny progesterone any fat to work with. Progesterone may be good at taking fat up into your fat cells, but not if you don't give it any to work with! That's why the premenstrual eating plan of the Woman's Advantage Diet emphasizes plenty of protein and low, low fat.

Estrogen and Your Metabolism

Estrogen works in your system in a very different way. First, it tends to help control your appetite.[7] The higher the level of estrogen in your system, the less hungry you feel. Second, estrogen tends to antagonize progesterone.[8] It does this primarily by inhibiting progesterone's effect on appetite. But, better yet, natural estrogen itself helps to increase those enzymes that are responsible for fat breakdown. [9]

The Woman's Advantage Diet is designed to use estrogen's natural benefits to enhance weight loss. The goal is to keep estrogen levels high throughout the ovulatory phase and even into the premenstrual phase of your cycle. [10] This helps control appetite. It even works to increase the body's ability to break down fat. The best way to keep estrogen levels high is to avoid dietary fiber. [11]

Fiber, which is found in carbohydrates (vegetables, fruits and grains), tends to lower estrogen levels. [12] Although scientists are not certain why, most believe fiber lowers estrogen levels as part of its general tendency to enhance the body's eliminatory processes. For this reason, the Woman's Advantage Diet recommends that you avoid high fiber carbohydrates during the ovulatory phase of your cycle. By doing so, you will avoid excreting estrogen and maintain your naturally high levels during this phase. As a result, your appetite will be decreased, and your body's natural ability to break down fat will be maintained. [13]

During the premenstrual phase of your cycle, you should eat only moderate amounts of fiber. That will help you avoid the loss of estrogen and retain that precious hormone's benefits. With that leftover estrogen in your system, you're better armed to counteract the appetite enhancing effects and potentiate the breakdown of fat. Of course, the progesterone in your system will not be completely neutralized. Progesterone will still easily dominate the remaining estrogen in your system. But avoiding high fiber carbohydrates in the ovulatory phase will at least give you some of estrogen's benefit in the premenstrual phase of your cycle.

Food and the Phases of Your Cycle

The Woman's Advantage Diet is a carefully balanced eating program that prescribes specific amounts of protein, high fiber carbohydrates, and low fiber carbohydrates to help regulate your naturally fluctuating hormonal levels for maximum weight loss. Many other diets recommend various combinations of protein, high and low fiber carbohydrates, and fat to achieve weight loss. Many even tell you to stick to only one kind of nutrient, like the well known pure protein or pure carbohydrate diets. Don't confuse these other programs with the Woman's Advantage Diet. Many of the other diets risk nutritional imbalance, and none is designed to take full advantage of your body's naturally changing hormonal levels and their effects on your metabolism. A pure protein diet will work very well during part of your cycle, but not so well during the rest of your cycle—and it won't work half as well as a diet that makes the most out of every phase of your cycle. The Woman's Advantage Diet is the only program that recommends specific combinations of nutrients to regulate the effects of hormones on appetite and metabolism for successful weight loss.

Let's review the roles the major nutrients play in the Woman's Advantage Diet:

Carbohydrates and Fiber. The major food groups that make up the nutrient we call carbohydrates are fruits, vegetables and grains. Fiber is only available in these foods, but not all fruits, vegetables and grains are high in fiber. For that reason, we'll be talking about high fiber carbohydrates and low fiber carbohydrates throughout the rest of the book. If you're uncertain about what I mean by these terms, you may feel more comfortable if you glance at the food group lists on pages 18–25, which specify exactly which foods are high fiber carbohydrates and which foods are low fiber carbohydrates.

The Woman's Advantage Diet recommends you eat a lot of high fiber carbohydrates during the postmenstrual phase of your cycle. This is a relatively neutral time for your estrogen and progesterone hormones, when high fiber carbohydrates can be especially satisfying. Most (although not all) of the fruits and vegetables that are high in fiber are also low in fat and calories. You can usually eat enough to curb your appetite without risking weight gain. The eliminatory efficiency that fiber produces also does not threaten to deplete your estrogen levels, as there is none of the extra amounts of that hormone in your system at the time, as there is in the ovulatory phase.

As we discussed, during the ovulatory phase of your cycle eating low fiber carbohydrates helps keep your estrogen levels high, and makes the most of that hormone's natural appetite suppressing and fat breakdown capabilities.

During premenstruation, the Woman's Advantage Diet asks you to limit both high and low fiber carbohydrates. You'll be keeping yourself busy eating protein in this phase of the menstrual cycle, and you won't have too much room left over to fill up on carbohydrates. For this reason, I recommend that you eat only enough of them to keep your diet nutritionally balanced.

During menstruation itself, you may eat as much of high and low fiber carbohydrates as you like. Since this is a time when your estrogen and progesterone levels are relatively neutral, no special dietary recommendations are made. Indeed, this is the time in your cycle when I think you can focus on eating the foods you most enjoy—but we'll talk more about that later.

Protein. The major food sources of this nutrient are poultry, meats, fish, seafood and dairy products. As we discussed, high amounts of protein are recommended during the premenstrual phase of your cycle to help control your appetite and minimize your body's fat storing tendencies.

During the menstrual and postmenstrual phases of your cycle, protein has a neutral effect on your hormones and metabolism. Accordingly, the Woman's Advantage Diet prescribes enough protein during these phases to keep your diet balanced, but not enough to risk weight gain.

Fat. Fat is the greatest source of calories in the foods we eat. Fat has about twice the number of calories as carbohydrates and protein. Many of the patients have asked me why, then, I include it in the Woman's Advantage Diet at all.

One reason I do this is because a certain amount of fat is essential for a healthy diet. Certain types of fat are not made in the body and are needed for a number of body functions. Fat is also necessary for the absorption of certain essential vitamins.

In 1988, the Surgeon General's *Report on Nutrition and Health* recommended that no more than 30 percent of your calories come from fat.[14] Of this, approximately one-fourth to one-third, or about 8 to 10 percent, of your total calories should come from polyunsaturated (essential) fatty acids. You should avoid saturated fats, especially if you're concerned about your cholesterol level. The lowest level of fat to be recommended is not known with certainty, but each person should have a diet that contains 1 to 2 percent of total calories as linoleic acid. This polyunsaturated fatty acid is found in certain vegetables and their oils that are recommended in the different phases of the Woman's Advantage Diet.

For you to lose weight, the amount of fat in your diet should be reduced to well below 30 percent of your daily calorie intake. If you've ever tried to diet before, you know there's plenty of fat in untrimmed meat, desserts, dairy products and most baked goods. But too few of us are aware of the fat that lurks in packaged foods. Also, fat sneaks into your diet in huge quantities when you cook. Here's an idea of how much fat can end up in food when you prepare it: [15]

Sautéed meat	½ teaspoon fat per ounce of meat
Breaded and sautéed meat	1 teaspoon fat per ounce of meat
Vegetables seasoned with fat	½ teaspoon fat per ½ cup vegetables
Breaded and fried vegetables	1 teaspoon fat per ½ cup vegetables
Stir fried vegetables	½ teaspoon fat per ½ cup vegetables
Fried eggs	1 teaspoon fat per egg
Potato salad	1 teaspoon fat per ½ cup salad
Gravy and sauce	1 teaspoon fat per 2 tablespoons gravy or sauce

The trick is to be sure of exactly where you're getting fat in your diet, so that you can choose not to get too much of it. Then, in conjunction with the Woman's Advantage Diet, you can be sure that the fat you eat does you the greatest good and the least harm.

For instance, I strongly advise avoiding fats during your premenstrual phase. As we discussed, that's when your progesterone is high, and it's natural efficiency in storing fat in your fat cells will lead to extra pounds for you.

During your postmenstrual, menstrual and ovulatory phases, your progesterone levels are relatively neutral, so you can be a little less stringent in your avoidance of fats than you are in the premenstrual phase.

The menstrual phase is a different story. I don't believe any diet can work if it's too strict. You just can't stay on a diet for the amount of time needed to achieve real weight loss if it is so rigid that it never allows a taste of chocolate cake or potato chips. I believe the menstrual phase of your cycle is the time for a little indulgence, a little reward for the successful dieting you've done in the preceding weeks. But, keep in mind, I said a *little* indulgence. This means either chocolate cake or potato chips, not both. And it means a small slice of cake (not the whole thing) or a few chips (not the whole bag). This is a time to celebrate your diet, not destroy it. But if you follow the guidelines of the Woman's Advantage Diet as they're explained later in the book, you can reward yourself during the menstrual phase of your cycle without risking weight gain.

The Advantage Food Groups

Now that you have an idea about how the various phases of the menstrual cycle are characterized by highs and lows in progesterone and estrogen, and the ways in which these hormones interact with important nutrients, let's examine in more detail how the foods you eat influence this interaction. Armed with an understanding of how certain foods work with your hormones at the different phases of the cycle, you will be able to maximize weight loss simply and effectively. Let me begin by further defining the nutrients the Woman's Advantage Diet concentrates on.

Years ago nutritionists grouped food into four basic categories:

Meats, fish, poultry, eggs and nuts
Milk and milk products
Fruits and vegetables
Breads and cereals

Today, while those basic food groups still exist, nutritionists have recognized that other groupings also have validity.

There are four special food groups that are used in the Woman's Advantage Diet. These four groups are directly related to your menstrual cycle and are used in varying combinations in the four parts of the Woman's Advantage Diet. They are:

High Fiber Carbohydrates
Low Fiber Carbohydrates
Proteins
Fats

I know that many of you may not be sure what foods are carbohydrates or proteins or fats. Even more of you may be confused about which carbohydrates are low in fiber and which are high in fiber. (Indeed, to a large extent a given food is "low" or "high" in fiber depending on how much of it you eat. In other words, even a food low in fiber will bring a lot of fiber into your system if you eat a large quantity of it.)

To help with these complicated issues, I've provided the following food lists. They are meant to define exactly what high fiber carbohydrates, low fiber carbohydrates, proteins, and fats are. At the very least, I hope they give you a general understanding of the food categories the Woman's Advantage Diet is based on. But, keep in mind that these lists do not include every food under the sun, and they are not necessarily made up of foods I recommend that you eat on the diet; for that information, see the later food plan lists. (Also, I am defining "low" and "high" fiber in these lists according to the portion size guidelines given in Chapter 3).

Take a look at the following Advantage Food Group lists, and I think you'll get a good understanding of the food categories that are important to the Woman's Advantage Diet.

HIGH FIBER CARBOHYDRATES

FRUITS

apple (any kind)	cherimoya	kumquat
apricot (any kind)	citron	lemon
avocado (any kind)	coconut	loquat
berry	dried fruit	mango
blackberry	apple	medlar
blueberry	apricot	nectarine
boysenberry	banana	orange (any kind)
cranberry	date	passion fruit
dewberry	orange	pear (any kind)
elderberry	pineapple	plantain
huckleberry	prune	pomegranate
ligonberry	raisins	prickly pear
mulberry	feijoa	quince
raspberry	figs	sapodilla
strawberry	guava	tamarind
carambola	kiwis	

VEGETABLES

alfalfa sprouts	bean sprouts	Brussels sprout
artichoke	beets	cabbage
bamboo shoots	broccoli	Chinese

green
red
cardoon
carrot
cassava
collard
eggplant*
green peas
heart of palm
jicama
kohlrabi
legume
  adzuki bean
  black or turtle bean
  black-eyed pea
  carob
  chickpea
  cranberry bean
  fava bean
  garbanzo bean

great northern bean
green bean
kidney bean
lentil
lima bean
marrow bean
mung bean
navy bean
pea bean
pink bean
pinto bean
red bean
split pea
tofu (soybean)
okra
parsnips
potatoes (any kind)
rhubarb
rutabaga
salsify

sea vegetable
  arami
  dulse
  hijiki
  nori
  wakame
snow pea
spinach
squash
  acorn
  butternut
  hubbard
  long cocozelle
  pumpkin
  yellow crookneck
  yellow straightneck
  zucchini
sweet potato
turnip
yam

GRAIN AND GRAIN PRODUCTS

barley
buckwheat (not a true
    grain)
cereal
  All-Bran, original
  All-Bran, with extra
    fiber
  barley
  Bran Buds
  Bran Chex
  bran flakes
  Fiber One
  Fruit & Fibre
  Müeslix Bran

Nutri-Grain, biscuits
Nutri-Grain, corn
Nutri-Grain,
  nuggets
Nutri-Grain, wheat
oat bran
100% Bran
Quaker Oats
  Squares
raisin bran
shredded wheat
Shredded Wheat 'n
  Bran
Toasted Wheat Bran

Weetabix
corn
corn starch
millet
oat
quinoa
rye
sorghum
triticale
wheat
  berry
  bulgur
  cracked

*Eggplant is listed under "vegetables," although technically it is a fruit. This is also the case for cucumbers, peppers, squashes and tomatoes.

BREADS AND BREAD PRODUCTS

bagel
  nut
  poppy seed
  pumpernickel
  raisin
  rye
  whole wheat
bread
  black
  bran
  cracked wheat
  oatmeal
  rye
  whole wheat

cracker
  bran
  rye
  whole wheat
muffin
  bran
  corn
  granola
  nut
  raisin
  whole wheat

pancake and waffle
  cornmeal
  fruit
  oatmeal
  whole wheat
pastries
  berry pie
  berry tart
  whole wheat cookie
roll and bun
  cracked wheat
  whole wheat

LOW FIBER CARBOHYDRATES

FRUITS

acerola
cherry (any kind)
genipap
grape (any kind)
lime
lychee
mangosteen

melon
  cantaloupe
  casaba
  Crenshaw
  honeydew
  Persian
  watermelon
papaya

pawpaw
peach (any kind)
persimmon
pineapple
plum (any kind)
tangelo (any kind)
tangerine (any kind)
ugli fruit

VEGETABLES

anise
arugula
asparagus
basil
cauliflower
celeriac
celery
cilantro
cucumber
dandelion
dill
endive

escarole
fiddlehead
garlic
hot pepper (any kind)
kale
leek
lettuce (any kind)
lotus
mushroom
mustard green
onion (any kind)
parsley

radish
scallion
sorrel
sweet pepper
  green
  red
  yellow
Swiss chard
tomato
truffle
watercress

GRAINS AND GRAIN PRODUCTS

cereal
  Corn Chex
  corn flakes
  Cream of Rice
  Cream of Wheat
  Crispix
  Crispy Wheats 'n
    Raisins
  Double Chex
  grits
  Just Right
  Life
  oatmeal
  Product 19
  puffed rice
  puffed wheat
  Rice Krispies
  Special K
  Team
  Total
  Wheat Chex
  wheat germ
  Wheatena
  Wheaties
pasta (refined flour
    varieties)
  capellini
  cellophane noodle
  couscous
  egg noodle
  elbow
  farfalle
  fedelini
  fettucine
  fusilla
  gnocchi
  lasagna
  linguine
  lo mein noodle
  macaroni bow
  manicotti
  orzo
  ravioli
  rotini
  shell
  spaghetti
  spaghettini
  tortellini
  vermicelli
  ziti
popcorn
rice
  brown
  cake
  long grain
  white
  wild
rye flour
wheat flour

BREADS AND BREAD PRODUCTS

bagel
  egg
  plain
bread
  French
  Italian
  pita
  white enriched
  cracker (except
    bran, rye or
    whole wheat)
muffin
  English
  plain
pancake and waffle
  buttermilk
  plain
pastry
  brownie
  cake
  cookie
  croissant
  cupcake
  doughnut
  flaky pastry
  pie, nonberry
  tart, nonberry
  torte
rolls
  plain

CANDY

chocolate
hard
soft

CONDIMENTS

chocolate extract
chutney
cranberry sauce
Cumberland sauce
honey
hot pepper sauce
   chili
   harissa
   horseradish
   Indian

Mexican salsa
nam prik
sambal
Tabasco
wasabi
jelly
ketchup
maple syrup
mayonnaise
miso

mustard
relish
soy sauce
steak sauce
tamari sauce
teriyaki sauce
vanilla extract
vinegar
Worcestershire sauce

SPICES AND HERBS

allspice
almond
angelica
anise
arrowroot
basil
bay leaf
bergamot
black pepper
caper
caraway
cardamon
cayenne pepper
chervil
chive
cinnamon
clove
coriander
cream of tartar
cumin
curry

dill
fennel
fenugreek
garlic
ginger
hyssop
licorice
mace
marjoram
melilot
mint
mugwort
mustard
nasturtium
nutmeg
oregano
paprika
parsley
peppermint
purslane
rocambole

rocket
rosemary
rue
saffron
sage
salad burnet
savory
scurvy grass
sesame
sorrel
star anise
stonecrop
sweet cicely
tamarind
tansy
tarragon
thyme
turmeric
vanilla
violet

PROTEIN FOODS

MEATS

beef
goat
lamb

pork
rabbit
turtle

veal
wild game

ORGAN MEATS

heart	liver	tongue
kidney	sweetbreads	tripe

POULTRY

chicken	goose	pheasant
Cornish hen	grouse	quail
duck	partridge	turkey

GELATIN (animal protein based)

EGGS

chicken	quail
goose	substitutes

FISH

amberjack	grouper	rockfish
anchovy	haddock	roe
arctic char	hake	sablefish
Atlantic cod	halibut	salmon
barracuda	herring	sardine
black sea bass	inconnu	sauger
bluefish	lake trout	sea trout
bonito	lingcod	shad
brook trout	mackerel	shark
buffalo fish or sucker	mahimahi	smelt
butterfish	monkfish	sole
carp	mullet	spot
cisco	ocean catfish	striped bass
cod	orange roughy	sturgeon
crevalle jack	perch	swordfish
croaker	pike	tilefish
cusk	pilchard	tuna
drum	pollock	turbot
eel	pompano	whitefish
flounder	porgy	white sucker
freshwater catfish	rainbow trout	whiting
frog's leg	red snapper	yellowtail snapper

SEAFOOD

abalone	lobster	periwinkle
clam	mollusk	scallop
crab	mussel	shrimp
crayfish	octopus	snail
langostino	oyster	squid

DAIRY PRODUCTS

cheese	Gouda	Swiss
American	Gruyère	Tilsit
blue	Liederkranz	milk
brick	Limburger	buttermilk
Brie	Monterey Jack	1% fat
Camembert	mozzarella	2% fat
caraway	Muenster	nonfat dry milk
Cheddar	Neufchâtel	skim milk
Cheshire	Parmesan	whole milk 3.3% fat
Colby	Port du Salut	whole milk 3.7% fat
Edam	provolone	yogurt
feta	ricotta	low fat
fontina	Romano	non fat
gjetost	Roquefort	whole milk

NUTS AND SEEDS

alfalfa seeds	cumin seed	pecan
almonds	dill seed	pignoli
anise seed	fennel seed	pistachio
Brazil nut	filbert	poppy seed
butternut	flaxseed	pumpkin seed
caraway seed	hickory nut	sesame seed
cardamon seed	Indian nut	star anise
cashew	macadamia nut	sunflower seed
chestnut	mustard seed	walnut
coriander seed	peanut	

FAT FOODS

ANIMAL FAT
chicken
lard

DAIRY
butter

OILS

almond	flaxseed	safflower*
coconut	hazelnut	sesame
corn*	olive	sunflower*
cottonseed*	peanut	walnut
fish oils	rapeseed	

VEGETABLE FAT
margarine

Foods High in Fat

You may find it useful to take a glance at the high fiber carbohydrate, low fiber carbohydrate, and protein foods that are also high in fats.

CANDY
chocolate bar
other chocolate candy

*These oils contain high amounts of polyunsaturated fats and are considered to be better for you than oils with saturated fats.

DAIRY PRODUCTS

cheese
  blue
  brick
  Brie
  Camembert
  caraway
  Cheddar
  Cheshire
  Colby
  cream
  Edam

  fontina
  gjetost
  Gouda
  Gruyère
  Monterey Jack
  Muenster
  Port du Salut
  processed
  provolone
  ricotta
  Roquefort

  Swiss
  Tilsit
butter
cream
  half-and-half
ice cream
sour cream
whipped topping
whole milk yogurt

FISH

amberjack
arctic char
butterfish
carp
chinook salmon
eel
herring

inconnu
lake sturgeon
lake trout
mackerel
pilchard
pompano (Atlantic
    only)

sablefish
sardine
shad (spiny dogfish)
turbot
whitefish

MEATS

bacon
barbecue loaf
blood sausage
bologna
braunschweiger
brisket of beef
chicken spread
corned beef
ham-and-cheese loaf

hard salami
headcheese
honey loaf
knockwurst (pork)
liver pâté
liverwurst
mortadella
old-fashioned loaf
olive loaf

pastrami
phrasky
pickle and pimento loaf
potted meat
salami
Spam
summer sausage

PASTRIES

brownie
cake
cheesecake
cookie

croissant
custard cream
doughnut
flaky pastry

pie
tart
torte

The Variety of the Woman's Advantage Diet

Sometimes when I start talking about the Advantage Food Groups to a new patient, I see a look of panic, and I'm asked: "Does that mean I can only eat one type of food during each phase of my cycle?"

I'm always quick to tell my patients that while each phase of the diet emphasizes a different Advantage Food Group, no one phase is absolutely limited to one type of food. The Woman's Advantage Diet is well balanced, and each phase contains nutrients from the other Advantage Food Groups as well. The following table is a broad explanation of what you may eat during each phase of the diet:

When and How to Use the Advantage Food Groups

MENSTRUATION	FORBIDDEN FOODS	LOTS OF CARBOHYDRATES AND PROTEIN and some fat
POSTMENSTRUATION	FABULOUS FRUITS AND VEGETABLES	LOTS OF HIGH FIBER CARBOHYDRATES with some protein (and low fat)
OVULATION	PASTA PLUS	LOTS OF LOW FIBER CARBOHYDRATES with protein (and low fat)
PREMENSTRUATION	PROTEIN POWER	LOTS OF PROTEIN with some carbohydrates (and very little fat)

Let's take a minute and review why each of the four eating plans is designed the way it is.

FORBIDDEN FOODS (during menstruation) recommends a lot of protein and carbohydrates (both with and without a lot of fiber) and even some fat, because this is the time to reward yourself for your successful dieting by indulging a little in your favorite foods. As long as you follow the diet guidelines, you don't run as much of a risk of gaining weight in this phase of your cycle as you do at other times.

FABULOUS FRUITS AND VEGETABLES (during postmenstruation) recommends a lot of high fiber carbohydrates because during this phase estrogen levels are low, so there's no risk of eliminating this important hormone. Most of these foods are low in calories, so you can eat enough to satisfy your appetite, which will help you avoid fats and the proteins that are high in calories.

PASTA PLUS (during ovulation) recommends a lot of low fiber carbohydrates to help you hold on to this phase's naturally high levels of estrogen. You should concentrate on these low fiber carbohydrates and protein and eat only enough fat to keep your menu nutritionally balanced. [16]

PROTEIN POWER (during premenstruation) recommends a lot of protein because this is the time progesterone levels are high, and protein is metabolized with extra efficiency. A lot of protein will also produce appetite control. [17] And if you take extra care to stay away from fat, you won't risk progesterone efficiently storing it in your fat cells. Deemphasize carbohydrates (both low and high fiber) in this phase of your cycle, as they don't contribute to the natural benefits you can get from your hormonal balance at this time.

Now that you have a good idea of how your menstrual cycle, your naturally fluctuating hormones, and the foods you eat all interact, it's time to concentrate on learning the mechanisms of the program so you can make it a part of your everyday life.

Let's begin by learning a little bit more about your individual menstrual cycle.

Figuring Out the Phases of Your Cycle

To use the Woman's Advantage Diet, you have to figure out when you personally experience each of the four phases of your menstrual cycle, so that you can match each of those phases to one of the four eating programs that I will tell you about in detail later.

Sometimes when I reach this point in describing the Woman's Advantage Diet to a new patient, she says, "That will never work for me. I don't have a regular twenty-eight-day cycle. I'll never be able to figure out the different phases of my cycle. It's too complicated."

Let me assure you, as I have assured my patients, you don't have to have a regular twenty-eight-day cycle for the Woman's Advantage Diet to work for you. And figuring out the different phases of your cycle is easy.

The Four Phases

The four phases of your menstrual cycle are:

1. The menstrual phase
2. The postmenstrual phase
3. The ovulatory phase
4. The premenstrual phase

There's no need to be medically precise about the lengths of the different phases of your cycle. You don't need to average out weeks of careful observation or take thermometer readings. If you're off by a day or two in your calculations, the diet will still work for you. That's why, if your cycle is somewhat irregular from month to month, the diet will still be effective.

In fact, for the purposes of the Woman's Advantage Diet, all women calculate their ovulatory and premenstrual phases the same way.

1) The first step in figuring out the phases of your menstrual cycle is to assume:

Your ovulatory phase is set at 6 days.
Your premenstrual phase is set at 14 days.

2) The next step is to figure out your menstrual phase. Most of you know how many days you actually menstruate each month. If the length of your menstruation tends to fluctuate, just pick the average number of days. For instance, if you menstruate for three days one month, but five days the next, you can say the length of your menstruation is four days. Now, fill in the blank below.

My menstrual phase is _____ days.

3) In order to figure out the length of your postmenstrual phase, you must first determine the overall length of your cycle. Most of you know this. How many days pass between the first day of your menstruation and the last day before your next menstruation begins? In other words, when did your last period begin? And when did the period before that begin? How many days passed between the two dates?

Again, if the length of your cycle changes each month, don't worry. Just pick the average number of days. If your cycle was 32 days last month, but 28 days the month before, and you feel that the length of your cycle fluctuates around that level all the time, for the purposes of the Woman's Advantage Diet you can say your cycle is 30 days long.

Also, don't worry if you can't remember exactly what day your last period began, much less the period before that. You won't need a medically precise measurement for the diet to work. If you're especially worried that your calculations are wrong, I recommend that you use your estimation to start the diet now anyway. Even if you're off in your calculations, you'll still be right about most of the days in your cycle, so you'll get the benefits of the diet. Write down the first and last days you project for your next period. Next month, you can reevaluate the phases of your cycle to begin the program anew, and get the full benefit of the Woman's Advantage Diet. In fact, for those of you who are especially irregular, I recommend you double-check your cycle calculations every month just to make sure you stay on track.

Once you've determined the overall length of your cycle, fill in the blank below:

My overall cycle is _____ days.

Now that you know the overall length of your cycle and the length of your menstrual phase, you can use the following chart to easily determine the length of your postmenstrual phase.

Locate the number in the left-hand column that represents the number of days of your overall cycle (the total length of all four phases of your cycle). Then find the number that represents the number of days you actually menstruate in the row at the top. Draw a straight line from each number to see where they meet. The number you zero in on is the length of your postmenstrual phase.

For example, if you have a 28-day cycle, and your menstruation lasts 3 days, your postmenstrual phase is 5 days. Or, if you have a 25-day cycle, and you menstruate for 4 days, your postmenstrual phase is 1 day. If you have a 38-day cycle and you menstruate for 4 days, your postmenstrual phase is 14 days.

Notice that if your overall cycle is between 22 and 28 days and your menstrual phase is between 2 and 8 days, you might end up zeroing in on a "0" for the length of your postmenstrual phase. You

| | Length of menstrual phase in days | | | | | | | |
	1	**2**	**3**	**4**	**5**	**6**	**7**	**8**
22	1	0	0	0	0	0	0	0
23	2	1	0	0	0	0	0	0
24	3	2	1	0	0	0	0	0
25	4	3	2	1	0	0	0	0
26	5	4	3	2	1	0	0	0
27	6	5	4	3	2	1	0	0
28	7	6	5	4	3	2	1	0
29	8	7	6	5	4	3	2	1
30	9	8	7	6	5	4	3	2
31	10	9	8	7	6	5	4	3
32	11	10	9	8	7	6	5	4
33	12	11	10	9	8	7	6	5
34	13	12	11	10	9	8	7	6
35	14	13	12	11	10	9	8	7
36	15	14	13	12	11	10	9	8
37	16	15	14	13	12	11	10	9
38	17	16	15	14	13	12	11	10
39	18	17	16	15	14	13	12	11
40	19	18	17	16	15	14	13	12
41	20	19	18	17	16	15	14	13

Length of overall cycle in days

will also find you don't have a postmenstrual phase if your cycle is less than 22 days. While this isn't common, I have found it to be the case with a couple of my patients. This is what I tell my patients who skip the postmenstrual phase: Always be sure you follow the premenstrual Protein Power eating plan for the full 14 days. Follow the ovulatory Pasta Plus eating plan for the remaining days between the end of one period and the beginning of the next. In other words, just skip the eating plan called Fabulous Fruits and Vegetables that's recommended for the postmenstrual phase.

If you have an unusually long cycle—that is, one in excess of 41 days—I recommend that you consult your doctor to help you determine the phases of your cycle.

Now that you know the length of your postmenstrual cycle, fill in the blank below.

My postmenstrual cycle is _____ days.

Your Scoreboard

Once you have determined the length of the different phases of your cycle, you may find it useful to summarize the information below, for easy reference:

> My menstruation lasts _____ days.
> My postmenstrual phase lasts _____ days.
> My ovulatory phase lasts ____6____ days.
> My premenstrual phase lasts ____14____ days.

When Can I Start the Diet?

Once you know the length of the different phases of your cycle, you can determine what phase you are currently in by using the Woman's Advantage Diet Calendar. Once you know that, you can start the Woman's Advantage Diet immediately.

To determine the current phase of your cycle, here's what to do:

(1) Turn to the Woman's Advantage Diet Calendar on page 33. (You'll find extra copies of the calendar at the back of the book.)

(2) Go to the "Day of Cycle" and "Cycle Phase" columns. Count off the numbers of days that you menstruate. (See your "score-card"). If it is less than eight, cross off the extra numbers in the "Menstrual" part of "Day of Cycle" column on the calendar. (For instance, if you menstruate for four days, you cross off numbers 5, 6, 7 and 8, as in the sample calendar on page 34.)

(3) Similarly, proceed down to the second group of numbers in the "Day of Cycle" column and count off the number of days in your postmenstrual phase. If there are fewer than 20 days in this phase of your cycle, cross off the extra numbers in that part of the column. (For instance, if there are four days in your post-menstrual cycle, cross off numbers 5, 6, 7, 8, 9, 10, 11, 12, 13, 14, 15, 16, 17, 18, 19 and 20, as in the sample calendar on page 34.)

(4) Since, for the purposes of the Woman's Advantage Diet, the ovulatory phase is always 6 days and the premenstrual phase is always 14 days, there is no need to adjust those sections.

(5) Now, go to the column marked "Day of the Month." In the first slot, write the actual date that your last period began (or as close to it as you can remember). (For instance, if your last period began on April 28, you write that date in the uppermost

Day of the Month	Day of Cycle	Cycle Phase	Food Group	Weight
	1	Menstrual	FORBIDDEN FOODS	
	2			
	3			
	4			
	5			
	6			
	7			
	8			
	1	Postmenstrual	FABULOUS FRUITS AND VEGETABLES	
	2			
	3			
	4			
	5			
	6			
	7			
	8			
	9			
	10			
	11			
	12			
	13			
	14			
	15			
	16			
	17			
	18			
	19			
	20			
	1	Ovulatory	PASTA PLUS	
	2			
	3			
	4			
	5			
	6			
	1	Premenstrual	PROTEIN POWER	
	2			
	3			
	4			
	5			
	6			
	7			
	8			
	9			
	10			
	11			
	12			
	13			
	14			

Day of the Month	Day of Cycle	Cycle Phase	Food Group	Weight
April 28	1	Menstrual	FORBIDDEN FOODS	
29	2			
30	3			
May 1	4			
	X			
	X			
	X			
	X			
May 2	1	Postmenstrual	FABULOUS FRUITS AND VEGETABLES	
3	2			
4	3			
5	4			
	X			
	X			
	X			
	X			
	X			
	X			
	X			
	X			
	X			
	X			
	X			
	X			
	X			
	X			
	X			
	X			
May 6	1	Ovulatory	PASTA PLUS	
7	2			
8	3			
9	4			
10	5			
11	6			
May 12	1	Premenstrual	PROTEIN POWER	
13	2			
14	3			
15	4			
16	5			
17	6			
18	7			
19	8			
20	9			
21	10			
22	11			
23	12			
24	13			
25	14			

left-hand corner slot of the calendar chart, as illustrated in the
sample on page 34.)

(6) Proceed down in the "Day of the Month" column, filling in all the
appropriate dates in the column's blank spaces. Be sure to skip
those spaces that correspond to the numbers you crossed off.
(For example, on our sample calendar chart, you fill in April 28
for day 1, April 29 for day 2, April 30 for day 3, May 1 for day 4,
and then skip down to the ninth blank slot to fill in May 2 for the
postmenstrual day 1).

You're Ready to Begin

You're now ready to start the Woman's Advantage Diet. For
instance, if you're in the third day of your postmenstrual phase (on
our sample calendar it's May 4) you should start with Fabulous Fruits
and Vegetables. If you're in the fourth day of your ovulatory phase
(it's May 9 on our calendar chart), it's time for Pasta Plus. And if
you're in the tenth day of your premenstrual phase (it's May 21 on
our sample calendar), use the Protein Power eating plan.

If you're currently menstruating and you want to start the diet,
you have two choices. You can wait until your menstrual phase has
ended, and go right into the postmenstrual program of the Woman's
Advantage Diet. Or, if you want to start the diet right away, you can
use the premenstrual diet program, Protein Power, for as long as
you're menstruating. Then proceed directly to the postmenstrual
Fabulous Fruits and Vegetables plan. Next month, you can go back
to the regular diet and enjoy Forbidden Foods while you're menstruating.

You'll notice that there is also a column on the Woman's Advantage Diet Calendar for you to record your weight. You'll find this
useful in keeping track of the progress you make on the diet.
Keeping this record will help you set realistic goals, and remind you
to get back on track if you're not following the diet carefully enough.
Don't get fanatical about weighing yourself. Many dieters have made
themselves miserable stepping on the scale two, three or even four
times a day. Such behavior doesn't give you any useful information.
Indeed, it's not necessary to weigh yourself more than once a week
to monitor the success of the Woman's Advantage Diet. In general,
my patients find it most useful to weigh themselves no more than
once a day and no less than on the first and last day of each phase of
their cycles. Be sure to weigh yourself on a dependable scale and to
do so at the same time of day each time (for instance, before

breakfast). Also, be sure you're wearing about the same amount of clothing each time. Wearing hiking boots one day and only underwear the next won't tell you how much weight you've lost—it will just tell you how much your boots weigh. Consistent weight measurements at reasonable intervals will help you stay on track with the diet and show you just how effective it is.

1. See Bibliography reference 54 (Steingrimsdottir, L., Brasel, J. and Greenwood, M.R.C. 1980).
2. See Bibliography reference 38 (Landau et al. 1955).
3. See Bibliography reference 37 (Landau et al. 1957).
4. Energy expenditure increases between 8 and 16 percent during the fourteen-day luteal phase of the menstrual cycle. Natural progesterone, secreted during the postovulatory time, is regarded as stimulating metabolism and resulting in the catabolism of amino acids in the liver. See Bibliography reference 59 (Webb 1986).
5. Eating protein adds amino acids to the body's metabolic amino acid pool. The body draws on these amino acids for building proteins or to use as an energy substrate. When this pool is enlarged through increased intake of dietary protein, progesterone catabolizes these amino acids to a greater extent. See Bibliography reference 41 (Landau and Lugibih 1961).
6. See Bibliography reference 28 (Hervey and Hervey 1967) and 54 (Steingrimsdottir et al. 1980).
7. Catechol estrogens increase epinephrine-induced lipolysis significantly more than other estrogen metabolites. See Bibliography reference 1 (Ackerman et al. 1981).
8. One of the reasons many women eat more during the premenstrual time is because of the high levels of progesterone during this phase of their cycles. Animal studies have shown that estrogen blocks this effect of progesterone on eating and appetite. A similar situation occurs during pregnancy when progesterone secretion is highest. During the late stages, estrogen secretion increases, causing eating to decrease and weight to stabilize. See Bibliography reference 30 (Hytten and Leitch 1971).
9. See Bibliography reference 57 (Wade et al. 1985).
10. The Woman's Advantage Diet achieves a change in the ratio of two estrogen metabolites: 2 OH estrogen (or catechol estrogen) and 16 alpha hydroxylated estrogen. What occurs is an increase in the ratio of the catechol estrogen to 16 alpha hydroxylated types. This effect comes about through changes in the metabolism of estrogen in the liver. The changes are brought about through the high protein levels of the diet. The catechol estrogen potentiate epinephrine-induced lipolysis in fat cells. See Bibliography references 20 (Fishman, Boyar and Hellman 1975) and 21 (Fishman and Martucci 1980).
11. See Bibliography reference 24 (Goldin et al. 1982).
12. See Bibliography references 3 (Aldercreutz et al. 1987), 23 (Goldin et al. 1981) and 26 (Goldin and Gorbach 1988).
13. See Bibliography reference 57 (Wade, Gray and Bartness 1985).
14. See Bibliography reference 46 (Public Health Service 1988).
15. See Bibliography reference 19 (Feldman 1983).
16. Moderate protein intake during this time works to produce the most favorable ratio of the catechol to 16 alpha hydroxylated estrogens. See Bibliography reference 6 (Anderson et al. 1984).
17. See Bibliography reference 43 (Mellinkoff et al. 1956).

3 HOW TO USE THE WOMAN'S ADVANTAGE DIET

Everyone likes to diet differently. Everyone has what I call an individual "dieting style." Some people don't want to have to think about food while they're trying not to eat it. They hate planning meals, and prefer weight loss programs that just tell them exactly what to eat and when to eat it with full menu plans. Many of my patients who prefer this method say it makes life easier, because they can just take their menus to the supermarket and do the shopping for an entire phase of the diet all at once. I think of these patients as Menu Style Dieters.

But other people hate being so regimented. They get hungry for foods not on the menu plan just because they know they're not supposed to eat them. These people prefer to design their own menus to adhere to the guidelines of the Woman's Advantage Diet, so that their meals can suit their tastebuds on each particular day. For some, it's not just a question of taste; many of my patients have special health concerns (such as high cholesterol, high blood pressure or allergies) that necessitate their being able to personalize their menus. Others are vegetarians and prefer to avoid meats, poultry, fish, seafood and even dairy products in their diets. Whether it's a question of taste or health, I think of such people as Designer Style Dieters.

Still others are somewhere in between. They start out preferring specific menu plans, but after having been on the Woman's Advantage Diet for one or two complete cycles, they want a little variety. They start out as Menu Style Dieters and end up as Designer Style Dieters.

As different as these two styles of dieting are, they are equally valid. My Menu Style Dieters lose just as much weight as my Designer Style Dieters. Everyone is happier losing weight in their own way.

For this reason, I've presented the Woman's Advantage Diet in both styles. For Designer Style Dieters, I've included Advantage Food Group lists and Advantage Food Plans. The Advantage Food Group lists tell you exactly what types of foods you have to choose from for each phase of your cycle. The Advantage Food Plan gives you guidelines about just how much of that food you may eat, and in what kind of serving sizes.

Those of you who are Designer Style Dieters might at first glance not be sure how to use the Advantage Food Group lists. Some of my patients have asked me why the lists are so long, and sometimes they're confused because they can't easily see the difference between one list and another. Indeed, some sections of the lists are identical in every phase of the diet.

One reason for this is because I wanted the lists to be easy reference guides. Each list contains all the foods you can eat during that particular phase of the diet. (That's why the lists contain so many exotic foods. I wanted to be sure to cover as many different individual tastes and ethnic cuisines as possible. I know that a food that might appear strange to one reader is a diet staple to another.) But this also means that these lists contain the *only* foods you can have during each phase of the diet. In other words, if you don't see it on the list you're currently using, you can't eat it!

I thought the easiest way for you to use such lists would be if you could find all the information you needed in one place. Some of you might even want to copy the lists and carry them with you in your purse, so I wanted them to be available to you in as compact a way as possible. As a result, however, the lists are repetitive. Many foods are "neutral" as far as the principles of the Woman's Advantage Diet are concerned, and so are allowed during all phases of the program. Other foods (such as protein) are always allowed, but you need to use the guidance of the Advantage Food Plans to tell you just what the appropriate quantity of that food might be during a particular phase of the cycle. Still other foods are allowed during some phases of the diet and not others; those are the obvious differences you'll see in the food group lists. For instance, you'll find a lot of high fiber carbohydrates on the Fabulous Fruits and Vegetables list, but not on the Pasta Plus list.

Don't worry about looking for these point-by-point differences on each list. Just consider each list the absolute guide to what you can and can not eat during each particular phase of the diet, and you should find a variety that makes the Woman's Advantage Diet both easy and fun to follow.

For Menu Style Dieters, I've provided specific, day-to-day and meal-by-meal (and snack time) menus for you to follow for an entire cycle. I've planned these menus with variety in mind. I don't think you should ever feel bored or frustrated by a weight-loss eating program. Since you can't indulge yourself in how much you eat, I want you to be able to indulge in what you eat. I've tried to provide you with a wide array of delicious gourmet meals that will show you just what a treat a healthful "diet" meal can be.

If you're using the menus, I'd like you to keep the following tips in mind. I believe leftovers are hidden land mines to dieters, and I don't think you should have them around or eat them. For this reason, I've planned the menus to leave you with as few leftovers as possible.

However, that also means the menus involve a lot of cooking and a lot of recipes. Don't be scared of these recipes; they're very simple and don't involve a lot of work to put together. They're not meant to be groundbreaking culinary inventions. Rather, I've designed them to help teach the habits of good, healthful dieting—how to reduce fat in cooking, how to use reduced calorie products in satisfying ways, how to measure appropriate serving sizes.

These tricks, and many of the recipes themselves, are so easy they should soon become second nature to you. But if they don't, and you find yourself thinking of the menus as just too much work, I recommend you switch over to Designer Style Dieting. You can always use the menus to help guide your meal choices when you don't feel like being creative. For instance, if you're not in the mood to choose which protein entrée to have for dinner during Protein Power, you can check the appropriate menu day (the day that corresponds to the time of your cycle) and see what I suggested.

However, remember to follow the Advantage Food Plans when designing your own meals. The food plans describe slightly different rules from the ones I followed in putting together the menus. Don't let this confuse you. Obviously, when I'm designing a menu myself, I can offer a greater variety of foods and still be confident that you'll lose weight. The price a Designer Style Dieter pays for her greater independence is a little less flexibility in the parameters of her food lists and meal plans.

Rules of the Game

No matter what style of dieter you are, let me tell you frankly that you will find no success in your weight loss efforts unless you follow what I call the "rules of the game." I think of these guidelines as the common sense of dieting, but in truth they are guidelines for healthful eating habits whether or not you want to lose weight. Certainly, unless you follow these "rules" you won't find the Woman's Advantage Diet or any other weight loss plan effective. Let me add that if you are a Designer Style Dieter these rules are especially important for you. With extra freedom comes extra responsibility, so read the following with care.

How to Diet—Behavior Tips

• Don't keep high calorie snack foods in the refrigerator or the kitchen cabinet. Remember what Grandma stitched on the sampler: "What the eye doesn't see, the heart doesn't grieve for."

• If you come home from work and you're really hungry, have a green salad before you sit down to dinner. A salad is filling, and you're less likely to overeat during the rest of the meal.

• Don't snack at night or before sleep. There is no need for calories when you are sleeping. Late night snackers are usually eating because of anxiety or depression. Often, it's a long-established habit. If you have this problem, you should work hard to change it. Make sure you stay out of the kitchen after supper. Examine your routine to see if activities such as watching television lead to snacking. Be aware of emotional problems that lead to snacking late at night. You may find taking a walk or reading a book, or even finishing household work before bed helpful.

• If you know that you're usually very hungry at a special hour—five or six, for example—have a plastic bag of washed carrots, celery, sweet peppers or other vegetables waiting for you in the refrigerator so that you can eat them immediately. (Be sure that the vegetables you choose have the appropriate amount of fiber for the phase of the cycle you're in.)

• You're a big girl now, and you don't have to worry about "cleaning your plate." It's all right to leave food, and it's even better to help yourself to smaller portions.

• Eat slowly. This will give your stomach time to signal your brain that you're full, and have had enough to eat. If you eat too quickly, you'll tend to overeat because your appetite control system won't have had time to send the message that you're no longer hungry. Have you ever noticed that the people who eat faster than anyone else at the table are usually overweight?

• Concentrate on *what* and *where* you're eating. If you eat in front of the TV set, you're liable to eat more because you're paying more attention to the program than to what you're eating. Don't nibble absentmindedly.

• Don't take a snack to bed, and don't eat while you're standing at the kitchen counter. Eat at the dining table or kitchen table, and when you've finished a meal, leave the table with the understanding that *you've finished eating.*

• Avoid the temptation to snack on free food, such as the samples offered at supermarkets or the candies offered after dinner at a restaurant. Such foods might not cost you money, but if you're trying to lose weight, they're not free!

• Going through an anxious period? Eating won't make the anxiety go away; it will just increase it. If you overeat because you're worried, you'll end up with two reasons to be anxious: the original reason, and the fact that you indulged in the wrong foods. When you're feeling uptight, try taking a walk (or getting another form of physical exercise), going shopping, seeing a movie, calling a friend, doing something other than eating until the anxiety attack lessens.

• Eat breakfast. Even if you're not much of a breakfast eater, try to have something at the beginning of the day. You'll burn up the calories during the day, and breakfast can prevent that feeling of starvation that might make you overeat at lunch time.

• Beware of *disinhibitors!* A disinhibitor is someone or something that disrupts your eating control. It can be a person (a friend with whom you're lunching who orders a gooey dessert) or a drink (alcoholic beverages can destroy a dieter's best intentions). Or maybe it's your mood—you're depressed, or sad, and you think food will make you feel better. Cope with such disinhibiting influences by remembering the goal you have set for yourself, and your motivations for wanting to lose weight.

• If you love the seasoning used in Chinese, or Mexican, or other ethnic foods, use that seasoning on steamed vegetables.

• When you're eating in a restaurant, ask the waiter or waitress not to bring you bread and butter. (If you're dining with friends who want the bread and butter, order a salad to eat while the others eat the bread and butter.)

• When eating out, order all meat and fish dishes broiled, and without sauce.

• If you're planning a plane trip, call the airline in advance to order a fresh fruit plate.

• Take a small bag of grapes or apple wedges to the movies, and stay away from candy bars and buttered, salted popcorn.

• When it's party time, or if you're at a restaurant and everyone is having a drink, order club soda with a wedge of lemon or lime.

• Have fruit for dessert or for a snack whenever possible.

How to Diet—Cooking Tips

• When you eat beef or veal, always choose lean cuts and trim away all visible fat. That means you'll have to forget those richly marbled porterhouse steaks, but I think you'll find a flank steak just as enjoyable. Also, be especially careful about the ground beef you buy. I allow hamburgers on the Woman's Advantage Diet, but only if you make them with the leanest ground beef you can find. Go for ground sirloin or ground round, not chuck; and ask your butcher to trim off as much fat as he can before he grinds it.

Be sure to broil, grill or roast both beef and veal. Don't fry.

• When you eat lamb, keep the same rules of the game in mind. Buy the leanest cuts; trim off all the fat; broil, grill or roast.

• When you eat pork, make an extra effort to avoid fatty cuts. You'll have to avoid pork roasts for now, unless it's a trimmed pork tenderloin. Pork chops need their fat trimmed as well, and avoid the richly marbled ones. While I don't advise eating fatty cured pork products like bacon, I do think you can enjoy some ham and Canadian bacon on occasion.

And remember to broil, grill or roast any meat you prepare at home.

• Chicken is a wonderful food for dieters. Remember to stick to the white meat, because that's leaner than the dark meat. Always trim off fat and skin before cooking. Broil, grill or roast your chicken—never fry it.

• Fish is also a wonderful food for dieters, and you'll see that I recommend a lot of it on the Woman's Advantage Diet. It's hard to trim the skin off fish before cooking it, but be sure not to eat it. Also, never fry your fish; enjoy it broiled, grilled or oven baked.

Eat only fresh or frozen fish. Avoid the canned or smoked varieties unless they're preserved in water or mustard. Avoid the kinds packed in oil.

• The Woman's Advantage Diet allows you to eat cheese, but let me add a special word of caution here. Cheese often contains lots of fat, calories and salt—three things you generally want to avoid on the diet. When you have cheese, stick to the low fat variety. Many cheeses are made with skim milk and low sodium, while others like feta cheese are naturally lower in calories.

Also, when you have cottage cheese or cream cheese, be sure to stick to the low fat brands.

• Similarly, when you have sour cream, use only the reduced calorie brands. Actually, I much prefer that you use plain yogurt instead of any kind of sour cream. And be sure to use low fat yogurt. When you're having yogurt alone, instead of as a condiment, try buying the plain kind and adding your own fresh fruits.

• When you use even small quantities of fat in cooking, try to use a reduced calorie margarine. Also, use this for a spread on bread, bagels and muffins rather than regular margarine or butter.

• If you're uncomfortable using reduced calorie products, but you enjoy sautéing, try doing so with only a teaspoon of oil in a nonstick pan along with a couple of tablespoons of defatted chicken or beef broth. Some of my patients even add Worcestershire sauce or wine (the calories in the alcohol burn off during cooking).

• Add flavor to your food by cooking with herbs and spices. That will help you avoid excess fat and salt in your diet.

• The Woman's Advantage Diet allows you to eat a variety of breads. I recommend looking for the reduced calorie brands whenever you can find them.

• You can even have a little pizza on this diet. But be careful to avoid the kind with meat toppings. There are lots of delicious vegetable toppings now—broccoli, spinach and eggplant as well as the more traditional mushrooms, peppers and onions.

• When you eat cereal on the Woman's Advantage Diet, I must ask you to be careful about your choices. When it comes to fat and calories, all cereals are not created equal!

Avoid the granola types and the packaged brands that have lots of added sugar. There are even some reduced calorie cereals that use sugar substitutes that you may want to try. If you don't like sugar or sugar substitutes, I encourage you to stick to the nonprocessed cereal varieties, like good old oatmeal.

• When you have a potato, I recommend baking, boiling and steaming as the best cooking methods. Whatever you do, don't fry! And don't lather on the sour cream and butter. Stick to reduced calorie margarine and reduced calorie sour cream, or better yet, just plain yogurt. Mix in some chopped chives or hot sauce for a change.

• When you have corn, feel free to enjoy it on the cob or in kernels. But remember to avoid butter and salt.

• When you have vegetables, be sure to boil or steam them. No frying, and don't smother vegetables in butter or oil at the table. I recommend a little lemon juice; it enhances the flavor of almost every vegetable.

• As we've discussed, during parts of the diet cycle, you're asked to avoid too much fiber. Keep in mind that a lot of the fiber in fruits and vegetables is in the skin. So, during the ovulatory phase of the diet, peel fruits and vegetables whenever you can. During the postmenstrual phase, leave the skins on.

• You'll see that the Woman's Advantage Diet plan is filled with fruits and vegetables. Sometimes, the menu plans may call for varieties that are out of season or otherwise unavailable in your area. If that happens, just consult the appropriate Advantage Food Group list, and you'll find a suitable substitute.

• Eat fresh fruit whenever possible. If you must have canned varieties, be sure they're packed in fruit juice with no added sugar.

• Let me add a word of caution about raisins, currants, dates and other dried fruits. They have more calories than fresh fruit, so use them sparingly and only where specifically called for in the menus. Even though they are technically fruits, they are not good snack foods.

• Enjoy fruit juices as much as possible on the diet. Look for low calorie cranberry juice and other reduced calorie varieties. Or, if you prefer regular kinds, I suggest having about an ounce of juice with a glass of carbonated water. I call these juice spritzers, and it is a great friend to a dieter. This trick will allow you to drink more fluids throughout the day. (I don't recommend that you drink glass after glass of pure fruit juice. It has more calories than you might think. As you'll see later in the book, I often treat fruit juices as side dishes or appetizers, rather than as simple beverages. Juice spritzers, on the other hand, you may drink as often as you like.)

• Let me add another special warning—about nuts. Avoid them! They're loaded with fat and calories, and I have yet to meet the dieter who can eat just one. It's best to get the nutrients that nuts offer from other sources while you're dieting. The Woman's Advantage Diet is designed to do that for you.

• Every now and then, on the Woman's Advantage Diet, I recommend hot chocolate. Please keep in mind that I mean only the reduced calorie cocoa drinks available at your supermarket. And be sure you make them with skim milk or water, not whole milk.

• I also occasionally suggest that you enjoy some frozen skim milk or frozen yogurt while you're on the diet. These can be delightful alternatives to ice cream. Please keep in mind that I mean only the low fat brands.

• Enjoy the soups I recommend, but make sure that none is cream based. Creamed soups are too high in fat and calories. Also, be sure to defat soups and broths before eating them or using them in cooking.

• The Woman's Advantage Diet does not strictly forbid alcoholic beverages, but I certainly do not advise drinking them regularly. Alcohol has a lot of calories, and it is the kind of disinhibitor that can trip you up on the best of diets. If you feel you must have alcohol, I recommend that you stick to only one or two drinks a week and limit them to the Forbidden Foods phase. Be sure to have only the reduced calorie beers or reduced calorie wine spritzers. And remember, even those drinks have a significant amount of calories, at least as much as a glass of juice or skim milk.

• One helpful hint to many a dieter is herbal tea. It's caffeine free, so even if you're sensitive to that chemical, you can drink it.

Water—A Dieter's Best Friend

One of the best friends you can have when dieting is *water*. Water is good for you—it flushes impurities out of your system naturally, it fills you up, and you can have as much of it as you want.

You'll notice on the diet that I suggest carbonated or mineral water with many meals. You can have tap water instead of these bottled waters if you wish, or you can have tap water in addition to bottled waters. Drink the kind of water you prefer, but *do* drink water. I recommend six to eight glasses of water a day.

Avoid Salt

Salt acts to retain water, which will add to your weight as well as contribute to symptoms of PMS. The Woman's Advantage Diet is low in salt, and to make sure that you keep your salt intake low—especially during your premenstrual phase—don't use it at the table. Also avoid the following foods:

• *cured meats:* ham, bacon, salami, sausage, frankfurter, bologna, pastrami, corned beef.

• *smoked fish:* salmon, trout, carp, bluefish, sablefish.

• *canned vegetables:* all canned vegetables, except those labeled "low sodium" or "salt free."

• *snacks:* salted pretzels, potato chips, corn chips, tortilla chips, popcorn, crackers, peanut butter, pork rinds, nuts.

• *dairy products:* cheese (unless it's low in sodium or low salt cheese), butter, margarine (unless it's low sodium margarine).

• *pickled foods:* herring, gravlax, pickles, relishes, sauerkraut, vegetables put up in brine.

When you're cooking, use herbs and spices instead of salt. Add dried or fresh dill, parsley, shallot, garlic, basil, oregano, tarragon, chili powder, cinnamon, cardamon, cumin, fennel, ginger, paprika, sage or rosemary. See the Advantage Food Group lists for additional suggestions.

A squeeze of fresh lemon in broth or on chicken or lamb is a delicious alternative to salt. If none of the above seems to do the trick, use light salt—a salt substitute—instead of regular salt.

Increasing Potassium

You may be especially sensitive to the effects of salt during your premenstrual phase. You can counteract this tendency both by avoiding salty foods and by emphasizing certain fruits and vegetables that are high in potassium. Remember to be careful. Protein Power is the time to de-emphasize carbohydrates. Some are allowed in order to keep your diet balanced. If salt is a problem for you, during

Protein Power you should concentrate on eating the following fruits and vegetables when you do allow carbohydrates into your diet:

Fruits: cherries, nectarines, plums, melons, mangos and pineapple.

Vegetables: tomatoes, lettuce, cucumbers, peppers, cauliflower, and asparagus.

What About Vitamin and Mineral Supplements?

The Woman's Advantage Diet is carefully planned to be fully balanced nutritionally. However, I do think it's a good idea to take a supplement while you're trying to lose weight, one that provides 100% of the recommended dietary allowance for vitamins and minerals. This is especially important for those of you who won't strictly be following the menu plans but will be instead designing your own meals.

A Word About Condiments

As you read through the menus for the Woman's Advantage Diet, you'll see that I do not always specify exactly when you may have condiments with a meal and the exact amounts you may have. That's because I've assumed you've read this chapter and understand the rules of the game.

You may use appropriate quantities of appropriate condiments when you want them. For instance, you may have something with your coffee—but skim milk and a reduced calorie sugar substitute, not cream and sugar. You may have something on your sandwich, but reduced calorie mayonnaise or mustard, not regular mayonnaise and butter. You may have something on your toast or muffin, but reduced calorie margarine, cream cheese or jelly, not the regular kind. You may put something on your chicken, but use lemon and spices, not salt. Stir your coffee with a cinnamon stick instead of adding sugar.

You get the idea. Refer to the rules of the game, and use the condiments—but use them within reason.

How to Diet—Portion Tips

There's a marvelously useful word that can be a big help when you're dieting, and that's the word *one,* as in:

One slice of bread
One muffin
One egg
One container of low fat yogurt
One waffle
One sandwich
One scoop of ice cream
One potato
One slice of bacon

You get the idea!

If *one* is the word that can make a big difference when you're dieting, *"Don't overeat"* is the short sentence that you should also commit to memory.

You won't be hungry if you follow the Woman's Advantage Diet, and there's no reason to keep eating when you're not hungry. Eat enough so that you feel satisfied, but not so much that you feel stuffed, full or uncomfortable from too much food.

There may be times when you know you've had enough, even though you haven't eaten every morsel of food listed on the menu or food plan for the day. *This is the moment to stop eating!* Even if, according to the plan, you may have dessert or a snack, don't eat if you're not hungry.

In addition to that important word *one,* and the essential rule to *never* overeat, the following will explain the quantities and serving sizes you may have of the foods on the Woman's Advantage Diet.

• *A SERVING OF MEAT or POULTRY* means you may have one lamb chop, one lean pork chop, a lean hamburger, two thin slices of roast beef or half a chicken breast. The meat (without bone) should weigh between four and six ounces. I don't recommend that you have red meat more than three times a week. As a dieter, you should emphasize poultry and fish.

• *A SERVING OF FISH* means a filet, steak, whole fish or portion of a large fish. The fish flesh should weigh between four and six ounces.

• *A SERVING OF SHRIMP* means about a cup of shrimp, which is usually three large ones, or six to eight medium ones, or a cup of small ones. Be careful with shrimp salad you don't make at home, it can be made with high fat ingredients; one-half cup is usually ample.

• *A SERVING OF SCALLOPS* means about four to six ounces.

• *A SERVING OF OYSTERS or CLAMS* means anywhere from

six to twenty plain oysters or clams. Oysters and clams themselves are low in calories, but most people like only a half dozen at a time. Also, be careful of recipes like oysters Rockefeller and clams casino that include lots of high fat, high calorie ingredients. Keep in mind, too, that these foods are high in cholesterol and you'll want to limit your intake if that is a concern of yours.

• *A SERVING OF PASTA* as a main dish means a moderate, filling amount, which is about two ounces of dry pasta. As most pasta comes in sixteen-ounce boxes, it's easy enough to figure out when you've taken approximately two ounces (or one-eighth) from the box.

When you're having pasta as a side dish, I think you should have only one-half to one ounce. That should be enough to accompany any main dish.

• *A SERVING OF PIZZA* means one quarter of a ten-inch-diameter pie.

• *A SERVING OF SOUP* means about a bowl, or twelve to sixteen ounces of soup, which is enough for a filling meal.

• *A SERVING OF BEAN SOUP* means about a cup, or eight to ten ounces.

• *A SERVING OF MEAT, FISH or CHEESE FOR A SAND-WICH* means approximately two ounces. If it's turkey or chicken breast, you may have as much as three ounces. Avoid those over-stuffed deli sandwiches.

• *A SERVING OF VEGETABLES* means . . . well, I've never met anyone who got fat from eating broccoli, Brussels sprouts, green beans, cabbage, asparagus, or similar vegetables. Just be sure you eat those vegetables without butter, margarine, oil or sauce. You may have as much as you want of the vegetables listed in the Advantage Food Groups; just be sure to eat only those vegetables allowed in the particular phase of the cycle you're in.

• *A SERVING OF POTATO* means one potato. Potatoes of all varieties (new potatoes, sweet potatoes, red bliss potatoes, Idahos) are special vegetables. You can't indulge in potatoes the way you can in other, less starchy vegetables. So, one serving of potato means only one. You may have it baked, steamed, or boiled. If you're having red bliss or new potatoes, you may have three small ones—the approximate equivalent of one baking potato.

• *A SERVING OF CORN* means one corn on-the-cob (without butter) or one-half a cup of kernels.

• *A SERVING OF BEANS* means about half a cup of beans.

Like potatoes, beans are higher in calories than most other carbo-hydrates.

• *A SERVING OF RICE* means one-half cup of cooked rice.

• *A SERVING OF COLESLAW* means one-half cup.

• *A SERVING OF SALAD* means you may have as much as you like of salad ingredients like lettuce, celery, onions, radishes. As with other vegetables, I haven't seen anyone get fat on salad—as long as you remember that eggs, cheese and meat are not considered salad ingredients! Also, stick to moderate amounts of low-in-fat, low-in-calories dressing.

• *A SERVING OF BREAD* means one slice, even if you're having a sandwich. If the bread is not presliced (as is often the case with Italian and French loaves), a serving means one half-inch slice.

If you're using reduced calorie bread, you can have two slices as a single serving or with a sandwich.

• *A SERVING OF A ROLL* means one roll.

• *A SERVING OF A MUFFIN* means one muffin. If it's the baked variety, it should weigh two and a half to three ounces. Avoid the super big muffins that weigh as much as five or six ounces.

If it's an English muffin, one serving includes both halves.

• *A SERVING OF BAGEL* means one bagel.

• *A SERVING OF CEREAL* means you may have one to one and one-half ounces of cereal.

• *A SERVING OF PANCAKES or FRENCH TOAST* means two pancakes (4″ × 4″ × ½″) or one piece of French toast.

• *A SERVING OF SKIM MILK ON YOUR CEREAL* means you shouldn't use so much that you turn your cereal into a soggy mush. Use one-third to one-quarter cup on your cereal.

• *A SERVING OF CREAM CHEESE* means you may have one ounce of a reduced calorie brand.

• *A SERVING OF YOGURT* means eight ounces of plain, low fat yogurt. Try adding a couple of ounces of fresh fruit if you want to flavor it.

• *A SERVING OF COTTAGE CHEESE* means about four ounces of a low fat brand.

• *A SERVING OF SOUR CREAM* means a tablespoon of a reduced calorie brand, to be used as a condiment.

• *A SERVING OF JELLY* means you may have one or two tablespoons of reduced calorie jelly.

• *A SERVING OF CRANBERRY SAUCE* or similarly naturally sweet condiment should be about 1 to 2 ounces.

• *A SERVING OF SYRUP* means you may have one or two tablespoons of reduced calorie syrup.

• *A SERVING OF MAYONNAISE* means you may use no more than one-half tablespoon of reduced calorie mayonnaise on a sandwich.

• *A SERVING OF MARGARINE* means one pat (about a teaspoon) of a reduced calorie kind. Again, it's better for you than the regular spread, but it's not calorie free.

• *A SERVING OF KETCHUP* means you may have up to two or three tablespoons.

• *A SERVING OF MUSTARD* means you may have as much mustard as you wish. This is a nice alternative for those of you who aren't comfortable using low calorie products on sandwiches, salads and the like.

• *A SERVING OF HORSERADISH* means you may have as much as you wish. This is another underappreciated, low-in-fat-and-calories condiment that's wonderful on sandwiches. Have half a teaspoon with turkey or cold beef and see what I mean.

• *A SERVING OF APPLESAUCE* means you may have half a cup of unsweetened applesauce. Don't have the regular, presweetened kind.

• *A SERVING OF SALAD DRESSING* means you may use one or two teaspoons of bottled reduced calorie salad dressing. It's not free, so don't pour it on.

• *A SERVING OF SAUCES* means that when you're putting sauce on spaghetti, use a light hand. I recommend one-third to one-half cup of meat sauce and one-half to three-quarters cup of vegetable or seafood sauce.

• *A SERVING OF CHEESE AS A CONDIMENT* means that when you're sprinkling Parmesan and Romano on spaghetti, don't overdo. One or two tablespoons should be enough.

• *A SERVING OF CHEESE AS A SNACK* means a slice of cheese that is low fat and preferably low salt. It should weigh about one ounce, which usually means one slice.

• *A SERVING OF POPCORN* means you may have one to two cups of unbuttered and unsalted popcorn.

• *A SERVING OF CRACKERS* means you may have two or three, not the whole box.

• *A SERVING OF RICE CAKES* means you may have one.

• *A SERVING OF RAISINS, PRUNES or other DRIED FRUIT* means no more than one-eighth cup.

• *A SERVING OF ICE CREAM, ICE MILK, FROZEN YO-GURT, TOFUTTI or SHERBET* means one two-ounce scoop. Most scoopers serve up just that amount.

• *A SERVING OF PIE OR CAKE* means only one slice. And one slice does not mean one-quarter of the pie or cake. You know what one slice means. A nine-inch pie divides nicely into eight pieces; that's what I mean by one slice. A slice of cake should be approximately the same size.

• *A SERVING OF FRUIT* means, in general, one piece of fruit. But this, like vegetables, is the place to overindulge. If you're feeling hungry, a second piece of fruit isn't going to ruin the diet.

If you're having berries, three-quarters to one cup is fine. But be more careful with cherries and grapes. Stick to one-half to three-quarters of a cup of these somewhat more calorie laden fruits.

Mangoes and papayas are exceptions. They're pretty rich in calories, so you should limit yourself to only half of one mango or papaya per serving.

Similarly, with pineapple, limit yourself to about half a cup.

• *A SERVING OF MELON* means half a cantaloupe, a quarter to an eighth of a honeydew, and a four-by-eight-inch wedge of watermelon. But, don't worry too much about melon. It's so low in calories and so filling, it would be awfully hard for you to eat enough to hurt your weight loss efforts. If you feel like overindulging, melons are a great way to do it.

• *A SERVING OF ANY FRUIT OR VEGETABLE JUICE* means a four to six ounce serving, the size of an average juice glass.

• *A SERVING OF JUICE SPRITZER* means you may have about as much as you want. Since they only contain about an ounce of fruit or vegetable juice, spritzers are a great way to quench your thirst through the day.

• *A SERVING OF SKIM MILK* means an eight-ounce serving, the size of an average water glass.

• *A SERVING OF WINE* means a three-and-a-half-ounce glass of wine or a twelve-ounce wine spritzer.

• *A SERVING OF BEER* means one bottle (twelve ounces) of low calorie beer.

• *A SERVING OF SKIM MILK IN YOUR COFFEE OR TEA* means you shouldn't turn these beverages white; after all, you want to retain that delicious coffee or tea flavor. Approximately one to two tablespoons of skim milk should do it.

• *A SERVING OF COFFEE OR TEA* means that, while there is no strict limit on the amount of coffee or tea you may drink (since these beverages contain no fat or calories that contribute to weight gain), I do recommend that you don't have more than two or three cups a day, and even less during your premenstrual phase. Many women have special health risks if they consume too much caffeine. You should consult your doctor before overdoing these beverages.

• *SODAS*. Stay away from regular sodas. They're loaded with sugar and calories. Diet sodas aren't fattening, and if they're caffeine free there's no strict limit on how many you can drink a day. However, the long term effects of sugar substitutes are still being debated, so you should consult your doctor before overdoing these beverages. Generally, I recommend no more than one or two diet sodas a day.

• *MINERAL OR CARBONATED WATER*. Enjoy! There are no health or weight gain risks here, and the lightly flavored carbonated waters can be truly delicious. (Be careful of those brands high in sodium.)

My E. and A. Lists

Whenever I start a new patient on the Woman's Advantage Diet, I give her a list of foods to emphasize and a list of foods to avoid. You'll find them useful, too.

Foods to emphasize:
cereals without sugar
chicken
fish
fruits
legumes
low fat, low sodium cheese
low fat yogurt
natural fruit and vegetable juices
pasta
seafood
skim milk
turkey
veal

vegetables
waters, mineral and carbonated

Foods to avoid:
alcohol
baked goods
breads
butter
candy
canned fruits in syrup
creamy soups
fatty meats
fried fish
fried meat
fried vegetables
fruit snack foods
high fat, high sodium cheeses
ice cream
jams
luncheon meats
nuts
peanut butter
potato chips
pretzels
whole milk

For Those of You with Special Health Concerns

I recommend you consult your doctor before you start any diet. The Woman's Advantage Diet is no exception. It has been designed to be completely safe and nutritionally sound for premenopausal women. It is not designed with special health concerns in mind. In general, I've found that those of my patients who do have health problems have been able to adapt the diet easily and safely to their needs. I feel confident that you can, too, but I must ask you to do so with your doctor's help. If you have a special health concern, such as high cholesterol, high blood pressure, diabetes or allergies, I must ask you to use the Woman's Advantage Diet as a Designer Style Dieter so that you can take your doctor's advice into account.

Recently, many of my patients have become especially concerned about cholesterol. If you are, too, let me first assure you that the Woman's Advantage Diet follows American Heart Association guidelines for cholesterol reduction. The menus have no more than 300 mg of cholesterol and no more than 30 percent of the total calories in the menus come from fat. Care has been taken to make sure that only 10 percent of the fats are saturated. The Woman's Advantage Diet will lower cholesterol for many readers who have not previously adjusted their diets with the American Heart Association guidelines in mind.

However, you may have a special problem with cholesterol, and your doctor may desire that you drastically lower your intake of cholesterol and saturated fats. The tips below should help you in following your doctor's advice:

(1) Use only egg whites in cooking.
(2) Use egg substitutes instead of eggs. These include powdered eggs, liquid eggs and egg yolk replacers.
(3) Use meat substitutes, such as products made with textured vegetable proteins and tofu. (I've provided plenty of tofu recipes later in the book for you to use during Protein Power.)
(4) Use poultry and fish instead of red meat or pork.

Some Questions and Answers

My patients often have questions when they first start the Woman's Advantage Diet. I'm sure you do, too. I've tried to anticipate what your questions might be, and provided the answers below.

Q May I drink decaffeinated coffee?

A Absolutely. Caffeine makes some people edgy and can even cause an upset stomach. If it affects you that way, or if your doctor has advised you to avoid caffeine, drink decaffeinated coffee or switch to another beverage. I strongly recommend decaffeinated beverages during your premenstrual phase, as caffeine can aggravate your PMS symptoms.

Q I don't like fish. May I have meat whenever you have fish on one of the menus?

A Yes, you may have a four- to six-ounce portion of meat or chicken (all fat trimmed, and skin removed from the chicken), whenever the menu offers fish. But keep in mind that fish tends to be lower in fat and calories than most meats. Try to substitute a lean meat or poultry. Check the Woman's Advantage Food Group lists and plans to be sure your substitute choice follows the guidelines of the diet.

Q You mention a number of spices, but not some of my favorites. May I use other spices on the diet?

A All spices are allowed on the Woman's Advantage Diet.

Q What happens if I can't find some of the foods you have listed on your diet?

A There's nothing unusual or strange about the required foods on any part of the Woman's Advantage Diet. You can easily follow the eating programs with foods available in supermarkets and grocery stores, and with dishes that are familiar ones in restaurants. If, however, for some reason you do have trouble finding a particular item, I recommend you consult the Advantage Food Group lists and the Advantage Food Plan to find a suitable substitute.

Q I like to put sugar in my coffee and on my cereal. What should I do?

A Use a sugar substitute, or try stirring your coffee with a cinnamon stick, or adding ground cinnamon to it. Fresh fruit can make your cereal deliciously sweet without your having to add anything else, but be sure you eat it according to the diet's guidelines.

Q If I eat less one day, may I eat more the next?

A That's not the way to diet. Stick to the menu for each day, or create your own menu using the Advantage Food Group lists and the Advantage Food Plans. Don't try to balance out amounts by eating less one day and more the next. The diet won't work.

Q May I eat your suggested lunch at dinner time, and vice versa?

A Yes, you may. The point is to eat a balanced portion at each meal, each day of the diet. Switching meals is fine. Just don't switch one day's lunch with another day's dinner. And please follow the Advantage Food Plans as a guide in order to keep your diet nutritionally balanced.

Q You say I should eat reduced calorie cheese, reduced calorie dressing, and so on. But what if I ate less of a regular food item instead of the reduced calorie stuff, would the diet work?

A No, it wouldn't work as well. The regular food items aren't just higher in calories, they're also higher in fat. They won't affect your body the same way foods low in fat do. Fat is not only "fattening" (high in calories), but it is also considered to be harmful to your overall health.[1] So don't try substituting less of a regular product for a normal portion of a reduced calorie product.

If you're uncomfortable eating some of the reduced calorie products, I recommend using equally low-in-calorie, low-in-fat substitutes. For instance, explore the list of condiments when you cook. Use defatted chicken stock for cooking instead of reduced calorie margarine. Use mustard or horseradish on your sandwich instead of reduced calorie mayonnaise. If you use your imagination, there's always a low-in-calorie, low-in-fat substitute for reduced calorie products.

Q My doctor has me on a low cholesterol diet, and I can't eat eggs or cheese. Does this mean I can't use the Woman's Advantage Diet?

A You can use the diet with your doctor's approval. Just use the Advantage Food Plan to substitute one of the other foods on the Advantage Food Group list whenever eggs or cheese are called for.

Q I've been taking a one-a-day vitamin supplement. May I continue doing this on the Woman's Advantage Diet?

A You certainly may. The diet is well balanced (and you'll probably be eating a more nutritionally sound menu than you were before), but it never hurts to take a one-a-day supplement. So many vitamins, minerals and trace elements are minimized or lost when foods are processed, it's a good idea to take a one-a-day supplement that provides the minimum daily requirements of these nutrients.

---

1. See Bibliography reference 46 (Public Health Service 1988).

4 FORBIDDEN FOODS

The Woman's Advantage Diet is really four eating programs rolled into one. It's this variety that will make it easy for you to continue on the Woman's Advantage Diet until you reach your goal weight. If no diet has ever worked for you because you got tired of the food plan after a couple of weeks, the Woman's Advantage Diet will be a welcome relief, as well as a healthful and nutritionally sound way of eating.

The Forbidden Foods Phase

Your menstrual phase is the time during your cycle when you can reward yourself. This is not the place to start the Woman's Advantage Diet (see Chapter 2). Your hormones are working in such a way that you can have some of your favorite foods without gaining weight.

I did say *some* of your favorite foods. If you're a dessert lover, have either ice cream or cake. If you yearn for potato chips, you can have some during this phase, but not every day. And if you're crazy about sausage, enjoy it, but not for breakfast, lunch and dinner.

The emphasis in Forbidden Foods is on carbohydrates (both high and low in fiber) combined with lots of protein and some fat. It's the extra, though small, allowance of fat that allows you to have such treats as ice cream and potato chips.

What do I Mean By "Forbidden" Foods?

Some of my patients have been confused by my calling the menstrual phase of the diet the Forbidden Foods eating program, so I want to take a minute to clarify what I mean by that name. I call this phase of the diet Forbidden Foods because it is the time you can eat some foods that are otherwise "forbidden" to a dieter. You'll find a specific list of these foods on page 71 in the "Special Forbidden Foods List." That list contains lots of goodies—bacon, doughnuts, fried chicken and the like. These are foods you can occasionally indulge in, according to the guidelines explained later in this chapter.

They are very different from the Advantage Food Group list for Forbidden Foods, which follow on pages 60–68. These foods are not "naughty" in the least; indeed, they are the foods I recommend you eat to lose weight. The Designer Style Dieter should use these foods in conjunction with the Forbidden Foods Advantage Food Plan to choose her meals. In other words, you should use the Forbidden Foods' Advantage Food Group list in just the same way you use the Advantage Food Group lists for Fabulous Fruits and Vegetables, Pasta Plus, Protein Power and the Stay Slim eating programs. The only thing that makes this phase of the diet different from the others is the "Special Forbidden Foods List," which is an auxiliary list with which you supplement the basic program.

Forbidden Foods for the Designer Style Dieter

Remember, the key to the Forbidden Foods phase of the diet (to be followed only during menstruation) is to eat

---

LOTS OF CARBOHYDRATES AND PROTEIN
and some fat

Following is the Advantage Food Group list for the Forbidden Foods phase of the Woman's Advantage Diet. Remember, you can eat any of the foods listed below according to the guidelines described in the Advantage Food Plan for Forbidden Foods, which follows the list. (Snack foods are listed in *italics*.)

FRUITS

acerola (any kind)
apple (any kind)
apricot (any kind)
avocado (any kind)
banana
berry
  blackberry
  blueberry
  boysenberry
  cranberry
  dewberry
  elderberry
  huckleberry
  lingonberry
  mulberry
  raspberry
  strawberry
carambola
cherimoya
cherry (any kind)
dried fruit
  apple
  apricot
  banana
  date
  orange
  pineapple
  prune
feijoa
fig
genipap
grape (any kind)
grapefruit
guava

kiwi
kumquat
lemon
lime
loquat
lychee
mango
mangosteen
medlar
melon
  cantaloupe
  casaba
  Crenshaw
  honeydew
  Persian
  watermelon
nectarine
orange (any kind)
papaya
passion fruit
pawpaw
peach (any kind)
pear (any kind)
persimmon
pineapple
plantain
plum (any kind)
pomegranate
prickly pear
quince
sapodilla
tamarind
tangelo (any kind)
tangerine (any kind)
ugli fruit

VEGETABLES

alfalfa sprouts
anise
artichoke
arugula
asparagus
bamboo shoots
basil
bean sprout
beets
broccoli
Brussels sprout
cabbage
  Chinese
  green
  red
cardoon
carrot
cassava
cauliflower
celeriac
celery
cilantro
collard
cucumber
dandelion
dill
eggplant
endive
escarole
fennel
fiddlehead
garlic
ginger
green peas
heart of palm
hot pepper (any kind)
jicama

kale
kohlrabi
leek
legume
  adzuki bean
  black or turtle bean
  black-eyed pea
  carob
  chickpea
  cranberry bean
  fava bean
  garbanzo
  great northern bean
  green bean
  kidney bean
  lentil
  lima bean
  marrow bean
  miso
  mung bean
  navy bean
  pea bean
  pink bean
  pinto bean
  red bean
  split pea
  tofu (soybean)
lettuce (any kind)
lotus
mushroom
mustard green
okra
onion (any kind)
parsley
parsnip
pea
potato (any kind)

VEGETABLES *(cont.)*

radish
rhubarb
rutabaga
salsify
savoy cabbage
scallion
sea vegetable
  arami
  dulse
  hijiki
  nori
  wakame
snow pea
sorrel
spinach
squash
  acorn
  butternut

hubbard
long cocozelle
pumpkin
yellow crookneck
yellow straightneck
zucchini
sweet pepper
  green
  red
  yellow
sweet potato
Swiss chard
tomato
truffle
turnip
watercress
yam

GRAINS AND GRAIN PRODUCTS

barley
buckwheat (not a true grain)
cereal
  All-Bran, original
  All-Bran, with extra fiber
  barley
  Bran Buds
  Bran Chex
  bran flakes
  Corn Chex
  corn flakes
  Cream of Rice
  Cream of Wheat
  Crispix
  Crispy Wheats 'n Raisins
  Double Chex

Fiber One
Fruit & Fibre
grits
Just Right
Life
Müeslix Bran
Nutri-Grain, biscuits
Nutri-Grain, corn
Nutri-Grain, nuggets
Nutri-Grain, wheat
oat bran
oatmeal
100% Bran
Product 19
puffed rice
puffed wheat

Quaker Oat Squares
raisin bran
Rice Krispies
shredded wheat
Shredded Wheat 'n Bran
Special K
Team
Total Wheat Bran
Total
Weetabix
Wheat Chex
Wheatena
wheat germ
Wheaties
corn
corn starch
millet
oat
pasta
  capellini
  cellophane noodle
  couscous
  egg noodle
  elbow
  farfalle
  fedelini
  fettucine
  fusilli
  gnocchi
  lasagna

  linguine
  lo mein noodles
  macaroni
  macaroni bow
  manicotti
  orzo
  ravioli
  rigatoni
  rotini
  shell
  spaghetti
  spaghettini
  tortellini
  vermicelli
  ziti
popcorn
quinoa
rice
  brown
  cake
  long grain
  white
  wild
rye
sorghum
triticale
wheat
  berry
  bulgur
  cracked

BREADS AND BREAD PRODUCTS

bagel
  egg
  fruit
  nut
  plain
  poppy seed
  pumpernickel
  raisin
  rye
  whole wheat
bread and rolls
  black
  bran
  cracked wheat
  French
  Italian
  oatmeal
  pita
  pumpernickel
  rye
  white enriched
  whole wheat

cracker
  Finn Crisp
  Norwegian Crisp
  Ry-Krisp
muffin
  bran
  corn
  English
  granola
  nut
  plain
  raisin
  whole wheat
pancake and French toast
  buttermilk
  cornmeal
  fruit
  oatmeal
  plain
  whole wheat

DAIRY PRODUCTS

buttermilk
cheese
  Camembert
  farmer
  feta
  low fat, low sodium
    American
  low fat cottage
  low fat Monterey Jack

  low fat mozzarella
  low fat ricotta
  Neufchâtel
  Parmesan
  Romano
frozen skim milk
low fat sour cream
low fat yogurt

MEATS, POULTRY AND EGGS

egg

egg substitute

meat

  beef

  goat

  hare

  lamb

  pork

  veal

poultry

  chicken

  Cornish hen

  grouse

  partridge

  pheasant

  quail

  turkey

reduced calorie gelatin

    (animal protein based)

FISH AND SEAFOOD

fish

  Atlantic sturgeon

  bass

  brook trout

  cod

  crevalle jack

  croaker

  cusk

  drum

  flounder

  grouper

  haddock

  hake

  halibut

  lingcod

  mahimahi

  monkfish

  orange roughy

  perch

  pike

  pollock

  red snapper

  rockfish

  sauger

  shark

  smelt

  sole

  tilefish

  tuna

  whiting

  yellowtail snapper

seafood

  abalone

  clam

  crab

  crayfish

  langostino

  lobster

  mussel

  octopus

  oyster

  scallop

  shrimp

  squid

SOUPS

barley
bean
beef
   broth
   consommé
   noodle
borscht
chicken
   broth
   consommé
   gumbo
   mushroom
   noodle
   rice
egg drop
fish

gazpacho
leek
lentil
Manhattan clam chowder
minestrone
mushroom
onion
Oriental noodle
split-pea
tomato
turkey noodle
vegetable
   bean
   beef
won ton

CONDIMENTS

chocolate extract
chutney (avoid any type with
    added sugar, dried fruits
    or nuts)
cranberry sauce (avoid any
    type with added sugar)
Cumberland sauce
honey
hot pepper sauce
   chili
   harissa
   horseradish
   Indian
   Mexican salsa
   nam prik
   sambal
   Tabasco
   wasabi

jelly (avoid any type with
    added sugar)
ketchup
maple syrup (reduced calorie
    brands)
mayonnaise (reduced calorie
    brands)
miso
mustard (avoid any sweet
    type)
relish
soy sauce
steak sauce
tamari sauce
teriyaki sauce
vanilla extract
vinegar
Worcestershire sauce

FATS

dairy
  butter
oils
  corn
  cottonseed
  olive

peanut
rapeseed
safflower
sunflower
vegetable
  margarine

SPICES AND HERBS

allspice
almond
angelica
anise
arrowroot
basil
bay leaf
bergamot
black pepper
caper
caraway
cardamon
cayenne pepper
chervil
chive
cinnamon
clove
coriander
cream of tartar
cumin
curry
dill
fennel
fenugreek
garlic
ginger

hyssop
licorice
mace
marjoram
melilot
mint
mugwort
mustard
nasturtium
nutmeg
oregano
paprika
parsley
peppermint
purslane
rocambole
rocket
rosemary
rue
saffron
sage
salad burnet
savory
scurvy grass
sesame
sorrel

SPICES AND HERBS *(cont.)*

star anise	tarragon
stonecrop	thyme
sweet cicely	turmeric
tamarind	vanilla
tansy	violet

ALCOHOL
(recommended for cooking purposes only)

beer	sherry
brandy	wine

BEVERAGES

apple juice	mineral water
carbonated water	orange juice
coffee	reduced calorie hot
cranberry juice	chocolate
decaffeinated coffee	skim milk
diet soda	tangelo juice
grape juice	tangerine juice
grapefruit juice	tea
herbal tea	tomato juice
juice spritzer	vegetable juice
lemonade	water

The Food Plans

(Remember to check the size of all portions, using the guidelines in Chapter 3).

THE ADVANTAGE FOOD PLAN
FOR THE FORBIDDEN FOODS
BREAKFAST
ALLOWS YOU TO HAVE

♀ **As a main dish, one of these:** one serving of cereal, muffin, bagel, pancake or French toast;

or, two servings of bread;

or, one serving of bread with one egg—*with*

♀ **As a side dish:** one serving of fruit, fruit juice, vegetable juice, skim milk,

or, reduced calorie hot chocolate—*with*

♀ **As a beverage:** coffee or tea.

THE ADVANTAGE FOOD PLAN
FOR THE FORBIDDEN FOODS
LUNCH
ALLOWS YOU TO HAVE

♀ **As a main dish, one of these:** a sandwich on any of the breads with meat, poultry, fish, seafood, cheese, eggs or tofu;

or, a salad with any of the vegetables and cheese, meat, poultry, fish, seafood, eggs or tofu;

or, a salad with any of the vegetables and a bowl of soup;

or, a bowl of bean soup with a serving of bread—*with*

♀ **As a dessert:** one serving of fruit—*with*

♀ **As a beverage:** coffee, decaffeinated coffee, tea, herbal tea, diet soda, juice spritzer, carbonated water, mineral water, or water.

THE ADVANTAGE FOOD PLAN
FOR THE FORBIDDEN FOODS
DINNER
ALLOWS YOU TO HAVE

♀ **As a main dish, one of these:** one serving of meat, poultry, fish, seafood or tofu;

or, one serving of pasta with a meat, poultry, fish, seafood or vegetable sauce—*with*

♀ **As a side dish one of these:** two servings of vegetables;

or, one serving of vegetable with a salad;

or, one serving of potato, rice or grain;

or, one small serving of pasta (only with meat, poultry, fish, seafood or tofu as a main dish)—*with*

♀ **As a dessert:** one serving of fruit—*with*

♀ **As a beverage:** decaffeinated coffee, herbal tea, diet soda, juice spritzer, carbonated water, mineral water, or water.

THE ADVANTAGE FOOD PLAN
FOR THE FORBIDDEN FOODS
SNACK
ALLOWS YOU TO HAVE

♀ One or two items as often as twice a day from any of the foods that are in italics. If you're not hungry, it's not necessary to eat a snack.

A Few Rules

We've gone over portion sizes and measurements in Chapter 3 so I'm not going to repeat them here. But because this is the Forbidden Foods phase, and it contains a very special list of foods, I do want to repeat a few cautionary words.

Again, the important word to remember is the word *one*. You may have *one* scoop of ice cream, *one* slice of cake, *one* piece of pie, *one* ice cream bar, *one* serving of French Fries, *one* doughnut, *one* brownie.

You get the idea. Indulge in *what* you eat, rather than in *how much* you eat. The diet will work better for you, and you will feel better if you don't overeat.

Special Forbidden Foods List

This is a very special list of foods that can be used only during the Forbidden Foods phase of your cycle and *only* every other day.

Don't overdo! Remember, these foods should not be in addition to your regular menu but *part* of it. Consult the menu plan for a guide as to when and how often you may indulge in the following Forbidden Foods:

1	slice bacon
1	12-ounce bottle of reduced calorie beer
1	brownie
1	slice cake
2	small cookies
1	croissant
1	cupcake
1	doughnut
1	serving (about 2 ounces) french fries
½	fried chicken breast
1	serving (about 2 ounces) fried clams
1	scoop ice cream
1	ice cream bar
1	ounce liqueur
1	pickle
1	slice pie
½	cup pudding
1	link breakfast sausage
1	waffle
1	glass (about 3½ ounces) wine

Forbidden Foods for the Menu Style Dieter

Your menstrual phase can vary from one to eight days. I have provided menus for six days because that will be enough for most of you. Those of you with shorter periods can simply use the appropriate number of days from the six day plan. For those of you with longer periods, I recommend that you repeat your two favorite days from the six day plan. Choose the days that look best to you; however, whether your period is shorter or longer than six days, please remember that you are allowed only one of the foods in the Special Forbidden Foods list every other day. So, don't cheat and pick two Forbidden Food treat days in a row. Be sure you alternate so that you have no more than one Forbidden Food snack, entree or beverage every two days.

What Does the Number Mean?

The number in parentheses following some items points you to the recipe for that entry, which is included in the back of the book.

DAY 1 Forbidden Foods

BREAKFAST
Cheese Omelet (6)
Orange juice
Coffee or tea

SNACK
Popcorn

LUNCH
Open Faced Turkey Sandwich (39)
Cucumber Rounds (162)
Frosty Spiced Tea (230)

SNACK
Grapes

DINNER
Roast beef
Broccoli in Cheese Sauce (125)
Forbidden food treat: strawberry ice cream
Pineapple Mint Spritzer (243)

DAY 2 Forbidden Foods

BREAKFAST
Low fat yogurt
Strawberries
Coffee or tea

SNACK
Plum

LUNCH
Warm Acapulco Salad (58)
Watermelon Cooler (249)

SNACK
Carrots

DINNER
Lamb Curry (86)
Baked Carrots (120)
Baked Fruit Cup (188)
Orange flavored carbonated water

DAY 3 Forbidden Foods

BREAKFAST
Banana Nut Muffin (4)
Cantaloupe
Skim Milk
Coffee or tea

SNACK
Cucumber

LUNCH
Cheese and Sprout Pitas (26)
Diet soda

SNACK
>   *Orange*

DINNER
>   Chicken Breast with Vegetables in Cheese Sauce
>   (71)
>   Zucchini and Carrots Julienne (148)
>   *Forbidden food treat:* chocolate cream pie
>   Iced herbal tea

DAY 4 Forbidden Foods

BREAKFAST
>   Soft boiled egg
>   Canadian bacon
>   English muffin
>   Coffee or tea

SNACK
>   *Kiwi*

LUNCH
>   Minestrone Soup (112)
>   Cherry tomatoes
>   Hard roll
>   Diet soda

SNACK
>   *Pear*

DINNER
>   Halibut steak
>   Artichokes in Mustard Sauce (119)
>   Mushroom Tossed Greens (170)
>   Vegetable juice

DAY 5 Forbidden Foods

BREAKFAST
Corn cereal
Blueberries
Reduced calorie cranberry juice
Coffee or tea

SNACK
Radishes

LUNCH
Vegetarian Pizza (57)
Celery Boats (156)
Skim milk

SNACK
Cantaloupe

DINNER
Sweet and Sour Vegetables (96)
Grilled Mushrooms (133)
Herbed Brussel Sprouts (134)
Blueberry Cloud (191)
Forbidden food treat: reduced calorie beer

DAY 6 Forbidden Foods

BREAKFAST
Oatmeal
Honeydew melon
Coffee or tea

SNACK
Tangelo

LUNCH
Ham and Tomato Pita (38)
Herbal tea

SNACK
> *Carrots*

DINNER
> Pork chop
> Potato au Gratin (138)
> Cauliflower Salad (155)
> Applesauce Mousse (186)
> Skim milk

Some Questions and Answers

I try to cover every aspect of the Forbidden Foods program when I explain it to my patients, but there are always questions. Here are the questions I hear most often, and my answers.

Q What should I do if my period goes on for more than six days?

A Just stay with the Forbidden Foods program until your period ends. But be sure not to have more than one food from the Special Forbidden Food list every other day.

Q I hate breakfast. Do I have to eat breakfast on the Forbidden Foods program?

A Maybe you've never given breakfast a fair chance. Try again. French toast? Yum! A banana nut muffin? Wow! Even if that doesn't do it for you, try to have one breakfast food before lunch, or you may be too hungry to stay on the diet.

Q I usually go to lunch at 2:00 P.M. Is that too late to follow the lunch menu?

A Not at all. You probably have dinner at a later hour, too. The time when you eat the meals on the Forbidden Foods menu plan should not interfere with the benefits of the diet.

Q I have an early breakfast, and then I'm starving way before lunch. Is there anything I can eat in the middle of the morning?

A No one has to starve on this diet. Have your snack when you get those midmorning hunger pangs.

Q How much meat, cheese or tuna should I put in my lunchtime salads?

A A salad is filling, and you won't want more than two ounces of meat, fish, or cheese to create a satisfying meal.

Q You promised that I could pamper myself when I got to the Forbidden Foods phase. May I use whole milk or half-and-half in my coffee?

A I'd always prefer it if you used skim milk, but if you truly love whole milk or half-and-half in your coffee or tea, this is the time to have it. Be sure not to use too much. Don't turn your coffee white with it. A tablespoon is more than enough. And remember, this indulgence in whole milk or half-and-half should be considered your Forbidden Food treat for the day.

Q I love the Forbidden Foods phase, but I just need more food than you recommend. Is there anything else I can eat and still have the diet work for me?

A Yes, don't despair; add more steamed vegetables and salads with reduced calorie dressing to the Forbidden Foods program. An extra portion of fresh fruit each day will also help you. (You can safely make additions of this kind during any phase of the diet.)

Q I'd like to change things around on the Forbidden Foods menu plan—have the lunch from Day One on Day Two, and move the dinner from Day Two to Day Three. May I do that?

A The menu plans are there to make dieting easier for you. You may create your own menus by using the Advantage Food lists and Advantage Food Plans. That's best if you're a Designer Style Dieter. But if you're a Menu Style Dieter, don't make any changes. You'll find yourself eating two dinners on one day, and two lunches on another, and the Forbidden Food program won't work for you.

Q I've just learned about the Woman's Advantage Diet, and I'm eager to start. I'm in my menstrual phase, and I want to know why I can't go on the Forbidden Foods program right away.

A The Forbidden Foods program is a reward diet, and comes along after you've followed the diet through one or more of the phases. You have two choices. You can wait until your menstrual phase has ended, and go right into the postmenstrual eating program, Fabulous Fruits and Vegetables. Or, if you want to start immediately, use the premenstrual phase eating program, Protein Power, until your period ends, and then continue with the postmenstrual plan.

5 FABULOUS FRUITS AND VEGETABLES

This phase of the Woman's Advantage Diet is the favorite of my patients who love vegetables and fruits. Most fruits and vegetables are low in fat and calories, so this is a time when you can enjoy especially filling, satisfying meals. Remember, no matter how much you love fruits and vegetables, you should use this eating plan only during your postmenstrual phase. (See Chapter 2 to find out how to determine the four phases of your menstrual cycle.)

It's High Fiber Time

This is the time of month when your appetite suppressing estrogens are low, and you need something else to keep you from feeling hungry. High fiber carbohydrates are the answer. In addition to fruits and vegetables, high fiber grains are recommended. You can't eat them in the same bulk as you can fruits and vegetables, but you'll find they're a great, natural, healthy way to satisfy your appetite.

But It's Not All High Fiber

For all of you who regard vegetables as something your mother made you eat, and you don't want to eat them anymore, don't get worried. Vegetables and fruits are not all that you'll find on this part of the Woman's Advantage Diet. In addition to the grains mentioned above, there's also a moderate amount of protein prescribed during this phase of the diet. Balance is an important part of every aspect of the Woman's Advantage Diet.

And even if you don't think you're especially passionate about vegetables and fruits right now, you may change your mind once you try the Fabulous Fruits and Vegetables program. The amounts of vegetables that you are allowed to eat means that you will never feel hungry, and that's a great plus in any diet.

Fabulous Fruits and Vegetables Diet for the Designer Style Dieter

Remember, the key to the Fabulous Fruits and Vegetables eating program (to be followed only during postmenstruation) is to eat

---

LOTS OF HIGH FIBER CARBOHYDRATES
with some protein
(and low fat)

Following is the Advantage Food Group list for Fabulous Fruits and Vegetables. Remember, you can eat only the foods listed below, and you must do so according to the guidelines described in the Advantage Food Plan, which follows the list. (Snack foods are listed in *italics*.)

FRUITS

apple (any kind)   elderberry
apricot (any kind)   huckleberry
avocado (any kind)   lingonberry
banana   mulberry
berry   raspberry
  blackberry   strawberry
  blueberry   carambola
  boysenberry   cherimoya
  cranberry   feijoa
  dewberry   fig

guava
kiwi
kumquat
lemon
loquat
mango
medlar
nectarine
orange (any kind)

passion fruit
pear (any kind)
plantain
pomegranates
prickly pear
prune
sapodilla
tamarind

VEGETABLES

alfalfa sprouts
artichoke
bamboo shoots
bean sprout
beet
broccoli
Brussels sprout
cabbage
  Chinese
  green
  red
cardoon
carrot
cassava
collard
cucumber
eggplant
ginger root
green peas
heart of palm
jicama
kohlrabi
legume
  adzuki bean
  black or turtle bean
  black-eyed pea
  carob

chickpea
cranberry bean
fava bean
garbanzo
great northern bean
green bean
kidney bean
lentil
lima bean
marrow bean
mung bean
navy bean
pea bean
pink bean
pinto bean
red bean
split pea
tofu (soybean)
lettuce (any kind)
okra
onions (any kind)
parsnips
potato (any kind)
rhubarb
rutabaga
salsify
savoy cabbage

VEGETABLES *(cont.)*

scallions	butternut
sea vegetable	hubbard
arami	long cocozelle
dulse	pumpkin
hijiki	yellow crookneck
nori	yellow straightneck
wakame	zucchini
snow peas	sweet potato
spinach	tomato
squash	turnip
acorn	yam

GRAINS AND GRAIN PRODUCTS

barley	Quaker Oat Squares
buckwheat (not a true grain)	raisin bran
cereal	shredded wheat
All-Bran, original	Shredded Wheat 'n Bran
All-Bran, with extra fiber	Weetabix
barley	corn
Bran Buds	corn starch
Bran Chex	millet
bran flakes	oat
Fiber One	quinoa
Fruit & Fibre	rye
Müeslix Bran	sorghum
Nutri-Grain, biscuit	triticale
Nutri-Grain, corn	wheat
Nutri-Grain, nuggets	berry
Nutri-Grain, wheat	bulgur
oat bran	cracked
100% Bran	

BREAD AND BREAD PRODUCTS

bagel
  poppy seed
  pumpernickel
  raisin
  rye
  whole wheat
bread
  black
  bran
  cracked wheat
  oatmeal
  rye
  whole wheat
cracker
  Finn Crisp
  Ry-Krisp

muffin
  bran
  corn
  granola
  raisin
  whole wheat
pancake and French toast
  buckwheat
  whole-wheat
roll and bun
  cracked wheat
  whole-wheat

DAIRY PRODUCTS

buttermilk
cheese
  Camembert
  farmer
  feta
  low fat cottage
  low fat, low sodium
    American
  low fat Monterey Jack

  low fat mozzarella
  low fat ricotta
  Neufchâtel
  Parmesan
  Romano
frozen skim milk
low fat sour cream
low fat yogurt

MEAT, POULTRY AND EGGS

egg
egg substitute
meat
  beef
  goat
  hare
  lamb
  pork
  veal
poultry
  chicken

Cornish hen
grouse
partridge
pheasant
quail
turkey
reduced calorie gelatin
    (animal protein based)

FISH AND SEAFOOD

fish
  Atlantic sturgeon
  bass
  brook trout
  cod
  crevalle jack
  croaker
  cusk
  drum
  flounder
  grouper
  haddock
  hake
  halibut
  lingcod
  mahimahi
  monkfish
  orange roughy
  perch
  pike
  pollock
  red snapper

  rockfish
  sauger
  shark
  smelt
  sole
  tilefish
  tuna
  whiting
  yellowtail snapper
seafood
  abalone
  clam
  crab
  crayfish
  langostino
  lobster
  mussel
  octopus
  oyster
  scallop
  shrimp
  squid

SOUPS

barley
beef broth
borscht
chicken broth
gazpacho
leek
minestrone
mushroom
potato
turkey noodle
vegetable
won ton

CONDIMENTS

chocolate extract
chutney (avoid any type with
    added sugar, dried fruits
    or nuts)
cranberry sauce (avoid any
    type with added sugar)
Cumberland sauce
honey
hot pepper sauce
  chili
  harissa
  horseradish
  Indian
  Mexican salsa
  nam prik
  sambal
  Tabasco
  wasabi
jelly (avoid any type with
    added sugar)
ketchup
maple syrup (reduced calorie
    brands)
mayonnaise (reduced calorie
    brands)
miso
mustard (avoid any sweet
    type)
relish
soy sauce
steak sauce
tamari sauce
teriyaki sauce
vanilla extract
vinegar
Worcestershire sauce

FATS

dairy
  butter
oil
  corn
  cottonseed
  olive
  peanut
  rapeseed
  safflower
  sunflower
vegetable
  margarine

SPICES AND HERBS

allspice
almond
angelica
anise
arrowroot
basil
bay leaf
bergamot
black pepper
caper
caraway
cardamon
cayenne pepper
chervil
chive
cinnamon
clove
coriander
cream of tartar
cumin
curry
dill
fennel
fenugreek
garlic
ginger
hyssop
licorice
mace
marjoram
melilot

mint
mugwort
mustard
nasturtium
nutmeg
oregano
paprika
parsley
peppermint
purslane
rocambole
rocket
rosemary
rue
saffron
sage
salad burnet
savory
scurvy grass
sesame
sorrel
star anise
stonecrop
sweet cicely
tamarind
tansy
tarragon
thyme
turmeric
vanilla
violet

ALCOHOL
(recommended for cooking purposes only)

beer	sherry
brandy	wine

BEVERAGES

apple juice	mineral water
carbonated water	orange juice
coffee	reduced calorie hot
cranberry juice	chocolate
decaffeinated coffee	skim milk
diet soda	tangelo juice
grape juice	tangerine juice
grapefruit juice	tea
herbal tea	tomato juice
juice spritzer	vegetable juice
lemonade	water

The Food Plans

(Remember to check the size of all portions, using the guidelines in Chapter 3.)

THE ADVANTAGE FOOD PLAN
FOR THE FABULOUS FRUITS AND VEGETABLES
BREAKFAST
ALLOWS YOU TO HAVE

♀ **As a main dish, one of these:** one serving of cereal, muffin, bagel, pancake or French Toast;

or, two servings of bread—*with*

♀ **As a side dish:** one serving of fruit, fruit juice, vegetable juice, skim milk or reduced calorie hot chocolate—*with*

♀ **As a beverage:** coffee or tea.

THE ADVANTAGE FOOD PLAN
FOR THE FABULOUS FRUITS AND VEGETABLES
LUNCH
ALLOWS YOU TO HAVE

♀ **As a main dish, one of these:** a sandwich on any of the breads with any of the vegetables;

or, a salad with any of the vegetables and a bowl of soup— *with*

♀ **As a dessert:** one serving of fruit—*with*

♀ **As a beverage:** coffee, decaffeinated coffee, tea, herbal tea, diet soda, juice spritzer, carbonated water, mineral water, or water.

THE ADVANTAGE FOOD PLAN
FOR THE FABULOUS FRUITS AND VEGETABLES
DINNER
ALLOWS YOU TO HAVE

♀ **As a main dish:** one serving of meat, poultry, fish or seafood—*with*

♀ **As a side dish, one of these:** two servings of vegetables;

or, one serving of vegetables with a salad;

or, one serving of potato or grain—*with*

♀ **As a dessert:** one serving of fruit—*with*

♀ **As a beverage:** decaffeinated coffee, herbal tea, diet soda, juice spritzer, carbonated water, mineral water, or water.

THE ADVANTAGE FOOD PLAN
FOR THE FABULOUS FRUITS AND VEGETABLES
SNACK
ALLOWS YOU TO HAVE

♀ One or two items as often as twice a day from any of the foods that are in italics. If you're not hungry, it's not necessary to eat a snack.

A Few Rules

As you can see, the emphasis during the Fabulous Fruits and Vegetables phase of the Woman's Advantage Diet is, indeed, on fruits, vegetables and grains. Keep your portions of fish, meat and poultry to a minimum. What do I mean by that? I don't mean that a single serving portion should be extra small. You may have four to six ounces as a main dish, as discussed in Chapter 3. However, the in Chapter 3. However, the important thing to remember during the Fabulous Fruits and Vegetables phase of the diet is that you should only have a protein like seafood, fish, meat, poultry or cheese once a day. That means if you have a chicken sandwich for lunch, don't have lamb chops for dinner. But if you have a salad for lunch, you should feel free to have some roast beef for dinner. Just limit yourself to one serving of fish, meat or poultry every day.

Fabulous Fruits and Vegetables for the Menu Style Dieter

As we saw in Chapter 2, most of you have a postmenstrual phase that is between one and twenty days long. I've provided seven days of menus because for the vast majority of you that will be enough. If your postmenstrual phase is shorter than seven days, just choose the days with menus that look best to you. If you have more than seven days in this phase, just repeat the menu cycle as long as you need to. If that becomes tiresome, take a look at the Designer Style Dieter's Advantage Food Groups and Food Plans for ideas about how to add a little variety to your schedule.

A word of caution—don't start mixing and matching days. For instance, if breakfast on Day Three looks good to you and lunch on Day Six looks great, too, you may be tempted to eat them both on one day. Don't do it. You'll end up muddling things so completely that the diet might not work for you. If you need additional days, select one specific day and use all the menus listed for it. If you turn to the Designer Style Dieter's information for some variety, be careful to pick only equivalent items. For instance, if you don't feel like red snapper for dinner on Day Five, be sure to check the Advantage Food Plan for Fabulous Fruits and Vegetables to see what an appropriate substitute for that specific item is.

What Does the Number Mean?

The number in parentheses following some item points you to the recipe for that entry which is included in the back of the book.

DAY 1 Fabulous Fruits and Vegetables

BREAKFAST
New England Buckwheat Pancakes (15)
Grapefruit juice
Coffee or tea

SNACK
Orange

LUNCH
Crispy Spinach Salad (159)
Neufchâtel cheese
Mint Iced Tea (239)

SNACK
Rice cake

DINNER
Chicken Ratatouille (74)
Flamed Strawberries (197)
Gingerade (231)

DAY 2 Fabulous Fruits and Vegetables

BREAKFAST
Bran Muffin (5)
Morning Berry Mix (14)
Coffee or tea

SNACK
Apple

LUNCH
Black Bean Soup (106)
Boston Brown Bread (23)
Tomato juice

SNACK
Apricot

DINNER
Lamb Chops Diablo (85)
Okra Salad (172)
Nectarine
Carrot Lime Drink (226)

DAY 3 Fabulous Fruits and Vegetables

BREAKFAST
Baked Cinnamon Apple (3)
Whole wheat toast
Reduced calorie cranberry juice

SNACK
Carrots

LUNCH
Pizza Sandwich (42)
Iced coffee

SNACK
Kiwi

DINNER
Sukiyaki (95)
Bean sprouts
Baked Banana (187)
Iced herbal tea

DAY 4 Fabulous Fruits and Vegetables

BREAKFAST
Bran cereal
Orange juice
Coffee or tea

SNACK
Peach

LUNCH
Tuna and Bean Salad (51)
Skim milk

SNACK
Ry-Krisp crackers

DINNER
Pasta Primavera (89)
Broccoli Vinaigrette (154)
Applesauce Sorbet (185)
Mineral water

DAY 5 Fabulous Fruits and Vegetables

BREAKFAST
Raisin bagel
Pomegranate
Coffee or tea

SNACK
Figs

LUNCH
Fruit Salad Delight (35)
Lemonade (237)

SNACK
Broccoli

DINNER
Red snapper
Country Vegetables (129)
Corn on the cob
Orange Sorbet (210)
Iced herbal tea

DAY 6 Fabulous Fruits and Vegetables

BREAKFAST
Shredded wheat
Prunes
Coffee or tea

SNACK
Apricots

LUNCH
Four Bean Salad (164)
Piña Colada Spritzer (242)

SNACK
Finn Crisp crackers

DINNER
Moussaka (88)
Raphael's Salad (174)
Citrus Delight (195)
Lemon flavored carbonated water

DAY 7 Fabulous Fruits and Vegetables

BREAKFAST
Oatmeal
Blueberries
Skim milk

SNACK
Apple

LUNCH
    Turkey Salad (56)
    Cracked wheat bread
    Raspberry flavored carbonated water

SNACK
    Orange

DINNER
    Barley Soup (105)
    Vegetarian Beans in Spicy Tomato Sauce (101)
    Melon Rings with Strawberries (207)
    Grapefruit Sling (233)

Questions and Answers

Here are the questions most frequently asked by my patients when they're on the Fabulous Fruits and Vegetables program during the postmenstrual phase of their cycles.

Q Is it possible to eat too much fiber?

A At this time, nutritionists have not decided on the absolute upper limit for fiber intake. In any case, the amount of fiber in the Fabulous Fruits and Vegetables diet doesn't approach a risk level and is both adequate and safe. However, if you have a health program that involves limiting your intake of fiber, talk to your doctor before starting on this, or any other diet.

Q There's a lot of cereal on this part of the Woman's Advantage Diet. That's all right, but may I put sugar on my cereal?

A Absolutely not. Use only artificial sweeteners on your cereal. Or, you might also try some cinnamon on your cereal; many of my patients find it's all the sweetening that cereal needs.

Q You say it's all right to put skim milk in my coffee. How about whole milk or a little half-and-half?

A This postmenstrual phase of your cycle calls for low fat, so don't use anything but skim milk. But don't worry, the Forbidden Foods phase will come around again and then you'll be able to indulge in whole milk or half-and-half.

Q Instead of tuna salad for lunch, I'd just like to use the tuna straight from the can without any dressing. Is that all right?

A That's fine. Use tuna packed in water, as we discussed in Chapter 3. Feel free to serve it on some lettuce, and have it with chopped celery and grated carrot.

Q I'm really not a cereal lover. May I have one of the breads you've listed, in place of a bowl of cereal?

A Yes, you may have any of the breads in place of cereal for breakfast. Take a look at the Advantage Food Group Plan for Fabulous Fruits and Vegetables to be sure you're making an appropriate substitution.

Q You have red snapper listed for one of the dinners. What if I can't find red snapper at the fish market?

A You may substitute any fresh fish on the Advantage Food Group list for the red snapper. Just make sure to broil or grill the fish. Don't fry or sauté it. (Again, consult the Designer Style Dieter's information to be sure you're making an appropriate substitution.)

Q I love your Fabulous Fruits and Vegetables program. May I stay on it past my postmenstrual phase?

A I'm glad you like this phase of the diet so much but, no, you can't stay on it past postmenstruation. It won't help you lose weight to do so. Go on to the next phase of the diet; you'll like that, too.

PASTA PLUS

The ovulation phase of your cycle is the time when your body receives the greatest surge of estrogen. Natural estrogen—the kind your body manufactures—acts to decrease appetite.[1] That's the key to losing weight during this phase of the Woman's Advantage Diet. If you follow the program, you will find you are simply not hungry enough during this time of the month to eat all your snack options or even finish every meal. Obviously, for the diet to work you must take advantage of your decreased appetite. *Don't overeat.* If you're careful to eat only when you're hungry—and stop eating when your appetite is satisfied—you'll find it easy to eat less and lose weight during this phase of your cycle.

But, remember, high fiber carbohydrates can act to curtail the effectiveness of estrogen. That's why the ovulatory eating plan, called Pasta Plus, emphasizes low fiber foods.

Why It's Called Pasta Plus

Because this phase of the diet is founded on low fiber carbohydrates, it emphasizes pasta dishes. My patients are so delighted to be able to enjoy their favorite pasta dishes that they've dubbed it Pasta Plus.

Of course, pasta won't be all you'll eat. During this phase of your cycle you'll also enjoy meals that contain other low fiber carbohydrates, as well as moderate amounts of protein.

How Many Days on the Pasta Plus Program?

The length of ovulation is always six days, and after completing your postmenstrual phase you won't have to consult any tables or charts. (See Chapter 2 for more information about how to determine the lengths of the four phases of your menstrual cycle.) Just stay on the Pasta Plus program for six days. You'll find it as enjoyable as the high fiber diet that you just completed.

Pasta Plus Diet for the Designer Style Dieter

Remember, the key to the Pasta Plus eating program (to be followed only during ovulation) is to eat

LOTS OF LOW FIBER CARBOHYDRATES
with protein
(and low fat)

Following is the Advantage Food Group list for Pasta Plus. Remember, you can eat only the foods listed below, and you must do so according to the guidelines described in the Advantage Food Plan, which follows the list. (Snack foods are in *italics*.)

FRUITS

acerola (any kind)
cherry (any kind)
genipap
grapes (any kind)
grapefruit
lime
lychee
mangosteen
melon
  cantaloupe
  casaba
  Crenshaw

honeydew
Persian
watermelon
papaya
pawpaw
peach (any kind, peeled)
persimmon
pineapple
plum (any kind)
tangelo (any kind)
tangerine (any kind)
ugli fruit

VEGETABLES

anise
arugula
asparagus
basil
cauliflower
celeriac
celery
cilantro
cucumber (peeled)
dandelions
dill
endive
escarole
fennel
fiddlehead
garlic
hot pepper (any kind)
kale

leek
lettuce (any kind)
lotus
mushroom
mustard green
onion (any kind)
parsley
radish
scallion
sorrel
sweet pepper
   green
   red
   yellow
Swiss chard
tomato
truffle
watercress

GRAINS AND GRAIN PRODUCTS

cereal
   Corn Chex
   corn flakes
   Cream of Rice
   Cream of Wheat
   Crispix
   Crispy Wheats 'n Raisins
   Double Chex
   grits
   Just Right
   Life
   oatmeal
   Product 19
   puffed rice
   puffed wheat

   Rice Krispies
   Special K
   Team
   Total
   Wheat Chex
   Wheatena
   wheat germ
   Wheaties
pasta (refined flour varieties)
   capellini
   cellophane noodle
   couscous
   egg noodle
   elbow
   farfalle

GRAINS AND GRAIN PRODUCTS *(cont.)*

fedelini
fettucine
fusilli
gnocchi
lasagna
linguine
lo mein noodle
macaroni bow
manicotti
orzo
ravioli
rotini
shell

spaghetti
spaghettini
tortellini
vermicelli
ziti
popcorn
rice
  brown
  cake
  long grain
  white
  wild
wheat flour

BREADS AND BREAD PRODUCTS

bagel
  egg
  plain
bread
  French
  Italian
  pita
  white enriched

muffin
  English
  plain
pancake and French toast
  buttermilk
  plain
roll and bun
  plain

DAIRY PRODUCTS

buttermilk
cheese
  Camembert
  farmer
  feta
  low fat cottage
  low fat, low sodium
    American
  low fat Monterey Jack

  low fat mozzarella
  low fat ricotta
  Neufchâtel
  Parmesan
  Romano
frozen skim milk
low fat sour cream
low fat yogurt

MEATS, POULTRY AND EGGS

egg
egg substitute
meat
  beef
  goat
  hare
  lamb
  pork
  veal

poultry
  chicken
  Cornish hen
  grouse
  partridge
  pheasant
  quail
  turkey
reduced calorie gelatin
    (animal protein based)

FISH AND SEAFOOD

fish
  Atlantic sturgeon
  bass
  brook trout
  cod
  crevalle jack
  croaker
  cusk
  drum
  flounder
  grouper
  haddock
  hake
  halibut
  lingcod
  mahimahi
  monkfish
  orange roughy
  perch
  pike
  pollock
  red snapper

  rockfish
  sauger
  shark
  smelt
  sole
  tilefish
  tuna
  whiting
  yellowtail snapper
seafood
  abalone
  clam
  crab
  crayfish
  langostino
  lobster
  mussel
  octopus
  oyster
  scallop
  shrimp
  squid

SOUPS

asparagus
beef
  broth
  consommé
  noodle
  celery
chicken
  broth
  consommé
noodle
cucumber
egg drop
mushroom
onion
Oriental noodle
turkey noodle
won ton

CONDIMENTS

chocolate extract
chutney (avoid any type with added sugar, dried fruits or nuts)
cranberry sauce (avoid any type with added sugar)
Cumberland sauce
honey
hot pepper sauce
  chili
  harissa
  horseradish
  Indian
  Mexican salsa
  nam prik
  sambal
  Tabasco
  wasabi
jelly (avoid any type with added sugar)
ketchup
maple syrup (reduced calorie brands)
mayonnaise (reduced calorie brands)
miso
mustard (avoid any sweet type)
relish
soy sauce
steak sauce
tamari sauce
teriyaki sauce
vanilla extract
vinegar
Worcestershire sauce

FATS

dairy
  butter
oil
  corn
  cottonseed
  olive

peanut
rapeseed
safflower
sunflower
vegetable
  margarine

SPICES AND HERBS

allspice
almond
angelica
anise
arrowroot
basil
bay leaf
bergamot
black pepper
caper
caraway
cardamon
cayenne pepper
chervil
chive
cinnamon
clove
coriander
cream of tartar
cumin
curry
dill
fennel
fenugreek
garlic
ginger

hyssop
licorice
mace
marjoram
melilot
mint
mugwort
mustard
nasturtium
nutmeg
oregano
paprika
parsley
peppermint
purslane
rocambole
rocket
rosemary
rue
saffron
sage
salad burnet
savory
scurvy grass
sesame
sorrel

SPICES AND HERBS *(cont.)*

star anise	tarragon
stonecrop	thyme
sweet cicely	turmeric
tamarind	vanilla
tansy	violet

ALCOHOL
(recommended for cooking purposes only)

beer	sherry
brandy	wine

BEVERAGES

apple juice	mineral water
carbonated water	orange juice
coffee	reduced calorie hot
cranberry juice	chocolate
decaffeinated coffee	skim milk
diet soda	tangelo juice
grape juice	tangerine juice
grapefruit juice	tea
herbal tea	tomato juice
juice spritzer	water
lemonade	

The Food Plans

(Remember to check the size of all portions, using the guidelines in Chapter 3.)

THE ADVANTAGE FOOD PLAN
FOR THE PASTA PLUS
BREAKFAST
ALLOWS YOU TO HAVE

♀ **As a main dish, one of these:** one serving of cereal, muffin, bagel, pancakes or French toast;

or, two servings of bread—*with*

♀ **As a side dish:** one serving of fruit, fruit juice, vegetable juice, skim milk or reduced calorie hot chocolate—*with*

♀ **As a beverage:** coffee or tea.

THE ADVANTAGE FOOD PLAN
FOR THE PASTA PLUS
LUNCH
ALLOWS YOU TO HAVE

♀ **As a main dish, one of these:** a sandwich on any of the breads with vegetables and cheese;

or, one serving of pasta and vegetables (a pasta salad);

or, one serving of salad and a bowl of soup—*with*

♀ **As a dessert:** one serving of fruit—*with*

♀ **As a beverage:** coffee, decaffeinated coffee, tea, herbal tea, diet soda, juice spritzer, carbonated water, mineral water, or water.

THE ADVANTAGE FOOD PLAN
FOR THE PASTA PLUS
DINNER
ALLOWS YOU TO HAVE

♀ **As a main dish, one of these:** one serving of pasta with meat, poultry, fish, seafood or vegetable sauce;

or, one serving of meat, poultry, fish or seafood—*with*

♀ **As a side dish, one of these:** two servings of vegetables;

or, one serving of vegetables and a salad;

or, a small serving of pasta (only with meat, poultry, fish, seafood or tofu as a main dish)—*with*

♀ **As a dessert:** one serving of fruit or frozen skim milk—*with*

♀ **As a beverage:** decaffeinated coffee, herbal tea, diet soda, juice spritzer, carbonated water, mineral water, or water.

THE ADVANTAGE FOOD PLAN
FOR THE PASTA PLUS
SNACK
ALLOWS YOU TO HAVE

♀ One or two items as often as twice a day from any of the foods that are in italics. If you're not hungry, it's not necessary to eat a snack.

A Few Rules

There are a lot of good things to eat on the Pasta Plus program. The important point is to limit your fiber intake, so that it doesn't eliminate the natural estrogen that your body is producing. Notice, though, that there is *some* fiber in this phase of the Woman's Advantage Diet. That's because a balanced diet is important during your entire cycle.

Don't try to eliminate all fiber; that wouldn't be healthy. Follow the diet plan and the menus for well rounded meals, and don't add fiber when it's not called for. Avoid bran cereals and bran muffins; peel fruits such as peaches.

This is the time during your cycle when you can enjoy that wonderful French or Italian bread—just make sure it isn't the whole wheat variety. And don't eat an entire loaf! If you're preparing a sandwich with this bread, make sure to use only one slice that is approximately one-half inch thick (see Chapter 3).

Pasta Plus for the Menu Style Dieter

Use the following menu guide for your six day ovulating phase. (See Chapter 2 to find out more about the lengths of the four phases of your cycle.)

What Does the Number Mean?

The number in parentheses following some items points you to the recipe for that entry, which is included in the back of the book.

DAY 1 Pasta Plus

BREAKFAST
Puffed rice cereal
Reduced calorie cranberry juice
Coffee or tea

SNACK
Celery

LUNCH
>   Rigatoni and Mushroom Salad (43)
>   Lime Cooler (238)

SNACK
>   *Peach*

DINNER
>   Vegetarian Lasagna (102)
>   Honeydew Melon
>   Herbal tea

DAY 2 Pasta Plus

BREAKFAST
>   Egg in a Nest (10)
>   Coffee or tea

SNACK
>   *Cantaloupe*

LUNCH
>   Cucumber Sandwich (31)
>   Onion Soup (113)
>   Iced Espresso (236)

SNACK
>   *Grapes*

DINNER
>   Baked Ziti with Meat Sauce (64)
>   Braised Endive (123)
>   Baked Peaches (189)
>   Hot Spiced Apple Cider (235)

DAY 3 Pasta Plus

BREAKFAST
Bagel
Orange juice
Coffee or tea

SNACK
Plums

LUNCH
Chicken Salad Pitas (29)
Cherry tomatoes
Chocolate soda (228)

SNACK
Cucumber

DINNER
Hearty Baked Macaroni (82)
Watercress and Bibb Salad (181)
Lime flavored carbonated water

DAY 4 Pasta Plus

BREAKFAST
Scrambled Eggs (16)
Grapefruit
Coffee or tea

SNACK
Cauliflower

LUNCH
Chicken noodle soup
Tomato and Cheese Layers (50)
Grapefruit Sling (233)

SNACK
Papaya

DINNER
Roast beef
Ziti with Grated Parmesan (103)
Lemon Soufflé (206)
Tangelo Delight (246)

DAY 5 Pasta Plus

BREAKFAST
Onion bagel
Cantaloupe
Coffee or tea

SNACK
Tangerine

LUNCH
Orzo and Shrimp Salad (40)
Orange Spritzer (241)

SNACK
Cantaloupe

DINNER
Angel Hair with Tomato-Basil Sauce (62)
Dandelion Greens Salad (163)
Peach Ambrosia (211)
Cherry Sling (227)

DAY 6 Pasta Plus

BREAKFAST
Cinnamon French Toast (7)
Peach
Coffee or tea

SNACK
Celery

LUNCH
Caesar's Pasta (25)
Spiced Coffee (244)

SNACK
Sweet pepper

DINNER
Lemon Chicken (87)
Rice
Pineapple-Lemon Dessert-in-a-Glass (216)
Skim milk

Questions and Answers

Here are some of the questions my patients ask when they're on the Pasta Plus program and my answers to their queries, which may help you as well.

Q Are you sure the ovulatory phase is only six days long? Can't it be longer or shorter for some people?

A The ovulatory phase is six days long for practically everyone. But in any case, for the purposes of the Woman's Advantage Diet, we assume it's the same for everyone.

Q If estrogen is so good for dieting, can I take estrogen pills during the rest of my cycle when estrogen is low?

A I definitely do not recommend it. The Woman's Advantage Diet is a natural eating plan; it is designed to work safely with your natural menstrual cycle. I cannot promise you it will be safe or effective if hormonal supplements are used.

Q Just how much pasta can I have on the Pasta Plus program?

A As we discussed in Chapter 3, a serving of pasta as a main dish is approximately two ounces of dry, uncooked pasta. When you have it as a side dish, I recommend only one-half to one ounce of dry, uncooked pasta. One way to figure this out is to remember that a pound of spaghetti (or other pasta) serves six to eight people. As a main course, you'll want one-eighth of a package; as a side dish, you'll want one-sixteenth.

Q I really like this phase of the diet because I really *love* pasta. In fact, I love it so much I have trouble eating just one serving when I have it. What should I do?

A Whenever you find yourself tempted to eat more than your fair share of pasta (or other foods), just remind yourself of the cardinal rule of dieting: *Only eat when you're hungry.* The greatest advantage of the ovulatory phase of your cycle is that your appetite is naturally low. The foods recommended during this phase are specifically designed to help you feel less hungry. Low fiber carbohydrates like pasta and the other foods emphasized during Pasta Plus tend to "stick to your ribs." If you concentrate on eating only until you feel full, you'll find you'll eat much less during ovulation and you'll lose weight. When you have trouble with overeating for reasons besides hunger (for instance, if you're feeling depressed or you just *love* that primavera sauce), just remind yourself of how much you have to lose—in pounds!—if you successfully take advantage of your decreased appetite during this phase of your cycle.

Q If I have only a small amount of meat at lunch time, may I also have meat at dinner?

A It's much easier to stick to the rule of having protein (such as meat, fish or chicken) only once a day. It's not really a hard rule to follow when you see all there is to eat during Pasta Plus.

Q As long as I'm eating low fiber bread, may I have as much of it as I want at each meal?

A As discussed in Chapter 3, one serving means only one slice of bread or one roll (unless it's a reduced calorie brand, in which case one serving means two slices). And don't have bread or a roll at every meal. Just because this phase of the diet is rich in starch doesn't mean you can overdo it.

Q I know the foods on Pasta Plus should be enough for me. But sometimes I'm still hungry at the end of the day, or during the late afternoon. Is there anything I can eat at those times?

A Yes, you may have another piece of fruit. However, try to have fruit that can be peeled, and do peel it. Also, be sure to check the Pasta Plus Advantage Food Group list to be sure the fruit you snack on is low in fiber.

Q I like cheese. May I have all the Parmesan or Romano cheese I want on my pasta?

A I recommend limiting yourself to about two tablespoons of grated cheese on a pasta dish. (See Chapter 3 for information on portions.) Parmesan and Romano are so flavorful you won't want more.

Q If I skip ice milk as dessert, may I have half-and-half in my breakfast coffee instead of skim milk?

A This borrowing from Peter to pay Paul just doesn't work in dieting. Stick with the skim milk. The Pasta Plus program is low in fat as well as low in fiber. Substitutions are allowed on Pasta Plus, but only when the items are equivalent. That is not the case here; half-and-half is much higher in fat than skim milk. When you have a question about substitutions, refer to the Advantage Food Group lists and Plans for Pasta Plus.

Q Are there other soups I can have besides the ones you have listed on the food plan? For instance, I make fish broth that I really like. Is that all right on the diet?

A A fish broth is fine. You can have any soup as long as it's low in fiber and fat.

Q Can I have a bowl of soup for supper instead of for lunch?

A Sounds to me as though you're a Designer Style Dieter trying to use the Menu Style Dieter version of the Woman's Advantage Diet. Take a look at the Designer Style Dieter information.

Q I forgot that broccoli is a high fiber vegetable, and I had it for lunch one day during Pasta Plus. Does that mean that I've ruined the entire diet?

A No, one serving of broccoli won't spoil the entire six days of this diet. Don't let yourself get too upset about your little mistake. You don't want one slip to turn into the kind of guilt that can lead to a binge. Just try not to violate the diet again and you'll be fine.

---

1. See Bibliography references 51 (Shoupe, Montz and Lobo 1985) and 57 (Wade, Gray and Bartness 1985).

7 PROTEIN POWER

The premenstrual phase of your cycle has one big plus and a few minuses that you have to cope with.

The plus is that your body is dominated by a big surge of progesterone during this phase of your cycle. This is the hormone that is known to burn up protein. That means that all you meat, fish, chicken and cheese lovers can eat more of these foods than at any other time of your cycles.

The minus is that the premenstrual phase is also the time when many women experience a variety of unpleasant PMS symptoms. Some say they are more anxious and irritable at this time, while others say they go from mad to sad in a matter of minutes. Others say that they suffer from headaches, breast tenderness, water retention and bloating, aches, pains and fatigue. Many of my patients tell me that this is the time in their cycles when cravings for no-no foods like chocolate and salt laden potato chips really hit them hard.

You're Not Alone

If you've gone through any or all of these symptoms, you should realize *you are not alone*. Most of the women I've worked with report that they experience the premenstrual syndrome known as PMS. There are so many women who suffer from PMS that I include a chapter dealing with just that problem later on in the book.

Good News

I have learned from research, and from observing my patients who are on the Woman's Advantage Diet, that following the Protein Power eating plan during the premenstrual phase can actually lessen the water retention, aches, pains, and emotional roller coaster of PMS. Indeed, some of my patients have told me that PMS is now a thing of the past for them.

And that's only part of the benefits of the Protein Power program. Not only can it help you feel better, it also acts to control both your appetite and cravings for certain foods. Naturally, with all that going on, you will lose weight.

Many of my patients have reported to me that the dread they used to feel when anticipating the premenstrual phase has now changed to a feeling of elation. Thanks to the Woman's Advantage Diet, they no longer fear PMS, and they look forward to losing weight during this phase.

How Many Days on the Protein Power Program?

For the purposes of the diet, you can assume the premenstrual phase is always fourteen days long; it follows immediately after the ovulation phase. Follow the Protein Power Diet for the full fourteen days. This high protein diet is well balanced with moderate amounts of high and low fiber carbohydrates. (Check Chapter 2 for more information about the length of the different phases of your cycle.)

Protein Power for the Designer Style Dieter

Remember, the key to the Protein Power eating program (to be followed only during premenstruation) is to eat

> LOTS OF PROTEIN
> with some carbohydrates
> (and very little fat)

Following is the Advantage Food Group list for Protein Power. Remember, you can eat only the foods listed below, and you must do so according to the guidelines described in the Advantage Food Plan, which follows the list. (Snack foods are listed in *italics*.)

FRUITS

acerola
cherry (any kind)
genipap
grape (any kind)
grapefruit
lemon
lime
lychee
mangosteen
melon
   cantaloupe
   casaba
   Crenshaw

honeydew
Persian
watermelon
papaya
pawpaw
peach (any kind)
persimmon
pineapple
plum (any kind)
tangelo (any kind)
tangerine (any kind)
ugli fruit

VEGETABLES

anise
arugula
asparagus
basil
cauliflower
celeriac
celery
cilantro
cucumber
dandelion
dill
endive
escarole
fennel
fiddlehead
garlic
hot pepper (any kind)
kale
leek

lettuce (any kind)
lotus
mushroom
mustard green
onion (any kind)
parsley
radish
scallion
sorrel
sweet pepper
   green
   red
   yellow
Swiss chard
tofu (soybean)
tomato
truffle
watercress

GRAINS AND GRAIN PRODUCTS

cereal
  Corn Chex
  corn flakes
  Cream of Rice
  Cream of Wheat
  Crispix
  Crispy Wheats 'n Raisins
  Double Chex
  grits
  Just Right
  Life
  oatmeal
Product 19
puffed rice
puffed wheat
Rice Krispies
Special K
Team
Total
Wheat Chex
Wheatena
wheat germ
Wheaties

BREADS AND BREAD PRODUCTS

bagel
  egg
  plain
bread
  French
  Italian
  pita
  white enriched
muffin
  English
  plain
pancake and French toast
  buttermilk
  plain
roll and bun
  plain

DAIRY PRODUCTS

buttermilk
cheese
  Camembert
  farmer
  feta
  low fat cottage
  low fat, low sodium
    American
  low fat Monterey Jack
low fat mozzarella
low fat ricotta
Neufchâtel
Parmesan
Romano
frozen skim milk
low fat sour cream
low fat yogurt

MEATS, POULTRY AND EGGS

egg
egg substitute
meat
  beef
  goat
  hare
  lamb
  pork
  veal
poultry
  chicken

Cornish hen
grouse
partridge
pheasant
quail
turkey
reduced calorie gelatin
      (animal protein based)

FISH AND SEAFOOD

fish
  Atlantic sturgeon
  bass
  brook trout
  cod
  crevalle jack
  croaker
  cusk
  drum
  flounder
  grouper
  haddock
  hake
  halibut
  lingcod
  mahimahi
  monkfish
  orange roughy
  perch
  pike
  pollock
  red snapper

  rockfish
  sauger
  shark
  smelt
  sole
  tilefish
  tuna
  whiting
  yellowtail snapper
seafood
  abalone
  clam
  crab
  crayfish
  langostino
  lobster
  mussel
  octopus
  oyster
  scallop
  shrimp
  squid

SOUPS

bean
beef
  broth
  consommé
  noodle
chicken
  broth

consommé
  noodle
egg drop
lentil
split-pea
turkey noodle

CONDIMENTS

chocolate extract
chutney (avoid any type with
    added sugar, dried fruits
    or nuts)
cranberry sauce (avoid any
    type with added sugar)
Cumberland sauce
honey
hot pepper sauce
  chili
  harissa
  horseradish
  Indian
  Mexican salsa
  nam prik
  sambal
  Tabasco
  wasabi

jelly (avoid any type with
    added sugar)
ketchup
maple syrup (reduced calorie
    brands)
mayonnaise (reduced calorie
    brands)
mustard (avoid any sweet
    type)
relish
soy sauce
steak sauce
tamari sauce
teriyaki sauce
vanilla extract
vinegar
Worcestershire sauce

FATS

dairy	peanut
butter	rapeseed
oils	safflower
corn	sunflower
cottonseed	vegetable
olive	margarine

SPICES AND HERBS

allspice	ginger
almond	hyssop
angelica	licorice
anise	mace
arrowroot	marjoram
basil	melilot
bay leaf	mint
bergamot	mugwort
black pepper	mustard
caper	nasturtium
caraway	nutmeg
cardamon	oregano
cayenne pepper	paprika
chervil	parsley
chive	peppermint
cinnamon	purslane
clove	rocambole
coriander	rocket
cream of tartar	rosemary
cumin	rue
curry	saffron
dill	sage
fennel	salad burnet
fenugreek	savory
garlic	scurvy grass

sesame	tansy
sorrel	tarragon
star anise	thyme
stonecrop	turmeric
sweet cicely	vanilla
tamarind	violet

ALCOHOL
(recommended for cooking purposes only)

beer	sherry
brandy	wine

BEVERAGES

carbonated water	juice spritzer
decaffeinated coffee	mineral water
diet soda (without caffeine)	skim milk
herbal tea	water

The Food Plans

(Remember to check the size of all portions, using the guidelines in Chapter 3).

THE ADVANTAGE FOOD PLAN
FOR THE PROTEIN POWER
BREAKFAST
ALLOWS YOU TO HAVE

♀ **As a main dish, one of these:** one serving of cereal;

or, two eggs;

or, cheese with one egg;

or, one serving of Canadian bacon with one egg;

or, one serving of Canadian bacon with one serving of bread;

or, one serving of bread with one egg;

or, one serving of low fat yogurt or low fat cottage cheese—*with*

♀ **As a side dish:** one serving of fruit, vegetable juice or skim milk—*with*

♀ **As a beverage:** decaffeinated coffee or herbal tea.

THE ADVANTAGE FOOD PLAN
FOR THE PROTEIN POWER
LUNCH
ALLOWS YOU TO HAVE

♀ **As a main dish, one of these:** a sandwich with meat, poultry, fish, seafood, cheese, egg or tofu;

or, a salad with any of the vegetables and meat, poultry, fish, seafood, cheese, egg, or tofu;

or, a salad with any of the vegetables and a bowl of soup;

or, a bowl of bean soup with a serving of bread—*with*

♀ **As a dessert:** one serving of fruit—*with*

♀ **As a beverage:** decaffeinated coffee, herbal tea, juice spritzer, diet soda (without caffeine), carbonated water, mineral water, or water.

THE ADVANTAGE FOOD PLAN
FOR THE PROTEIN POWER
DINNER
ALLOWS YOU TO HAVE

♀ **As a main dish:** one serving of meat, poultry, fish, seafood or tofu—*with*

♀ **As a side dish, one of these:** two servings of vegetables;

or, one serving of vegetable and a salad;

or, one serving of cheese—*with*

♀ **As a dessert:** one serving of fruit—*with*

> ♀ **As a beverage:** decaffeinated coffee, herbal tea, juice spritzer, diet soda (without caffeine), carbonated water, mineral water, or water.

THE ADVANTAGE FOOD PLAN
FOR THE PROTEIN POWER
SNACK
ALLOWS YOU TO HAVE

♀ One or two items as often as twice a day from any of the foods that are in italics. If you're not hungry, it's not necessary to eat a snack.

A Few Rules

As you can see, there are a lot of good things to eat on the Protein Power program, especially if you love meats, poultry, fish, seafood, cheese and eggs, as many of my patients do.

My advice is not to overdo. As we discussed in Chapter 3, make sure that all the wonderful cheeses, yogurts, and other dairy products that you eat are low in fat (made with skim milk). Be sure to trim off every bit of visible fat before you grill your steak or chop. Remove the skin from the chicken or turkey breast before you cook it. Don't eat the skin on fish, either.

While eggs are great protein food, they are also high in cholesterol, and I don't recommend eating them more than twice a week. (The yolk is the problem; you could have egg whites more frequently). If you have an egg for breakfast, don't have an egg salad sandwich for lunch. If cholesterol is a problem for you, skip the eggs, cut down on the cheese, and have one of the other protein rich foods instead. (See the discussion on cholesterol in Chapter 3.)

You'll also notice this is the one phase of the diet where I ask you not to drink coffee or tea in the morning. I do this because the caffeine can aggravate your PMS symptoms. Most of you will find decaffeinated coffee or herbal tea satisfying, but if you feel you must cheat and have a little caffeine please don't exceed more than *one* cup of coffee or tea a day.

Protein Power for the Menu Style Dieter

Use the following menu guide for the fourteen days of your premenstrual phase. As we discussed earlier, for the purposes of the Woman's Advantage Diet, all women have a fourteen day premenstrual phase. (See Chapter 2 to find out more about the lengths of the four phases of your cycle).

What Does the Number Mean?

The number in parentheses following some items points you to the recipe for that entry, which is included in the back of the book.

DAY 1 Protein Power

BREAKFAST
Shirred Eggs with Cheese (18)
Skim milk

SNACK
Watermelon

LUNCH
Tangy Cottage Cheese (48)
Pineapple
Lime flavored carbonated water

SNACK
Grapes

DINNER
Tofu Chow Mein (98)
Cherries
Iced herbal tea

DAY 2 Protein Power

BREAKFAST
Cottage Cheese Blintzes (8)
Herbal tea

SNACK
Peach

LUNCH
Grilled Tofu Sandwich (37)
Skim milk

SNACK
Low fat cottage cheese

DINNER
Halibut
Spinach
Green Salad with Asparagus Tips (165)
Grapefruit Sling (233)

DAY 3 Protein Power

BREAKFAST
Low fat yogurt
Wheat germ
Herbal tea

SNACK
Pineapple

LUNCH
Tofu Miso Soup (115)
Pita bread
Skim milk

SNACK
Feta cheese

DINNER
>Salmon
>Tomato-Mozzarella Salad (180)
>Tangelo
>Lemon flavored carbonated water

DAY 4 Protein Power

BREAKFAST
>Scrambled Egg with Tomato and Basil (17)
>Decaffeinated coffee

SNACK
>*Plum*

LUNCH
>Seafood Chowder (114)
>Hearts of Palm, Radish and Bibb Lettuce Salad
>   (166)
>Iced herbal tea

SNACK
>*Skim milk*

DINNER
>Grilled Beef Kebabs (81)
>Watercress, Romaine and Radish Salad (182)
>Peach Shortcake (212)
>Tangerine Spritzer (247)

DAY 5 Protein Power

BREAKFAST
Low fat yogurt
Peach
Herbal tea

SNACK
Celery

LUNCH
Chicken and Tomato Sandwich (27)
Lime Cooler (238)

SNACK
Low fat cottage cheese

DINNER
Shrimp Creole (91)
Cauliflower
Fluffy Puff (198)
Skim milk

DAY 6 Protein Power

BREAKFAST
Corn cereal
Banana
Decaffeinated coffee

SNACK
Feta cheese

LUNCH
Tuna Salad (53)
Orange flavored carbonated water

SNACK
Cantaloupe

DINNER
Barbecue Chicken (65)
Herbed Tomato and Crouton Salad (167)
Cucumber Rounds (162)
Frozen Orange Yogurt (200)
Mineral water

DAY 7 Protein Power

BREAKFAST
Reduced calorie white bread
Grapefruit
Herbal tea

SNACK
Cucumber

LUNCH
Greek Salad (36)
Hard roll
Skim milk

SNACK
Low fat American cheese

DINNER
Sole
Creamy Asparagus Soup (109)
Sliced Tomatoes and Red Onions (178)
Grapefruit Mold (203)
Reduced calorie cranberry juice

DAY 8 Protein Power

BREAKFAST
Tofu Rancheros (19)
Decaffeinated coffee

SNACK
Tangerine

LUNCH
Cheese and Sprout Pita (26)
Diet soda

SNACK
Celery

DINNER
Almond Chicken (61)
Nasturtium-Leaf Salad (171)
Peach Ambrosia (211)
Lemonade (237)

DAY 9 Protein Power

BREAKFAST
Reduced calorie white bread
Mango
Herbal tea

SNACK
Honeydew melon

LUNCH
Tofu Sloppy Joe (49)
Tomato juice

SNACK
Low fat cottage cheese

DINNER
>Tofu Burger (97)
>Endive with Cheese Sauce (130)
>Tangerine Sorbet (221)
>Lime Cooler (238)

DAY 10 Protein Power

BREAKFAST
>Puffed rice cereal
>Peach
>Decaffeinated coffee

SNACK
>*Low fat American cheese*

LUNCH
>Vegetable Beef Soup (117)
>French bread
>Skim milk

SNACK
>*Celery*

DINNER
>Turkey breast
>Cranberry sauce
>Cauliflower au Gratin (127)
>Watermelon
>Iced herbal tea

DAY 11 Protein Power

BREAKFAST
>Low fat yogurt
>Cherries
>Orange juice

SNACK
> *Sweet peppers*

LUNCH
> Tuna Salad (53)
> Pita bread
> Iced herbal tea

SNACK
> *Low fat cottage cheese*

DINNER
> Chicken Florentine (73)
> Tofu Parmesan (99)
> Tangerine Whip (220)
> Skim milk

DAY 12 Protein Power

BREAKFAST
> Bagel
> Grapefruit
> Herbal tea

SNACK
> *Plum*

LUNCH
> French-Toasted Ham and Cheese (33)
> Orange flavored carbonated water

SNACK
> *Grapes*

DINNER
> Onion Soup (113)
> Chinese Pepper Steak (75)
> Pineapple
> Tropical Fizz (248)

DAY 13 Protein Power

BREAKFAST
Canadian bacon
Whole wheat bread
Herbal tea

SNACK
Ugli fruit

LUNCH
Chicken and Tomato Sandwich (27)
Cucumber Mint Frappe (229)

SNACK
Low fat calorie mozzarella

DINNER
Fillet of Flounder Amandine (78)
Shrimp with Cold Cilantro Sauce (93)
Mixed Green Salad with Radishes (168)
Tofu Lemon Pie (222)
Tangerine Spritzer (247)

DAY 14 Protein Power

BREAKFAST
Egg White Omelet with Herbs (11)
Sourdough bread
Decaffeinated coffee

SNACK
Low fat American cheese

LUNCH
Shrimp Salad (46)
Skim milk

SNACK
Persimmon

DINNER
Red snapper
Sliced Tomatoes and Red Onions (178)
Sesame Asparagus (141)
Tangerine Sorbet (221)
Mineral water

Questions and Answers

Many of my patients have questions about the Protein Power phase of the diet. Here's what I tell them:

Q May I continue with the Protein Power program after my period starts?

A If you're a Menu Style Dieter, I advise you to stick with the menus for Forbidden Foods. If you're a Designer Style Dieter, you can eat nearly anything you want—Forbidden Foods is, after all, reward time. If you follow the Food Plan for Forbidden Foods, you'll be able to eat a lot of protein and still lose weight.

Q I think I have a premenstrual phase that is longer than fourteen days. Should I be on the Protein Power program for more than fourteen days?

A For the purposes of losing weight on the Woman's Advantage Diet, you can assume your premenstrual phase remains at a constant fourteen days.

Q I've been told that nuts are a good source of protein. May I eat nuts as a snack?

A Nuts are a good source of protein but they're also a good source of fat, and it's hard to stop eating nuts once you get started. That's why I don't include nuts on the Protein Power eating plan. You can get all the protein you need from other foods.

Q I think tofu is bland and boring. Do I have to eat it?

A No. You can substitute another protein; just be sure to check the Designer Style Dieter's information to be sure you make an appropriate choice. But, I really think that if you give tofu a chance you may learn to love it. Tofu marries well with many other flavors, and it doesn't have to be either bland or boring.

Q With all that progesterone, will I lose more weight during my premenstrual phase than at any other time in my cycle?

A Some of my patients do, but most enjoy an even loss of weight during the entire menstrual cycle.

Q I love the Protein Power program, but isn't it terribly rich in fats?

A The Protein Power program is actually low in fat, and it will remain that way if you use reduced calorie products, trim all visible fat off meats and discard poultry skin.

Q I like tuna canned in olive oil. May I use that instead of tuna packed in water?

A No. As we discussed in Chapter 3, stay with the water packed tuna. It's rich in protein and doesn't have any added fat.

Q Instead of one of the snacks you have listed on the menu, may I have celery?

A Yes, you may have celery and some other vegetables in place of any snack. But remember that the goal of this phase of the diet is to emphasize protein and not overdo carbohydrates with a lot of fiber. Stick to protein or low fiber carbohydrates for snacks. And don't overindulge. Even a vegetable with low fiber will end up giving you a lot of fiber if you eat a lot of it.

Q Do you really think this diet will help me? I've always been troubled with PMS. Mainly, I gain weight. Can Protein Power do anything about that?

A I think you'll be pleasantly surprised at how very much Protein Power can help you. Your weight gain may be caused by a combination of craving—and eating—foods that are loaded with fat and calories, and retained water. Protein Power will do two major things for you: it will help you to control your appetite, so you won't crave foods so intensely. And it will alleviate many of your PMS symptoms. You won't retain water, so your weight loss efforts won't be handicapped.

Q The Protein Power program is so great, I'd like to stay on it all the time. But if I can't do that, can I take progesterone pills during the rest of my cycle?

A The Woman's Advantage Diet works because of the hormones that your body secretes *naturally*. I definitely do not recommend that you take progesterone pills. I cannot promise you that the Woman's Advantage Diet will be safe or effective if you use hormonal supplements.

8

HOW YOU CAN OVERCOME PREMENSTRUAL SYNDROME

I'm surprised when a new patient tells me that she has a physician who is still telling her that PMS is a myth and that her bloated feeling, aches, pains, depression and anger have nothing to do with her menstrual cycle. I'm not saying that those symptoms, as well as others, are always directly attributable to PMS. But they can be, because the premenstrual syndrome certainly does exist. The first scientific paper that recognized PMS appeared in 1931.[1] Until that time, many doctors were even more unsympathetic than some of them are today.

For the most part, the medical community now fully acknowledges PMS as a real and common problem. In fact, it is generally agreed that at least 70 percent of all premenopausal women experience one or more of the symptoms of PMS. Women that I've spoken to say that every woman they know has some of the symptoms. Indeed, although the medical community is just catching up to them, women have always known about PMS—even if they didn't have a scientific name for it.

What Exactly Is PMS?

PMS occurs only during the premenstrual phase of the cycle. Whereas for the purposes of the Woman's Advantage Diet we assume the premenstrual phase is always fourteen days long, a measurement concerned with precise medical accuracy may find individual variations. Most PMS symptoms seem to strike women during the last six days before the onset of menstruation, although they can occur at any time during the premenstrual phase.

PMS is generally defined as manifesting one or more symptoms during the premenstrual phase that are experienced for two or more cycles. More than 150 symptoms have been attributed to PMS, and the most familiar ones are:

PMS SYMPTOMS CHART

Body
headache
breast tenderness
breast enlargement
joint/muscle pain
backache
weight gain, fluid retention
acne

Emotion
irritability
anger
sadness
mood swings

Thinking
poor concentration
indecision
thoughts of harming yourself

Digestion and Heart
nausea, vomiting
diarrhea, constipation
cold sweats
heart pounding

Balance and Coordination
dizziness
fainting, lightheadedness
seizures
clumsiness
trembling
numbness

Energy
fatigue
lethargy
sleepiness
agitation

Eating
loss of appetite
bingeing
food allergies
food craving

Behavior
avoidance of socializing
decreased motivation
decreased efficiency
change in sexual activity

Clearly, PMS is a problem that can affect body, mind and spirit. From headaches to oily hair, PMS can alter and often complicate every aspect of a woman's life. But probably the one aspect most vulnerable to the influences of PMS is a woman's weight. Water retention makes her feel as though she's gained weight; depression makes her feel that, since she's gained weight despite her best efforts, she will never be able to lose it; her food cravings are so powerful she becomes convinced that her only response is to give in to them. For too many women for too long, PMS has meant failure for even the best diets. The Woman's Advantage Diet will put an end to this sabotage of women's weight loss efforts once and for all.

Do You Have PMS?

If you experience any of the above symptoms, or others, during your premenstrual cycle, you may have PMS. The only reason I qualify this by saying you *may* have PMS is because it's important to make sure that your symptoms are not caused by another condition. Chronic headaches, to name just one of the PMS symptoms, can be caused by a serious medical condition. You should always check with your doctor rather than assume that a medical problem is PMS related.

I use a special chart with my patients to help them keep track of all their PMS symptoms. Many women find tracking their symptoms reassuring, because they know what to expect and are less worried. One patient told me she often gets sudden crying spells just before her period. My tracking chart has helped her because it indicates she almost always has a crying jag one or two days before her period. She knows now not to worry when she gets weepy at that time because it is PMS, not a problem, that is causing her tears. Now she knows things will look better in a couple of days.

I've included a sample Woman's Advantage Diet Calendar for PMS on the next page that you may use if you think tracking your PMS symptoms may be helpful to you. (There are additional calendar blanks at the back of the book). If your symptoms are part of PMS, remember that they will occur at some time during your premenstrual phase and will reoccur in at least two cycles.

All you need to do to use the Woman's Advantage Diet Calendar for PMS is review the symptoms listed on page 138, and note the day of your cycle on which they occur. You'll want to use the blanks

Day of the Month	Day of Cycle	Cycle Phase	Food Group	PMS Symptoms
	1	Menstrual	FORBIDDEN FOODS	
	2			
	3			
	4			
	5			
	6			
	7			
	8			
	1	Postmenstrual	FABULOUS FRUITS AND VEGETABLES	
	2			
	3			
	4			
	5			
	6			
	7			
	8			
	9			
	10			
	11			
	12			
	13			
	14			
	15			
	16			
	17			
	18			
	19			
	20			
	1	Ovulatory	PASTA PLUS	
	2			
	3			
	4			
	5			
	6			
	1	Premenstrual	PROTEIN POWER	
	2			
	3			
	4			
	5			
	6			
	7			
	8			
	9			
	10			
	11			
	12			
	13			
	14			

offered at the back of the book to adjust the calendar according to your individual cycle. (See Chapter 2 for instructions.)

The calendar works in two specific ways:

(1) When you list a symptom and you see that it reoccurs month after month during your premenstrual phase, you know that you have PMS. *And you also know that the troubling symptom will disappear when your premenstrual phase ends.*

I think that most women can cope with pains and depression they know that they will be suffering these symptoms for a finite time. It's not so hard to keep from turning to food for solace when you know your weight gain or depression is only temporary.

(2) And, after a time, your PMS symptoms will for the most part disappear if you follow the Woman's Advantage Diet. Almost all my patients no longer suffer any PMS related weight gain, and they find that their other symptoms lessen or even disappear.

Protein Power and the Physical Symptoms of PMS

There's a lot going on in your body during the premenstrual phase. Some studies have suggested that low levels of certain hormones at this time can cause PMS, but as yet this hypothesis has not been proven. What I do know is that when my patients follow the Protein Power eating plan, they report that many of their PMS symptoms have completely disappeared, and the severity of others has been considerably lessened. Here's how Protein Power will help you.

• *You have that bloated feeling:* This is caused by the excess water that your body has retained during the premenstrual phase. You've gained weight (it could be two pounds, it could even be ten pounds), your clothes don't fit, and you feel terrible physically and mentally. Excess water retention is the culprit behind many PMS symptoms. You'll also find it's one of the symptoms the Woman's Advantage Diet is most effective in counteracting.

Why does this happen? Your body tends to store more water with the carbohydrates you eat than with the protein. Emphasizing protein, as you do with the premenstrual Protein Power eating plan, in itself lessens the water you retain. In addition, the diet is low in salt, another water retaining villain. It all adds up to leaving you feeling much less bloated.

• *You have pains in your muscles and joints, headaches and backaches:* These pains can also be caused by water retention. The

Woman's Advantage Diet gets rid of the water, and the pain goes with it.

• *You feel nauseated at this time:* Nausea is caused by the change in the way your digestive tract works during the premenstrual phase. Food actually takes longer to digest, and certain foods that may not have troubled you at any other time can now cause heartburn, constipation and nausea. Protein Power foods won't cause these problems. As we discussed earlier, progesterone is especially efficient at metabolizing protein, which should help greatly in your PMS related digestive problems. [2]

• *You suffer from either diarrhea or constipation:* Most of my patients have found that the foods in the various phases of the program help regulate bowel movements and relieve these types of distress.

• *Your breasts are tender and enlarged:* This uncomfortable condition may be due to a sensitivity to the chemicals in such caffeine-filled foods as coffee, tea or chocolate. [3] The foods in Protein Power contain very little caffeine. If you avoid coffee, tea and chocolate (using the Advantage Food Group lists to find appropriate substitutes) these symptoms may be eliminated. The water retention, which can also cause this condition as we discussed, will be relieved by the diet.

• *You get dizzy at this time in your cycle, and you're afraid you might faint:* The foods that are part of the Protein Power plan and other phases of the diet insure well balanced meals. They will stabilize your blood sugar, which should also help you with dizziness, fainting or trembling.

• *You are overtired at this time. Not only do you have trouble working, you don't enjoy being with friends, and just can't seem to get out of bed in the morning:* You need the extra burst of energy that you will get from protein—that's why I call it Protein Power! My patients have told me that the severe bouts of lethargy and fatigue that they experienced before they embarked on the Woman's Advantage Diet are now gone. They have energy for work and play.

Protein Power and the Emotional Symptoms of PMS

From what my patients tell me, they are more upset by their emotional ups and downs than by their physical symptoms during the premenstrual phase.

Psychological problems may actually be alleviated by Protein

Power. Some of my patients with no need to lose weight have gone on the diet because it has made them feel so much better emotionally and psychologically. And all my patients, once they have reached their goal, have continued to enjoy freedom from PMS by using the Stay-Slim Maintenance Plan discussed later in the book.

At this point, neither doctors nor scientists know why the premenstrual phase affects the emotions. One cause could be low blood sugar, which can cause dizziness, fatigue, anxiety and irritability. It's possible that some women do suffer from low blood sugar during the premenstrual phase, and this could explain why they eat excessive amounts of sugar laden foods.

If you suffer from emotional problems during your premenstrual phase, the Woman's Advantage Diet may relieve your symptoms. Here's how it works:

• The protein this phase of the diet emphasizes can work to modulate your blood sugar level. Once your blood sugar level is raised, you may find the worst of those anxious, irritable feelings disappear.

• Eating foods in tune with the harmony of the menstrual cycle keeps your body from suffering from hormonal imbalance. This helps you to cope better with emotional problems.

• Protein Power also contains important levels of such amino acids as tryptophan, which can decrease anxiety, lift depression, and improve your state of mind. [4]

• With less anxiety and a better mood, you won't want to eat as much—which will keep you from being depressed about your weight.

• You'll find the meals recommended on the diet are satisfying, and you won't feel the need to binge.

• All in all, you'll find your emotions are on an even keel. You'll feel better about yourself as you lose pounds and your self-esteem reaches a new high.

• With all those good things happening in your life, you'll suddenly be amazed to discover your anxiety and anger are gone. And when problems do come up, you'll find you have the emotional strength to deal with them with a smile.

Questions and Answers

I think I've covered most of the important points about PMS, but I'd like to include some of the questions that I've heard from my patients and my answers to them.

Q If it's just a question of raising my blood sugar, why don't I eat a candy bar or a piece of chocolate when I get those awful PMS symptoms?

A The answer to raising your blood sugar is definitely not a quick fix of candy or chocolate. This is the worst thing you can do. Any of these refined sugars will give you a quick sugar high and an even quicker low-sugar low. Hypoglycemic patients know enough never to rely on instant remedies, but anyone who indulges in quick sugar fixes will feel depressed as soon as the short-term blood sugar spurt is over. Follow the diet; you'll find it's the best way to counteract PMS related blood sugar lows.

Q I've just started the Woman's Advantage Diet, and I hope that it will rid me of PMS symptoms. My doctor recently prescribed magnesium; he said that would help with my PMS. Should I take magnesium tablets while I'm on the diet?

A The level of magnesium in the body is affected by stress,[5] and if you are greatly stressed, you could be losing magnesium that you need to stave off the anxieties and angers common to PMS. That is probably why your doctor prescribed it.

The Woman's Advantage Diet has adequate amounts of magnesium, and for most patients, I would say they need not take supplements. If you have special health needs, though, I do advise you to follow the advice of your doctor. You can also make sure to eat foods rich in magnesium, such as dark green leafy vegetables, seafood, cereal, chicken, veal, and most spices.

Q I always used to shrug when my friends told me that they have PMS. It never bothered me. Not until this past year. I'm thirty and now I seem to have every symptom I've ever heard about.

A PMS can appear at any age. You may not have it when you first start menstruating, but it can appear later in life. Don't succumb to anxieties about the onset of PMS. Instead, cope with it by going on the Woman's Advantage Diet.

Q I've charted my menstrual cycle as you suggested but this really bad headache that I get comes at different times during my cycle. Some months it doesn't even appear during the premenstrual phase. What does that mean?

A It probably means that your headaches are not related to PMS. Check out those headaches with your doctor.

Q I'm not a big drinker, and when I'm not in my premenstrual phase, I can have a drink before dinner and it doesn't seem to affect me. But during my premenstruation—wow! One drink and I feel drunk. Why is that?

A Your body is going through definite changes during premenstruation, and your ability to handle alcohol is different than it is at other times. Alcohol does have a more potent effect during the premenstrual phase, and many women find they're more comfortable not drinking at that time.[6] In any case, I don't recommend that you drink during this phase of your cycle.

Q I'm slightly allergic to fish and bananas, but I've noticed that I'm especially sensitive to these foods during my premenstrual time. Have you ever heard of anything like this?

A I certainly have heard about allergies getting worse during premenstruation, and I've seen it in my patients. You're not alone; just do your best during premenstruation to avoid all the foods you're allergic to. If you need to, consult the Advantage Food Groups and Food Plans to find whatever appropriate substitute food you might need.

Q I love the way you call your diet the Woman's Advantage Diet. You've given me another way of looking at menstruation. I was brought up to call that time of month "the curse." I've had really bad PMS ever since I started menstruation. Do you think your diet will help me?

A I definitely think it can. My experience has been that women who have been brought up to dread menstruation are those who suffer the most with PMS. If you can learn to think of it differently, you may find that your new attitude, plus the diet, will help you rid yourself of the most unpleasant of your symptoms.

Q I've heard that vitamin B_6 can cure PMS. Should I take B_6 supplements in addition to following the diet?

A There's been a great deal of controversy surrounding the use of vitamin B_6 supplements. Some studies have indicated that B_6 can relieve some PMS symptoms such as depression, dizziness, nausea, and poor social and business performance. However, B_6 can also cause health problems that affect the nerves of the body. Vitamin B_6 supplements should not be taken without medical supervision, and I don't recommend them for long term use.[7]

Rather, I recommend that you increase your intake of vitamin B_6 naturally through the food you eat. The Woman's Advantage Diet has excellent sources of this vitamin, which can be found in chicken, oatmeal, eggs, tuna, salmon, wheat germ and cauliflower.

Q I love salty foods and I seem to need salt especially during my premenstrual time. Can salt have any effect on PMS?

A The bloated feelings of water retention will be increased by a high intake of salt. Indeed, water retention is believed to be behind many common PMS symptoms, like headaches, joint aches, and loss of concentration. Cut down on salt and salty foods. If you find that especially difficult, consult Chapter 9 on food cravings.

Q Why is it called Premenstrual Syndrome?

A Doctors and scientists call a condition a *syndrome* when it is evidenced by many different symptoms, each of which probably has its own cause. When the exact causes of a condition are not known, it's called a syndrome. For example, PMS could be caused by low blood sugar; it could be caused by hormonal changes; and so on. The exact causes of PMS are not known at this time.

---

1. See Bibliography reference 22 (Frank 1931).
2. See Bibliography reference 13 (Castro 1967), 12 (Bruce and Behsudi 1979) and 58 (Wald et al. 1981).
3. A number of studies have shown that breast tenderness, for example, decreases with a diet low in caffeine and methylxanthines. See Bibliography reference 44 (Minton et al. 1979).
4. See Bibliography references 29 (Hullin 1976) and 15 (Conlay and Zeisel 1982).
5. See Bibliography reference 49 (Seelig 1980).
6. See Bibliography reference 32 (Jones and Jones 1976).
7. See Bibliography references 9 (Biskind 1943) and 36 (Kendall and Schurr 1987).

9 FREE YOURSELF OF FOOD CRAVINGS

What is a *craving*? The dictionary says it's "an urgent need for instant gratification." Applied to a craving for food, this could mean that at a certain moment you feel that you *must* have a chocolate bar right then and there or you'll just die. (Emotionally, you think you'll die, though you certainly won't perish for lack of a piece of candy.) A craving isn't a response to hunger. When you give in to a food craving, you will most likely eat too much of it.

I have had women tell me that they crave spinach or fresh fruit during certain times in their menstrual cycle, but those are not the cravings that can sabotage your diet.

The four most familiar food cravings that are dangerous if you want to lose weight are cravings for:

(1) Chocolate, and foods made with a lot of chocolate. These foods are usually high in fat and calories.

(2) Sugar, and foods made with a lot of sugar. These foods are always high in calories and usually high in fat.

(3) Starchy foods plus margarine, butter, sour cream and other condiments that are usually added on. Most of these add-ons are high in fat and calories.

(4) Salt, and foods made with a lot of salt.

When Do Food Cravings Strike?

Food cravings can hit at any time, but for a great percentage of women, these cravings peak during the premenstrual phase.

Scientific studies have confirmed that the menstrual cycle plays an important role in creating cravings. Hormonal activity during the premenstrual phase can stimulate the appetite, and create strong urges for eating all the wrong foods. Maybe you can stay away from high calorie foods during the rest of your cycle, but you find it positively painful to keep away from foods that are bad for your diet when you're in your premenstrual phase. And once you eat foods that are loaded with calories, you feel guilty, and are disgusted with your lack of self-control.

If this problem is familiar to you, I'd like to tell you what I tell my patients: *Don't feel guilty*. Guilt will only make you feel worse, and feeling bad about yourself may cause you to eat still more. Besides, feeling guilty won't do anything to stop those terrible cravings for the wrong kinds of food. Experiencing such cravings during the premenstrual phase is not your fault. You are not yearning for chocolates or french fries because you're a weak, undisciplined person, but because the changes in your body at this time create an atmosphere of need for certain foods.

The Reasons for Your Food Cravings

You'll feel better about yourself if you know *why* you have these cravings.

• You are more anxious, tense, or depressed during the premenstrual phase, and you look to food for comfort.

• You feel so tired all the time, you're more likely to give in to a craving.

• Your senses of taste and smell reach a peak during ovulation and premenstruation, and your appetite is increased.[1]

• You have aches and pains due to PMS, and you think foods that please you will make you feel better.

The System to End Food Cravings

You have dreaded those times in your cycle when you know you will be attacked by cravings for all the wrong foods, but you will find that these cravings will lessen and gradually be eliminated altogether thanks to my system to end food cravings.

The first part of the system is the Woman's Advantage Diet. You will find as you follow this diet that your cravings may be completely gone after just one cycle. I have had patients tell me that their cravings for large quantities of all the wrong foods have disappeared completely after a short time on the Woman's Advantage Diet. Others have said that while their cravings have lessened, their desires for the wrong foods are still with them to a degree.

Because of this, in conjunction with the diet, I also recommend *the second part of the system, which is the substitution program.*

Just as I recommend that you use a chart to make note of your PMS symptoms, I also feel that you should chart your food cravings. Tracking your cravings will help you recognize their real cause. You'll know that they'll only last a few days, and it will be easier for you to overcome them. Use the Woman's Advantage Diet Calendar for Food Cravings to record the days when you feel cravings for chocolate, sugar, salt or add-ons. A sample is provided on page 150 but you will want to personalize your calendar blanks at the back of the book. (See Chapter 2 for instructions.)

The calendar will help you determine just when food cravings occur, and the role they play in your weight problem. As you follow the Woman's Advantage Diet, the calendar will reveal the pleasing fact that the cravings are becoming a problem of the past.

Free Yourself from Chocolate

Chocolate heads the list when it comes to food cravings. More people crave chocolate and foods made with chocolate than any other type of food.

Chocolate has a lot going for it to make it seductive: it has caffeine, and if you're a coffee drinker, you already know about your need for caffeine. It also contains chemicals that can affect many different body processes. That's why recent studies have said that the good feeling you get from chocolate is similar to the good feeling you get from falling in love. Chocolate also has a strong taste, an aroma that is pleasing, and something that food manufacturers call a good "mouth feel," which means it's pleasant to the palate and is easily and smoothly swallowed. But chocolate also contains more than its fair share of fat, sugar and calories.

When you crave chocolate cake, brownies, chocolate chip cookies, chocolate ice cream, chocolate candy—send in the substitutes!

Day of the Month	Day of Cycle	Cycle Phase	Food Group	Food Cravings
	1	Menstrual	FORBIDDEN FOODS	
	2			
	3			
	4			
	5			
	6			
	7			
	8			
	1	Postmenstrual	FABULOUS FRUITS AND VEGETABLES	
	2			
	3			
	4			
	5			
	6			
	7			
	8			
	9			
	10			
	11			
	12			
	13			
	14			
	15			
	16			
	17			
	18			
	19			
	20			
	1	Ovulatory	PASTA PLUS	
	2			
	3			
	4			
	5			
	6			
	1	Premenstrual	PROTEIN POWER	
	2			
	3			
	4			
	5			
	6			
	7			
	8			
	9			
	10			
	11			
	12			
	13			
	14			

Chocolate Substitutes

If you're craving the caffeine in chocolate, and your doctor hasn't asked you to avoid caffeine, I recommend the following substitutes:

- Coffee with reduced calorie sweetener, skim milk and a touch of cinnamon
- Diet soda with caffeine
- Diet chocolate soda with skim milk

(I know some chocolate slipped through on that last one, but at least it won't bring a lot of fat and calories with it. Combined with an ounce of skim milk, diet chocolate soda can make a delightfully frothy dessert treat.)

If you need or want to avoid caffeine (and you know I recommend that you do avoid it during your premenstrual phase), you might also try overcoming your chocolate craving with the following spices sprinkled or poured on fresh or canned (in reduced calorie syrup) fruits:

- Ground ginger on pineapple
- Ground cloves on peaches or pineapple
- Liquid anise on peaches or pineapples

Free Yourself from Sugar

On the list of foods that are craved the most, those with refined sugar come right after chocolate. Sugar itself isn't harmful to health, but it's loaded with calories. Dishes prepared with sugar are also often loaded with fat.

The craving for sweet food is, in part, psychological. Most of us think of sugar as a reward food. When you were good as a child, you were given candy. As you grew older, dessert was emphasized as the best part of any meal. We are conditioned to like and want sugary foods. It's also true that sugar gives a quick lift—but when your burst of energy comes from refined sugar, it lasts a very short time. That is why it's best to get sugar from the complex carbohydrates that are found in other foods.

When you crave ice cream, cookies, nondiet soda, pastries or cake—it's time to send in the substitutes!

Sugar Substitutes

The easiest answer for sugar cravings is to turn to those foods with artificial sweeteners:

- Diet soda
- Sugarless gum
- Reduced calorie popsicle
- Reduced calorie gelatin
- Reduced calorie pudding
- Reduced calorie powdered drinks
- Presweetened reduced calorie tea

Some people don't feel comfortable eating large quantities of sugar substitutes. For those of you who feel that way, the best substitutes when you're craving sweets is fruit. It's good for you, and naturally sweet. When you're hit with a craving, your diet won't be ruined by an extra fruit snack or even two. Here are some especially sweet varieties of fruit my patients find very satisfying:

> cherry
> grape
> grapefruit
> melon
> papaya
> peach
> pineapple
> plum
> tangerine

If the fruits by themselves don't satisfy you, add spices to them that will make these naturally sweet fruits taste even sweeter. Use the following spices sprinkled on the fruits listed in this table:

cinnamon	peach, tangerine, papaya, watermelon, cantaloupe, grapefruit and grapes
nutmeg	peach, pineapple, watermelon, cantaloupe, plum, papaya, and ugli fruit
allspice	peach, pineapple, tangerine, watermelon, cantaloupe, grape and papaya

Free Yourself from Starchy Foods and Their Add-Ons

Starchy foods are craved almost as much as foods made with sugar. Foods that are starchy are usually comfort foods—mashed potatoes or slices of white bread. Those are the foods that made you feel good as a kid so, if you're like most of us, you assume they'll make you feel good now, too. Foods that have a great deal of starch are also filling, and they're a quick satisfier when hunger pangs hit. But starch-laden foods can also be high in calories. Even when a starchy food is not too bad by itself, you may still have a problem because you are probably craving starchy foods because of what is added to them.

Do you want a baked potato? Or do you want a baked potato because you're going to eat it with butter and sour cream? Do you really crave french fries? Or do you want them because they're loaded with fat and salt? How about that roll? Would you eat it if it wasn't slathered with butter or margarine?

This is one time when you must call upon your will power. To make that just a little easier, the following table will be of some help.

To overcome the damage starchy foods can do to your weight loss efforts, I have found it most effective to trick your appetite. My patients find that the following substitutes (which address the symptom but not the cause of this particular craving) are effective satisfiers.

So, when you crave baked potato, cereal, popcorn or crackers—send in the substitutes!

Starchy Food Substitutes

craved starchy foods	*food substitutes*
baked potato with butter or sour cream	plain baked potato
roll with butter	plain roll
french fries	plain baked potato
buttered popcorn	unbuttered popcorn
sugared cereal	cereal with fruit
crackers	rice cakes
bread or roll	carrot or celery sticks

Free Yourself from Salt

Salt does not contain calories, but it's usually combined with foods that do. Even if you crave salt for its own sake, you will still want to avoid the water retention it causes.

When you crave potato chips, tortilla chips, cheese curls, pretzels, peanut butter, cheese, crackers, nuts, popcorn, preserved meat or other salty foods, but you want to avoid excess salt—send in the substitutes!

Salt Substitutes

When you're craving a salty snack, try

> asparagus
> cauliflower
> celery
> cucumber
> pear
> tangelo
> tangerine
> skim milk

A lot of salt slips into your diet without your knowing it in the packaged foods you eat. Try to cut down by using it sparingly at the table. Never cook with it. Instead try cooking with

chopped shallot	lemon
green onion	pepper
parsley	oregano
cilantro	thyme
basil	tarragon
garlic	

Questions and Answers

Here are some of the questions my patients have asked me about food cravings, and my answers to them:

Q I'm not troubled with cravings for any of the foods you mentioned so far. What I do crave during my premenstrual phase is Chinese food—and I mean a lot of Chinese food. What can I do about that?

A You may be craving one or more of the spices used in Chinese cooking. I've heard much the same thing from other women who crave Indian, Chinese, Thai, Vietnamese, Korean, Mexican, Tex-Mex, Caribbean, African and Cajun foods. They're all cuisines involving the heavy use of spices.

The way to handle this craving is to use the spices you crave on foods that are low in fat and calories. Put the cilantro that's used in Mexican cuisine in a salad. Try the ginger in Thai foods with some steamed carrots. Put some of the hot sauce in Cajun cuisine into vegetable-based soups. With a little imagination, you'll find it easy to satisfy your craving for spices without going near fattening foods.

Q I don't crave any particular food when I'm in my premenstrual phase; I crave all foods. I get so hungry. I don't care what I eat—steak, salad, my desk—just so long as I eat. Can this craving be controlled?

A Yes, it can be controlled. What you're describing isn't technically a food craving; it's just a ravenous appetite! You'll find the Woman's Advantage Diet wonderfully effective in controlling your appetite. You'll also find the following will help: have cereal for breakfast every morning, but use only those cereals on the Advantage Food List. Add cubes of tofu to soup, salads and vegetable dishes. Add a tossed green salad (with a reduced calorie dressing) to your dinner. This should satisfy your appetite; if you're still hungry, have fresh fruit as a snack.

Q Once I substitute fruit and spices for chocolate, won't I start to crave them?

A If you should develop such a craving, it would be one that's all right to indulge. This is not the kind of food that will cause you to gain weight.

Q If I get rid of my cravings for chocolate and foods made with sugar, do you think I'll stop being overweight?

A It depends on whether these are the only areas of excess in the diet that led to your weight problem in the first place. Certainly, chocolate and foods made with sugar can make you gain weight. Once you end your craving problem, you may also end your weight problem. I've seen this happen with many of my patients.

Q Something really strange happens to me during my premenstrual cycle. I drink one glass of wine, and then I just can't stop myself from eating desserts! What can I do?

A This happens to many women. The premenstrual phase can magnify the effects of alcohol. It's best if you avoid alcohol during this phase. For some women, alcohol at this time creates an intense craving for sweets—and the calories add up!

Q You told me to eat low fat and low salt cheese, and I've been doing that. But once I start eating cheese of any kind, I just can't stop. What should I do?

A I've recommended low fat cheese because it's lower in calories, and low salt cheese because of the problems salt can cause you. But you must remember that even the cheese I recommend is not calorie and fat free, and it should be eaten in small quantities. I think you crave large amounts of cheese because you need more protein. Add tofu to soups, salads, and vegetable dishes. That will provide protein with fewer calories.

Q I get food cravings but not during my premenstrual phase. Those cravings hit me when I'm menstruating. What can I do about that?

A Your menstruation phase coincides with the Forbidden Foods program, which should help you with your cravings. But you'll still need to eat chocolate, sugar, salt and starchy foods in moderation. The substitution program will help you.

Q I do get intense cravings for chocolate. I'll try the substitution program, but does this mean I'll never want to eat chocolate again?

A The substitution program works in such a way that, instead of that intense craving for chocolate you now have, you will want only one or two pieces of chocolate occasionally, when you're hungry and have an appetite for chocolate. It's not that you'll never be able to eat it again, only that you'll have a normal desire to eat it.

Q I do crave sweets during my premenstrual phase, but I can usually control that craving—except when I'm alone in the house. What can I do?

A If the craving hits when you're alone in the house, go for a walk—head for a park or a mall, not a supermarket. Also, don't keep the foods you know you will crave in the refrigerator or kitchen cabinet at home.

Q What's going to happen to my weight while I use your substitution program? I've been doing great on your diet, but will I stop losing weight while I fight my food craving?

A The wonderful thing about the Woman's Advantage Diet is that you continue to lose weight during your entire cycle. You will continue to lose weight at the same time that you fight your food cravings with the diet and the substitution program.

Q Since I started the Woman's Advantage Diet, I no longer have food cravings. Do I have to do anything else?

A As long as the diet has worked to rid you of those weight gaining food cravings, you don't have to do another thing. The substitution program is for those people and those occasions when the diet isn't sufficient.

Q I get food cravings at all different times. Will the substitution program work for me?

A The substitution program works no matter when those food cravings hit. Be sure to follow the Woman's Advantage Diet as well.

Q I seem to have a strange reaction to foods prepared with MSG. If I use MSG when I'm cooking, I develop cravings for everything I've cooked. Why is that?

A MSG is a flavor enhancer, and it can certainly increase cravings for food cooked with it. Don't use MSG when you cook, and when you eat in a restaurant where MSG is used (this could be a Chinese restaurant or an American steak house), request that your food be prepared without it.

---

1. See Bibliography references 8 (Barris, Dawson and Theiss 1980), 17 (Diamond and Mast 1972), 18 (Doty et al. 1981), 27 (Henkin 1974), 42 (Mair et al. 1978), and 61 (Wong and Tong 1974).

10 EXERCISE AND THE WOMAN'S ADVANTAGE DIET

First, let me say that you don't have to exercise when you follow the Woman's Advantage Diet. You will lose weight without exercise.

Then let me add that if you do exercise, you will lose body weight faster, because exercise burns up body fat. I can't tell you exactly how many more pounds you will lose, because that depends on how frequently you exercise and the type of exercise you do. However, I can tell you that you will lose anywhere from 10 percent to 20 percent more weight during each cycle if you combine the diet with exercise.

Why You Should Volunteer

Exercising is strictly a volunteer activity when you're on the Woman's Advantage Diet, but you should opt to do it because:

• As I've said, exercise burns up body fat, and you'll lose weight faster.

• Moderate exercise can decrease the appetite.

• Exercise can lessen food cravings. [1]

• Exercise affects metabolism and will help you keep weight off after you've lost it.

• Exercise will make you look better as flab is replaced by muscles and connective tissue.

159

• Exercise reduces stress and worry, and this helps eliminate anxiety induced eating.

• Exercise makes you feel better about yourself, and it will help you stop looking to food for comfort.

• Exercise is great for the cardiovascular system.

• Exercise can lower cholesterol.

• Exercise is a great shield against osteoporosis.

Exercise and Your Premenstrual Phase

You will find exercise most beneficial to your weight loss efforts during the premenstrual phase of your cycle.[2] If you plan to do a limited amount of exercising, I strongly recommend that you do it during this phase. Exercise at this time works in conjunction with your natural hormones to help you shed pounds even faster.

Exercise will also help rid you of PMS symptoms. You'll see that food cravings, angers and irritations will lessen, and aches and pains will disappear even more quickly when you combine exercise with the Woman's Advantage Diet.

When I describe the marvelous results of diet and exercise during the premenstrual phase, I'm frequently asked to recommend "the best exercise" for this phase.

There is no best exercise! All exercise works equally well at this time. You can walk, do calisthenics, swim, jog—whatever you prefer. Any exercise will help you lose weight, and the good news is that the exercise doesn't have to be strenuous. Walking twenty minutes each day during the premenstrual phase will improve weight loss just as much as a fast game of racquetball. The important thing is to emphasize exercise during your premenstrual phase.

I don't see how you can resist exercising during your premenstrual phase when you know it will rid you of weight and many of the troubling symptoms of PMS as well.

There's an Exercise Program That's Made for You

If the word *exercise* scares you, don't let it. There are many levels of exercise. Take a look at the following list. There may be an exercise that you haven't as yet thought of, but that you would really enjoy.

Aerobics
Backpacking
Badminton
Bicycling
Calisthenics
Canoeing
Cross country skiing
Dancing
Downhill skiing
Golf
Hiking
Ice skating
Jogging
Roller skating
Rope skipping
Rowing
Running
Swimming
Table tennis
Tennis
Volleyball
Walking

You can do almost all these exercises either alone or with friends. Local health clubs offer many facilities and group classes, or if you prefer, you can exercise in the privacy of your own home using rowing, bicycle or cross country ski machines, or doing simple calisthenics. If nothing I've mentioned appeals to you, there is still a way that you can make exercise a part of your life, and you'll only have to change your daily routine a little bit.

The Activity Program

To create an activity program that will work for you, examine what you do every weekday and weekend. If you go to work, how do you get there? How do you do the marketing? Do you take the kids to school? How do you get to a friend's house? How do you run errands? When you take notice of all the things that you get done in one week, you will realize that you are a more active person than you thought you were.

Now, take all those activities that you are already involved in and make them work for you as a form of exercise.

Walking Whenever You Can

Walking is one of the best and easiest forms of exercise, and you can easily make it part of a daily activity program.

• If you take a bus to work, get off the bus five streets before your usual stop. Walk those five blocks to and from the bus every day, and you will have walked a total of ten blocks. You can work up gradually to walking more every day.

• If you take the train to work, don't take any other form of transportation after you get off the train. Walk the distance from the train station to your place of employment.

• When you go to lunch, spend half your lunch break eating, and half your lunch break walking.

• If you drive to work, don't park your car at the nearest garage. Choose one a few blocks away and walk to your place of employment.

• Ride a bicycle to work instead of driving or taking public transportation.

• Instead of driving your kids to school on nice days, walk them there.

• If you're running two or three errands, walk from one place to the next rather than drive.

• Planning to have dinner out? Walk to and from the restaurant.

• Going to a movie? Walk there, or if it's too far and you drive, don't park your car near the entrance to the movie theatre. Park it a few streets away and walk the rest of the way.

• Invite a friend to join you for a walk on a pleasant Saturday or Sunday afternoon. Go to a popular park, a zoo, or a botanical garden—somewhere that calls for walking if you want to see the sights. But, remember, your goal is to get exercise, so *walk,* don't saunter. The more you stop the less valuable the exercise will be.

• Spend time in a museum. You'll have to walk to get from one exhibit to another. Remember, to be most valuable, your exercise should be continuous.

• If you live near a beach, take a walk by the water.

• Walk up and down flights of stairs instead of taking an elevator.

Sometimes when I get to this point in my list of walking opportunities, I'm told that none of the walking options will work:

"My office is too far away for me to walk to it, and I park my car in the building garage because the surrounding area isn't safe for my car—or me."

There's always *someplace* to walk. Suburban malls are wonderful places for a walk. They're distracting because of the shop windows (but don't window shop; your walk has to be continuous to be fully beneficial). They're indoors, which means that you can walk on cold or wintry days.

If walking doesn't appeal to you, it's probably because you've never done much of it, and it may take you a while to learn to like it. Start a walking program by walking around the block for ten minutes. Walk at every opportunity, and set a definite goal of a ten minute walk every day to start with. After you've done that for a week or two, raise your sights to a twenty minute walk every day, and eventually an hour of walking three times a week.

You can actually walk away the craving for a snack. If you suddenly want something to eat after supper, try a five minute walk instead. You'll be pleasantly surprised to discover that the yearning for food will disappear, because walking lowers the appetite.

Aerobic Exercise

You've learned to love walking, and now you want to do *more*. You've heard the word *aerobic*, and you're planning to do aerobic exercises—whatever they are. Let me explain:

Aerobics are any type of exercise that uses the large muscle groups and requires large amounts of oxygen. Any of the exercises (except for golf) listed on page 161 can become an aerobic exercise if it's done at a fast and continuous pace. Aerobic exercise is designed to increase your endurance, and improve your cardiovascular system. (Golf is not aerobic because the exercise is not continuous, and there are too many pauses between activities.)

I'm all for aerobic exercising, though I advise a visit to your doctor if you're planning to embark on any strenuous program after living a sedentary lifestyle. I also recommend a series of warm-up and stretching exercises to precede strenuous aerobics.

If you've ever been to a professional studio, you've seen dancers do warm-ups before they start their practice. Warm-ups make the body limber, strengthen the muscles, and gradually increase heartbeat, blood circulation and body temperature. A proper series of warm-ups done *before* aerobic exercising helps prevent strains and sprains, and enables your body to cope with the stress of strenuous exercise. Many people also advise having a cool-down and stretching period immediately following strenuous aerobic activities.

The following are common exercises that I've recommended to my patients for both warm-up and cool-down periods. Do these exercises for about ten minutes before and after aerobics.

Ten Warm-Up Exercises

Lower Back Muscle Stretch: Lie on your back, with your legs stretched out and your arms at your sides. Bring your right leg up to your chest, knee bent. Lower your leg to the floor. Repeat with your left leg. Alternate knee bends. Repeat ten times for each leg at first. Work up to thirty times for each leg.

Upper Back Muscle Stretch: Stand two feet away from a wall, extend your arms, and press your palms flat against the wall. Lean forward toward the wall, and press palms firmly against it as though you were trying to push it away from you. Count to ten. Now lean away from the wall, pushing out against it with your hands; take a deep breath, and repeat the exercise. When you first start, do it five times. Work gradually up to thirty.

Waist Stretch: Stand straight, arms extended out from your shoulders. Your hands should end up not in front of you, but out to each side, parallel to your shoulder line. Twist your body to the left as far as you can, and then twist your body to the right. Don't move your hips; just twist your upper body. Repeat twist ten times at first. Work up to thirty.

Push-up Stretch: Lie on your stomach, legs together, with your hands under your shoulders, palms flat on the floor. Push your body from your knees up off the floor until your arms are straight. Repeat five times, and work gradually up to thirty times.

Standing Leg Stretch: Hold on to any piece of stable furniture that is approximately waist high. Point toe of your outside leg (the leg farthest from the furniture) and slowly raise it straight out in front of you until it is waist high. Lower. Repeat five times. Turn and face the other way, and repeat the exercise with the other leg. Do this five times to start. Work up to thirty gradually.

Sit-ups: Lie on your back with knees bent and hands clasped behind the neck. Raise your head and shoulders off the floor, lifting with your stomach and not your back muscles. Hold for count of two, and return to the lying position. Start with five, and work up to repeating thirty times.

Toe-stands: Stand, placing feet astride by about two feet. Slowly, raise your body until your weight is on your toes. Hold for count of five and lower to standing position. Start with five and build up to thirty times.

Hip-lifts: Sit up on the floor with your arms at your sides and your legs extended straight out in front of you. Raise your hips off the floor, while supporting your body with your arms and heels. Start with five and build to thirty.

Hurdles: Sit on the floor with one leg extended straight out in front of you, and the other leg out to your side at a right angle with the knee bent and your foot behind you. Keeping your back as straight as possible, lean forward, reaching for your toes with your extended arms. Reach as far as you can comfortably and hold for a count of five. Gradually build up your flexibility each time you do this exercise, so that you can eventually touch your nose to your knees. Repeat five times for each leg, building up to thirty.

Jumping Jacks: Stand straight, with feet together and hands at your sides. Jump, so that your feet are spread about shoulder width and at the same time swing your arms up over your head so that you clap your hands. Jump again, returning to the original position of feet together and arms at your sides. Repeat at a fast and continuous pace fifteen times; work up to thirty times.

Starting Slowly

If you haven't exercised recently, I recommend that you start doing so slowly. Whether it's calisthenics, dancing or tennis, don't try to do too much at first. If you do, you may cause injury and discourage yourself from exercising. It's important, also, to use different exercises to improve your strength and endurance.

Day of the Month	Day of Cycle	Cycle Phase	Food Group	Exercise
	1	Menstrual	FORBIDDEN FOODS	
	2			
	3			
	4			
	5			
	6			
	7			
	8			
	1	Postmenstrual	FABULOUS FRUITS AND VEGETABLES	
	2			
	3			
	4			
	5			
	6			
	7			
	8			
	9			
	10			
	11			
	12			
	13			
	14			
	15			
	16			
	17			
	18			
	19			
	20			
	1	Ovulatory	PASTA PLUS	
	2			
	3			
	4			
	5			
	6			
	1	Premenstrual	PROTEIN POWER	
	2			
	3			
	4			
	5			
	6			
	7			
	8			
	9			
	10			
	11			
	12			
	13			
	14			

You should aim to build up your exercising frequency to three times per week. If you have not exercised in the past, you may want to start with five to ten minutes every day until your body gets conditioned. No matter how long your workout, you should always do warm-up and cool-down exercises. Start with about ten minutes of each at first, and build up your strength to do twelve to twenty minutes.

Build yourself up gradually. If you find that you are in pain, stop exercising for that session. The ideas "no pain, no gain" and having to "go for the burn" have been discredited. A slow, steady pace building up gradually to more strenuous exercise is the right way to do it.

Keeping Track of Your Exercising

Use the Woman's Advantage Diet Calendar for Exercise to record the days that you exercise. That will help show you just how beneficial exercise can be, and will help motivate you to do it. You'll want to use the calendar blanks offered at the back of the book; see Chapter 2 for instructions on how to personalize the calendar according to your individual cycle.

Questions and Answers

I've been asked many questions about the relationship of exercise to the Woman's Advantage Diet. Here are the most important queries and my answers to them:

Q Is it all right to exercise while I'm menstruating? My mother always said to take it real easy during that time.

A It's perfectly fine to exercise while you're menstruating or at any other time during your cycle. The idea of not exercising during menstruation is an old-fashioned one and has no basis in scientific fact.

Q I just don't have the time to embark on any exercise program or sport, but I am willing to walk. Will it help to walk during the premenstrual phase?

A It certainly will help you lose weight if you walk. Walking is a perfectly legitimate exercise. In time, you may want to go into aerobic walking, which is rapid walking that increases the heartbeat rate.

Q I've always been afraid to exercise because I thought it would increase my appetite. Are you now saying it works in just the opposite way?

A While heavy and extended exercise may make you hungry, the kind of exercise you do in a normal fitness program actually *decreases* the appetite. Some studies have shown that inactive people have greater appetites than people who are active.

Q Would I lose weight if I just exercised and didn't diet?

A Perhaps, but in nowhere near the efficient manner you would if you combined exercise with the Woman's Advantage Diet. In fact, if you exercised only and you were out of shape when you started, you would run the risk of losing fat but building up the muscle and connective tissue that weighs so much. You'd be in better shape, but you wouldn't have lost pounds.

That's not a bad thing—you'd certainly be healthy—but you might get discouraged about your weight loss efforts. After a while, this muscle weight will stabilize and you'll see normal weight loss accompanying your dieting and exercising efforts. And you'll look much better!

Q I haven't exercised for a lot of years, but I'm inspired by what you've said, and I'm all set to go. Is it all right if I get involved in really strenuous aerobics right away?

A I'm glad you're so enthusiastic, but if you haven't done any exercise for many years, it's really better to start slowly. You have to exercise your muscles to make them strong enough to cope with strenuous exercising. Don't overdo it and injure yourself so that you're forced to stop. Also, don't push yourself on exercises that are hard to do; that will just make you not want to do them. Rather, build yourself up gradually until what was once a difficult exercise is easy for you.

Q My family laughed the first time they saw me do your warm-up exercises. Then they got intrigued, and they want to join in. Is that a good idea?

A I think it's a great idea. It's nice to have a supportive group around you when you're exercising. That's why many people go to a gym instead of exercising at home.

Q You recommend walking, but it's not that easy to walk either where I work or where I live. The neighborhoods aren't completely safe, and I certainly couldn't take a walk at night to take my mind off having a snack. What do you suggest?

A I certainly don't recommend walking where it's not safe. But have you tried walking around a shopping center or shopping mall? You can have an enjoyable walk in an area that's usually safe because there are many other people walking about as well. You might also consider just using the stairs in your house or apartment building.

You could also purchase exercise equipment. There are stationary rowing machines, cross country ski machines, bicycling machines, treadmills for jogging, Nautilus and stretching apparatus that can be used in the safety of your own home.

Q Is it best to exercise at any special time of the day? Someone told me that if I don't exercise in the morning before I go to work, the exercise won't have any effect. Is that true?

A That absolutely isn't true. You can exercise whenever it fits in with your schedule. Some people enjoy exercising first thing in the morning, but some of my patients have told me that they like to exercise at night before dinner because this really cuts down on appetite. If you decide to exercise before dinner or before any meal, you'll get another benefit: The exercise will increase your rate of metabolism, and the calories you consume during that meal will be burned up faster.

Q Will exercise have any effect on my hormones during my postmenstrual phase?

A Unless you do very strenuous exercise, your hormones won't be affected by exercise during your postmenstrual phase.

Q Is there any time during the cycle when I shouldn't exercise?

A There is no special time during the cycle when you shouldn't exercise, but I don't think it's a good idea to exercise on a day when your schedule is already crammed with activities. If you have a sixteen hour workday ahead of you, or if each hour is filled with work and other obligations, it's probably not a good idea to exercise. Exercise is meant to relieve stress, not to create more of it. But, remember, a short exercise session in the midst of a tense day can let off critical steam. In general, just try to do twenty minutes of aerobic exercise three times a week, or an hour of walking a week.

Q I plan to do your stretch exercises while I'm on the Woman's Advantage Diet, but after I lose ten pounds I'm going off the diet. Can I stop exercising then, too?

A It's a good idea to exercise even when you're not on a diet. Exercise can make you feel better, and it's good for your health. The choice is yours.

---

1. For further information on food intake, body weight and body composition, see Bibliography reference 50 (Segal and Pi-Sunyer 1989).
2. See Bibliography references 33 (Jurkowski et al. 1981) and 34 (Jurkowski et al. 1978).

11 THE WOMAN'S ADVANTAGE DIET AND YOUR FAMILY

It's a good idea to tell your family and close friends that you're on a diet. People who are close to you and who love you can be a marvelously supportive backup to all your diet plans.

You know that what other people say about your weight and shape means a lot to you. Frankly, most women want to lose weight because they're displeased with their image, and because they believe that they see some measure of that displeasure in the eyes of others.

I always ask each new patient why she wants to lose weight. The *first* thing I hear is, "I don't like the way I look." The *second* thing I'm told is, "I know it's not healthy to be overweight."

I believe you should go on a diet—first of all—to improve your health. But we both know you are also going on a diet because you would like to be more attractive to other people. That's why I recommend that you involve the most important *other* person in your life in your diet plans.

Tell your husband or boyfriend all about the Woman's Advantage Diet. Once he knows how it works, he won't be puzzled when you emphasize eating certain foods during the various phases of your cycle.

When the people close to you understand that you have certain eating problems, they can help you solve them. Let's say you're starving when you get home from work, and the first thing you do is run to the refrigerator for a fattening snack. If your husband—and kids, too—know that you're working hard to lose weight, they could have the refrigerator stocked with carrot sticks, celery stalks, and rounds of freshly cut cucumber. Maybe you can't resist snacking after dinner as you watch TV. Talk about this problem, and the person who lives with you—and loves you—might make sure that available snacks are fresh fruit, rice cakes, and other snack foods that are recommended on the Woman's Advantage Diet.

If you've dieted before—and who hasn't?—your family will appreciate that this is one diet that doesn't ask you to serve them weird foods at mealtime. There's no reason why everyone who joins you for a meal can't eat the same foods that you're eating. As I've explained before, this is a Woman's *Advantage* Diet, and the advantage of your hormonal cycle will not apply to a man or to young children. Eating the same food that you do will not mean that your husband or young children will lose weight. Just remember, other members of your family will probably eat more than you do. Don't try to keep up with them in terms of serving sizes and number of servings. You're trying to lose weight, and you have to be careful not to overeat. If the other members of your family don't have to or aren't trying to lose weight, they don't have to follow the "rules of the game."

Your husband, boyfriend, or children may want to eat more than you do, but this doesn't mean that you have to prepare one array of foods for them and another menu of foods for yourself. The Woman's Advantage Diet is well balanced, and can be eaten and enjoyed by everyone. If you do want to modify the diet for children, add one or two extra items to your menu—a baked potato, a pasta dish, or another vegetable. My patients find the Woman's Advantage Diet controls their appetites so effectively, they have no trouble forgoing such extra side dishes.

If you're concerned that the diet is going to affect others in your house—don't be! I have never had anyone who has been on the program complain that it is interfering with the lifestyle of other members in the family. In fact, most of the time it actually improves the eating habits of husbands and children. It is not uncommon for a husband to remark that the family is eating better, and enjoying a wider variety of foods now than before his wife started the diet.

On the other hand, your husband or children may be overweight, and they may not want to do anything about the problem. Let me assure you that even in a situation like that, you can be successful in losing weight. The Woman's Advantage Diet gives you the excellent appetite control you need to avoid temptations. In fact, patients have remarked to me that even though others around them are overeating—something that often takes the typical dieter off her diet—that does not occur for those on the Woman's Advantage Diet.

What About My Daughter?

One excellent benefit for those mothers concerned about a teenage daughter's overweight condition is that here, finally, is a weight loss method that your daughter can use to solve her weight problem. As long as your daughter has reached puberty, she can diet with you. It is not uncommon for a previously distraught mother to tell me that for the first time her daughter has been able to lose weight, and rid herself of the terrible habit of eating junk foods.

On the other hand, you might have a daughter who doesn't want or need to lose weight. Maybe she even needs to gain some. If she's reached puberty and eats primarily at home, you'll have to take care to supplement her diet to make sure she doesn't lose weight because of the Woman's Advantage Diet menus she is sharing with you. While there's a potential for a problem here, frankly it couldn't be easier to solve. Just make sure your daughter eats generous servings. Also, add the following supplementary foods to her menu as side dishes.

To Protein Power (during premenstruation), add a carbohydrate (a vegetable, fruit or grain) to her menu.

To Fabulous Fruits and Vegetables (during postmenstruation), add a protein (meat, poultry, fish, seafood, tofu or cheese).

To Pasta Power (during ovulation), add a protein (meat, poultry, fish, seafood, tofu or cheese).

You won't have a problem with the Forbidden Foods phase, as long as your daughter eats generous portions.

Getting Your Husband Involved

Most husbands are delighted with the program because it does not interfere with the way they eat. As you know by now, the Woman's Advantage Diet is four eating programs rolled into one. The variety helps keep your husband from getting bored. One patient even told me her husband didn't notice she was on a diet!

Certainly, the Woman's Advantage Diet never asks you to serve only one kind of food or a restricted menu to your husband every night. The special menu you eat changes every few days.

Since your husband will be happy with his meals, I think you'll find he'll be more than willing to help you with your dieting efforts. How can he do this? The complaining he's *not* doing is a great first step. You might also find shopping together very helpful. He can help you make sure that the right foods are purchased. You may also start to exercise together. Whether it be the activity or the aerobic program, exercising together can be fun, and serve as a further aid to motivating you.

In general, I offer these tips to those of my patients who are married or involved with someone.

• Take time out of your busy schedule to talk about your diet with each other.

• Make sure that both of you work to keep only the right foods in the house.

• Be honest with each other; if you have violated the diet, tell your husband.

• Be supportive of each other. Remind your husband that a little praise goes a long way when you've been faithful to the diet.

• Work together to preplan meals.

• Any time you have to go to a party, wedding or other social occasion where food is present, stay together. Even the silent support of your partner will remind you of your diet goals.

You, Your Diet, and Casual Friends

I do recommend that you tell people close to you about your diet, and enlist their support and their help. I don't recommend that you go into great detail about dieting to casual acquaintances.

If you're at a party and you see that most of the food being offered is too fattening, you'll only make the party-goers uncomfortable if you tell them that you can't eat a thing because you're on a diet. There's enough of a choice on the Woman's Advantage Diet so that you can usually find something to eat when you're at a party. Instead of demanding attention by stating, "I can't eat that, I'm on a diet," just eat those foods that are permissible on the diet.

The most gratifying way to attract attention when you're dieting is to lose weight and then hear someone say, "You look marvelous! Have you been on a diet?"

12 THE WOMAN'S ADVANTAGE DIET STAY-SLIM MAINTENANCE PLAN

For many of my patients, the most difficult part of dieting confronts them when they reach their goal weight. Losing the weight was easy, they say; they had a specific goal, and they were motivated to carefully follow the guidelines for either Menu Style Dieters or Designer Style Dieters. But once they lost the weight, they became uncertain. They look great, they feel great, and they don't ever want to be overweight again, but they're afraid they'll slip back into their old eating patterns that led to their weight gain in the first place.

I don't blame them. We all know too many people (including ourselves!) who have successfully lost weight only to put it back on in the weeks and months after completing a diet. Many people believe this happens because the ex-dieter is so hungry from long-term starvation that she binges until the weight is back. If you've been on the Woman's Advantage Diet, you don't have that problem because you didn't feel as though you were "starving" while you lost weight. But I know you still might be nervous, believing that you'll binge or, worse, just make the kind of day-to-day food choices that slowly but steadily lead to weight gain.

I sympathize with your fears, but let me assure you that I think your only real problem is that you're not quite ready yet to trust yourself around food again. All you need is a little help in learning how to relax about eating. To give you that help, I've developed the Stay-Slim maintenance plan. The Woman's Advantage Diet Stay-Slim Maintenance Plan is a well-balanced, evenhanded approach to eating. It is designed to help you incorporate the good eating habits you learned while on the Woman's Advantage Diet into your everyday life. Instead of emphasizing either forbidden foods, high fiber carbohydrates, low fiber carbohydrates, or protein during the four phases of the menstrual cycle, the Stay-Slim Plan offers fairly equal amounts of foods containing those nutrients every day.

There are only two significant exceptions to this rule. The first has to do with Forbidden Foods. Because you're not trying to lose weight, these foods are not as "forbidden" as they were before. But they are still high in fat and calories, and you should not overindulge in them. This can be an especially tricky area for the recent dieter, so I think you need to be extra careful. I recommend indulging in a Forbidden Food treat only during your menstruation, and then only on non-consecutive days.

The other exception to the basic Stay-Slim Maintenance Plan has to do with the week before you start your period, when I recommend you use a Protein-Power-like eating plan. I call this eating plan Stay-Slim II. When combined with a regular menu the rest of the month, Stay-Slim II won't lead to weight *loss*. You're allowed more food during the week before your period during maintenance than you were during the original Protein Power eating plan. While this balance prevents weight loss, the good eating habits you learned during the diet that are now the basis of Stay-Slim will prevent weight gain.

(If you find your weight sneaking up a little, try returning to the original Protein Power for the two weeks before your period. You'll find this is a quick, easy and safe way to shed any extra pounds that may be creeping up on you. If that's insufficient, I recommend you return to the Women's Advantage Diet for your full cycle).

The best part is that, by sticking with Stay-Slim II the week before your period, you can continue to enjoy the *advantages* the Woman's Advantage Diet gave you in terms of PMS and food cravings. Stay-Slim II, because of its modified version of Protein Power, will keep you from ever again being burdened with PMS. Stay-Slim II will also help keep you free of food cravings. But if you're ever tempted, you'll find the substitution program from Chapter 9 will be just as effective during Stay-Slim as it was while you were losing weight.

The Rules of the Game

You are on the Stay-Slim maintenance plan, but there are some good ideas from the Women's Advantage Diet that you should follow:

Don't overeat. Yes, you can have toast or a bagel every morning, if you wish, but make sure that's *one* slice of toast or *one* bagel. In general, the portion size instructions in Chapter 3 still hold true.

Keep fat intake low. This is a good idea not just for dieters, but for everyone. Stick to low fat yogurt and cottage cheese; and use reduced calorie spreads and salad dressings, or their naturally low in calorie whole food alternatives.

Don't gorge on sugar rich foods. Use artificial sweeteners in beverages and on cereal, drink only naturally sweetened fruit juices, and stick to diet sodas, water or juice spritzers. Cookies, cakes, pies, candies and other sweets should still only be occasional treats and never a regular part of your diet.

As before, trim all visible fat from meat and remove the skin from chicken. Broil or roast meat, and steam or boil vegetables. Never fry.

The Stay-Slim maintenance plan allows a greater variety of food every day than the Woman's Advantage Diet did; you'll have even more choices than before. But, in general, the good eating habits described in Chapter 3 still hold true. Indulge in *what* you eat, rather than *how much* you eat. Choose *what* you eat sensibly—and I think you'll find your weight problems are permanently things of the past.

Stay-Slim Maintenance Plan for the Designer Style Dieter

There are two phases to the Stay-Slim Plan. The first will help you incorporate into your everyday life the good eating habits you learned while on the diet. It's called Stay-Slim I, and you'll use it for three-quarters of your cycle (from the first day of menstruation until a week before the first day of your next period).

The menstrual phase of Stay-Slim I is the time to have your Forbidden Foods treats. Remember to have them only then, and never to have them on two consecutive days. See the Special Forbidden Foods List later in this chapter for guidelines as to what these foods are.

The second phase of the maintenance plan, called Stay-Slim II, is for you to follow the week before your period. Remember, this is not a weight loss food plan. Stay-Slim II is designed to keep you free of PMS symptoms and food cravings.

Stay-Slim I for the Designer Style Dieter

Remember, the key to the Stay-Slim I maintenance plan (to be followed from the first day of menstruation until the week before your period begins again) is to eat

LOTS OF CARBOHYDRATES AND PROTEIN
and some fat

Following is the Advantage Food Group list for Stay-Slim I. Remember, you should use these lists to guide your food choices, and you should do so according to the Advantage Food Plan, which follows the list. (Snack foods are in *italics.*)

FRUITS

acerola
apple (any kind)
apricot (any kind)
avocado (any kind)
banana
berry
  blackberry
  blueberry
  boysenberry
  cranberry
  dewberry
  elderberry
  huckleberry
  lingonberry
  mulberry
  raspberry
  strawberry
carambola
cherimoya
cherry (all kinds)
dried fruit
  apple
  apricot
  banana
  date
  orange
  pineapple
  prune
fijoa
fig
genipap
grape (any kind)
grapefruit
guava
kiwi

kumquat
lemon
lime
loquat
lychee
mango
medlar
melon
  cantaloupe
  casaba
  Crenshaw
  honeydew
  Persian
  watermelon
nectarine
orange (any kind)
papaya
passion fruit
pawpaw
peach (any kind)
pear (any kind)
persimmon
pineapple
plantain
plum (any kind)
pomegranate
prickly pear
prune
quince
sapodilla
tamarind
tangelo (any kind)
tangerine (any kind)
ugli fruit

VEGETABLES

alfalfa sprouts
anise
artichoke
arugula
asparagus
bamboo shoots
basil
bean sprout
beet
broccoli
Brussels sprout
cabbage
  Chinese
  green
  red
cardoon
carrot
cassava
cauliflower
celeriac
celery
cilantro
collard
cucumber
dandelion
dill
eggplant
endive
escarole
fiddlehead
garlic
green peas
heart of palm
hot pepper (any kind)
jicama
kale
kohlrabi

leek
legume
  adzuki bean
  black or turtle bean
  black-eyed pea
  carob
  chickpea
  cranberry bean
  fava bean
  garbanzo
  great northern bean
  green bean
  kidney bean
  lentil
  lima bean
  marrow bean
  mung bean
  navy bean
  pea bean
  pink bean
  pinto bean
  red bean
  tofu (soybean)
  split pea
lettuce (any kind)
lotus
mushroom
mustard green
okra
onion (any kind)
parsley
parsnip
potato (any kind)
radish
rhubarb
rutabaga
salsify

savory cabbage
sea vegetable
  arami
  dulse
  hijiki
  nori
  wakame
snow pea
sorrel
spinach
squash
  acorn
  butternut
  hubbard
  long cocozelle

pumpkin
yellow crookneck
yellow straightneck
zucchini
sweet pepper
  green
  red
  yellow
sweet potato
Swiss chard
tomato
truffle
turnip
watercress
yam

GRAINS AND GRAIN PRODUCTS

barley
buckwheat (not a true grain)
cereal
  All-Bran, original
  All-Bran, with extra fiber
  barley
  Bran Buds
  Bran Chex
  bran flakes
  Corn Chex
  corn flakes
  Cream of Rice
  Cream of Wheat
  Crispix
  Crispy Wheats 'n Raisins
  Double Chex
  Fiber One
  Fruit & Fibre
  grits
  Just Right

Life
Müeslix Bran
Nutri-Grain, biscuits
Nutri-Grain, corn
Nutri-Grain, nuggets
Nutri-Grain, wheat
oat bran
oatmeal
100% Bran
Product 19
puffed rice
puffed wheat
Quaker Oat Squares
raisin bran
Rice Krispies
shredded wheat
Shredded Wheat 'n Bran
Special K
Team
Total

GRAINS AND GRAIN PRODUCTS *(cont.)*

Weetabix
Wheat Chex
Wheatena
wheat germ
Wheaties
corn
corn starch
millet
oat
pasta
  capellini
  cellophane noodle
  egg noodle
  elbow
  farfalle
  fedelini
  fettucini
  fusilli
  gnocchi
  lasagna
  linguine
  lo mein noodle
  macaroni
  macaroni bow
  manicotti

  orzo
  ravioli
  rigatoni
  rotini
  shell
  spaghetti
  spaghettini
  tortellini
  vermicelli
  ziti
popcorn
quinoa
rice
  brown
  cake
  long grain
  white
  wild
rye
sorghum
triticale
wheat
  berry
  bulgur
  cracked

BREADS AND BREAD PRODUCTS

bagel
  egg
  fruit
  nut
  plain
  poppy seed
  pumpernickel
  raisin
  rye
  whole wheat

bread and roll
  black
  bran
  cracked wheat
  French
  Italian
  oatmeal
  pita
  pumpernickel
  rye

white enriched
whole wheat
crackers
  Finn Crisp
  Ry-Krisp
muffin
  bran
  corn
  English
  granola
  nut

plain
raisin
whole wheat
pancake and French toast
  buckwheat
  buttermilk
  cornmeal
  fruit
  oatmeal
  plain
  whole wheat

DAIRY PRODUCTS

buttermilk
cheese
  Camembert
  farmer
  low fat, low sodium
    American
  low fat cottage
  low fat Monterey Jack
  low fat mozzarella

  low fat ricotta
  Neufchâtel
  Parmesan
  Romano
frozen low fat yogurt
frozen skim milk
low fat sour cream
low fat yogurt

MEATS, POULTRY AND EGGS

egg
egg substitute
meat
  beef
  goat
  hare
  lamb
  pork
  veal

poultry
  chicken
  Cornish hen
  grouse
  partridge
  pheasant
  quail
  turkey
reduced calorie gelatin
  (animal protein based)

FISH AND SEAFOOD

fish
  Atlantic sturgeon
  bass
  brook trout
  cod
  crevalle jack
  croaker
  cusk
  drum
  flounder
  grouper
  haddock
  hake
  halibut
  lingcod
  mahimahi
  monkfish
  orange roughy
  perch
  pike
  pollock
  red snapper

  rockfish
  sauger
  shark
  smelt
  sole
  tilefish
  tuna
  whiting
  yellowtail snapper
seafood
  abalone
  clam
  crab
  crayfish
  langostino
  lobster
  mussel
  octopus
  oyster
  scallop
  shrimp
  squid

SOUP

artichoke
barley
bean
beef
  broth
  consommé
  noodle
borscht
carrot
chicken
  broth

consommé
gumbo
mushroom
noodle
rice
cucumber
egg drop
fish
gazpacho
hot and sour
leek

lentil
Manhattan clam chowder
minestrone
mushroom
onion
Oriental noodle
spinach and shrimp broth
split pea
strawberry

tomato
tropical fruit
turkey noodle
vegetable
  bean
  beef
  plain
vichyssoise
won ton

CONDIMENTS

chocolate extract
chutney (avoid any type with
    added sugar, dried fruits
    or nuts)
cranberry sauce (avoid any
    type with added sugar)
Cumberland sauce
honey
hot pepper sauce
  chili
  harissa
  horseradish
  Indian
  Mexican salsa
  nam prik
  sambal
  Tabasco
  wasabi

jelly (avoid any type with
    added sugar)
ketchup
maple syrup (reduced calorie
    brands)
mayonnaise (reduced calorie
    brands)
miso
mustard (avoid any sweet
    type)
ponzu sauce
relish
soy sauce
steak sauce
tamari sauce
teriyaki sauce
vanilla extract
vinegar
Worcestershire sauce

FATS

dairy
  butter
oils
  corn
  cottonseed
  olive

peanut
rapeseed
safflower
sunflower
vegetable
  margarine

SPICES AND HERBS

allspice	hyssop
almond	licorice
angelica	mace
anise	marjoram
arrowroot	melilot
basil	mint
bay leaf	mugwort
bergamot	mustard
black pepper	nasturtium
caper	nutmeg
caraway	oregano
cardamon	paprika
cayenne pepper	parsley
chervil	peppermint
chive	purslane
cinnamon	rocambole
clove	rocket
coriander	rosemary
cream of tartar	rue
cumin	saffron
curry	sage
dill	salad burnet
fennel	savory
fenugreek	scurvy grass
garlic	sesame
ginger	sorrel

star anise	tarragon
stonecrop	thyme
sweet cicely	turmeric
tamarind	vanilla
tansy	violet

ALCOHOL
(recommended for cooking purposes only)

beer	sherry
brandy	wine

BEVERAGES

apple juice	mineral water
carbonated water	orange juice
coffee	reduced calorie hot
cranberry juice	chocolate
decaffeinated coffee	skim milk
diet soda	tangelo juice
grape juice	tangerine juice
grapefruit	tea
herbal tea	tomato juice
juice spritzer	vegetable juice
lemonade	water

The Food Plans for Stay-Slim I

(Remember to check the size of all portions, using the guidelines in this chapter and Chapter 3.)

THE ADVANTAGE FOOD PLAN
FOR THE STAY-SLIM I
BREAKFAST
ALLOWS YOU TO HAVE

♀ **As a main dish, one of these:** two servings of Canadian bacon;

or, two servings of eggs;

or, one serving of Canadian bacon and one egg;

or, one serving of either low fat yogurt or low fat cottage cheese;

♀ **As a side dish, one of these:** one serving of cereal, muffin, bagel, pancake or French toast;

or, two servings of bread—*with*

♀ **As a side dish:** one serving of fruit—*with*

♀ **As a side dish:** one serving of fruit juice, vegetable juice, skim milk or reduced calorie hot chocolate—*with*

♀ **As a beverage:** coffee, decaffeinated coffee, tea or herbal tea.

THE ADVANTAGE FOOD PLAN
FOR THE STAY SLIM I
LUNCH
ALLOWS YOU TO HAVE

♀ **As a main dish, one of these:** a sandwich on any of the breads with meat, poultry, fish, seafood, cheese, tofu or vegetables;

or, a salad with any of the vegetables and meat, poultry, fish, seafood, cheese or tofu;

or, one serving of pasta and vegetables (a pasta salad)— *with*

♀ **As a side dish:** one serving of vegetables;

or, a bowl of soup—*with*

♀ **As a dessert:** one serving of fruit— *with*

♀ **As a beverage:** decaffeinated coffee, tea, herbal tea, diet soda, juice spritzer, mineral water, carbonated water, or water.

THE ADVANTAGE FOOD PLAN
FOR THE STAY-SLIM I
DINNER
ALLOWS YOU TO HAVE

♀ **As an appetizer:** one serving of either salad with any of the vegetables or soup—*with*

♀ **As a main dish, one of these:** one serving of meat, poultry, fish, seafood or tofu;

or, one serving of pasta with a meat, poultry, fish, seafood or vegetable sauce—*with*

♀ **As a side dish, one of these:** two servings of vegetables;

or, one serving of potato, rice, or grain;

or, one small serving of pasta (this is appropriate only if you've chosen a serving of meat, poultry, fish or seafood as a main dish)—*with*

♀ **As a dessert:** one serving of fruit, frozen skim milk or frozen low fat yogurt—*with*

♀ **As a beverage:** decaffeinated coffee, tea, herbal tea, diet soda, juice spritzer, mineral water, carbonated water, or water.

THE ADVANTAGE FOOD PLAN
FOR THE STAY-SLIM I
SNACK
ALLOWS YOU TO HAVE

♀ One or two items as often as twice a day from any of the foods that are in italics. If you're not hungry, it's not necessary to eat a snack.

Special Forbidden Foods List

These are the special foods you can indulge in on nonconsecutive days of your menstrual phase. Refer to the Stay-Slim menus for guidelines about when and how to eat these foods. Remember, they should be part of your regular menu, not an addition to it.

I have listed here the Forbidden Foods we discussed in Chapter 4. However, you should consider these foods only a partial list. I think you've learned enough to know a Forbidden Food when you see one. It's high in fat and calories, and does not belong as a regular part of any healthful diet. If you have a particular love for such a food that is not listed here, I think it is safe to say you can indulge in it during the menstrual phase of Stay-Slim I. Just remember, have such foods only once every other day during menstruation.

1	slice bacon
1	12-ounce bottle of reduced calorie beer
1	brownie
1	slice of cake
1	croissant
1	doughnut
1	serving (about 2 ounces) of french fries
½	fried chicken breast
1	serving (about 2 ounces) fried clams
1	scoop ice cream
1	ice cream sandwich
1	ice cream bar
1	ounce liqueur
1	pickle
1	slice pie
½	cup pudding
1	link breakfast sausage
1	waffle
1	glass (about 3½ ounces) wine

Stay-Slim II for the Designer Style Dieter

Remember, the key to the Stay-Slim II maintenance program (to be followed only the week before your next period starts) is to eat

LOTS OF PROTEIN
some carbohydrates
(and very little fat)

Following is the Advantage Food Group list for Stay-Slim II. Remember you should use these lists to guide your food choices, and you should do so according to the Advantage Food Plan, which follows the list. (Snack foods are in *italics*.)

FRUITS

cherimoya
cherry (any kind)
genipap
grape (any kind)
grapefruit
lime
lychee
mangosteen
melon
   cantaloupe
   casaba
   Crenshaw

honeydew
Persian
watermelon
papaya
pawpaw
peach (any kind)
persimmon
pineapple
plum (any kind)
tangelo (any kind)
tangerine (any kind)
ugli fruit

VEGETABLES

anise
arugula
asparagus
basil
cauliflower
celeriac
celery
cilantro
cucumber
dandelions
dill
endive
escarole
fiddlehead
garlic
hot pepper (any kind)
kale
kohlrabi
leek

lettuce (any kind)
lotus
mushroom
mustard green
onion (any kind)
parsley
radish
scallion
sorrel
sweet pepper
  green
  red
  yellow
Swiss chard
tofu (soybean)
tomato
truffle
watercress

GRAINS AND GRAIN PRODUCTS

cereal
  Corn Chex
  corn flakes
  Cream of Rice
  Cream of Wheat
  Crispix
  Crispy Wheats 'n Raisins
  Double Chex
  grits
  Just Right
  Life
  oatmeal
  Product 19
  puffed rice
  puffed wheat

  Rice Krispies
  Special K
  Team
  Total
  Wheat Chex
  Wheatena
  wheat germ
  Wheaties
popcorn
rice
  brown
  cake
  long grain
  white
  wild

BREADS AND BREAD PRODUCTS

bagel
  egg
  plain
bread
  French
  Italian
  pita
  white enriched

muffin
  English
  plain
pancake and French toast
  buttermilk
  plain
roll and bun
  plain

DAIRY PRODUCTS

buttermilk
cheese
  Camembert
  farmer
  feta
  low fat cottage
  low fat, low sodium
    American
  low fat Monterey Jack

  low fat mozzarella
  low fat ricotta
  Neufchâtel
  Parmesan
  Romano
frozen low fat yogurt
frozen skim milk
low fat sour cream
low fat yogurt

MEATS, POULTRY AND EGGS

egg
egg substitute
meat
  beef
  goat
  hare
  lamb
  pork
  veal

poultry
  chicken
  Cornish hen
  grouse
  partridge
  pheasant
  quail
  turkey
reduced calorie gelatin
  (animal protein based)

FISH AND SEAFOOD

fish
  Atlantic sturgeon
  bass
  brook trout
  cod
  crevalle jack
  croaker
  cusk
  drum
  flounder
  grouper
  haddock
  hake
  halibut
  lingcod
  mahimahi
  monkfish
  orange roughy
  perch
  pike
  pollock
  red snapper
  rockfish
  sauger
  shark
  smelt
  sole
  tilefish
  tuna
  whiting
  yellowtail snapper
seafood
  abalone
  clam
  crab
  crayfish
  langostino
  lobster
  mussel
  octopus
  oyster
  scallop
  shrimp
  squid

SOUP

bean
beef
  broth
  consommé
  noodle
chicken
  broth
  consommé
  noodle
egg drop
lentil
split pea
tropical fruit
turkey noodle
won ton

CONDIMENTS

chocolate extract
chutney (avoid any type with
    added sugar, dried fruits
    or nuts)
cranberry sauce (avoid any
    type with added sugar)
Cumberland sauce
honey
hot pepper sauce
  chili
  harissa
  horseradish
  Indian
  Mexican salsa
  nam prik
  sambai
  Tabasco
  wasabi

jelly (avoid any type with
    added sugar)
ketchup
maple syrup (reduced calorie
    brands)
mayonnaise (reduced calorie
    brands)
mustard (avoid any sweet
    type)
relish
soy sauce
steak sauce
tamari sauce
teriyaki sauce
vanilla extract
vinegar
Worcestershire sauce

FATS

dairy
  butter
oils
  corn
  cottonseed
  olive

peanut
rapeseed
safflower
sunflower
vegetable
  margarine

SPICES AND HERBS

allspice	mint
almond	mugwort
angelica	mustard
anise	nasturtium
arrowroot	nutmeg
basil	oregano
bay leaf	paprika
bergamot	parsley
black pepper	peppermint
caper	purslane
caraway	rocambole
cardamon	rocket
cayenne pepper	rosemary
chervil	rue
chive	saffron
cinnamon	sage
clove	salad burnet
coriander	savory
cream of tartar	scurvy grass
cumin	sesame
curry	sorrel
dill	star anise
fennel	stonecrop
fenugreek	sweet cicely
garlic	tamarind
ginger	tansy
hyssop	tarragon
licorice	thyme
mace	turmeric
marjoram	vanilla
melilot	violet

ALCOHOL
(recommended for cooking purposes only)

beer	sherry
brandy	wine

BEVERAGES

carbonated water	lemonade
decaffeinated coffee	mineral water
diet soda	skim milk
herbal tea	water
juice spritzer	

The Food Plans for Stay-Slim II

THE ADVANTAGE FOOD PLAN
FOR THE STAY-SLIM II
BREAKFAST
ALLOWS YOU TO HAVE

♀ **As a main course, one of these:** two eggs;

or, one serving of Canadian bacon and one egg;

or, one serving of egg with one serving of cheese—*with*

♀ **As a side dish, one of these:** one serving of cereal, muffin, bagel, pancake or French toast;

or, two servings of bread;

or, one serving of low fat yogurt or low fat cottage cheese—*with*

♀ **As a side dish:** one serving of fruit—*with,*

♀ **As a side dish:** one serving of fruit, fruit juice, vegetable juice or skim milk—*with*

♀ **As a beverage:** decaffeinated coffee or herbal tea.

THE ADVANTAGE FOOD PLAN
FOR THE STAY-SLIM II
LUNCH
ALLOWS YOU TO HAVE

♀ **As a main dish, one of these:** a sandwich on any of the breads with meat, poultry, fish, seafood, cheese or tofu;

or, a salad with any of the vegetables and meat, poultry, fish, seafood, cheese or tofu;

or, a bowl of bean soup with one serving of bread—*with*

♀ **As a side dish:** one serving of vegetables—*with*

♀ **As a dessert:** one serving of fruit—*with*

♀ **As a beverage:** decaffeinated coffee, herbal tea, diet soda, juice spritzer, mineral water, carbonated water, or water.

THE ADVANTAGE FOOD PLAN
FOR THE STAY-SLIM II
DINNER
ALLOWS YOU TO HAVE

♀ **As a main dish:** one serving of meat, poultry, fish, seafood, tofu—*with*

♀ **As a side dish, one of these:** a salad with meat, poultry, fish, seafood, tofu or cheese;

or, two vegetables and a salad—*with*

♀ **As a dessert:** one serving of fruit, frozen skim milk or frozen low fat yogurt—*with*

♀ **As a beverage:** decaffeinated coffee, herbal tea, diet soda, juice spritzer, mineral water, carbonated water, or water.

THE ADVANTAGE FOOD PLAN
FOR THE STAY-SLIM II
SNACK
ALLOWS YOU TO HAVE

♀ One or two items as often as twice a day from any of the foods that are in italics. If you're not hungry, it's not necessary to eat a snack.

Stay-Slim Maintenance Plan for the Menu Style Dieter

Stay-Slim has two phases for the Menu Style Dieter, too. I've provided three weeks' worth of menus for Stay-Slim I, which you should use from the first day of menstruation until a week before the first day of your next period. If your cycle is longer than twenty-one days, just repeat your favorite days from the Stay-Slim I menus. Following these menus, you will find seven days' worth of menus for Stay-Slim II.

What Does the Number Mean?

The number in parentheses following some items points you to the recipe for that entry, which is included in the back of the book.

DAY 1 Stay-Slim I

BREAKFAST
Corn cereal
Raspberries
Orange juice
Coffee or tea

SNACK
Carrots

LUNCH
Tuna and Bean Salad (51)
Hard roll
Cantaloupe
Skim milk

SNACK
Apple

DINNER
London broil
Baked Potato (121)
Salad with Parsley Dressing (177)
Frozen Nectarine Yogurt (199)
Lemon flavored carbonated water

DAY 2 Stay-Slim I

BREAKFAST
Cinnamon French Toast (7)
Canadian bacon
Pear
Coffee or tea

SNACK
Apple

LUNCH
> Chicken noodle soup
> Vegetarian Pizza (57)
> Baked Fruit Cup (188)
> Lemonade (237)

SNACK
> *Camembert cheese*

DINNER
> *Forbidden Food Treat:* fried chicken
> Oven French Fries (137)
> Coleslaw Bowl (158)
> Cocoa Angel Food Cake (196)
> Herbal tea

DAY 3 Stay-Slim I

BREAKFAST
> Herbed Zucchini 'n' Eggs (13)
> Orange juice
> Coffee or tea

SNACK
> *Pear*

LUNCH
> Salmon salad (44)
> Celery
> Ry-Krisp crackers
> Grapefruit spritzer

SNACK
> *Peach*

DINNER
> Chicken and Spinach Manicotti (70)
> Tomato-Mozzarella Salad (180)
> Corn-Stuffed Tomatoes with Basil (128)
> Carrot Cake (193)
> Apple Cider Spritzer (224)

DAY 4 Stay-Slim I

BREAKFAST
Oatmeal
Strawberries
Grapefruit juice
Coffee or tea

SNACK
Nectarine

LUNCH
Ham and Tomato Pitas (38)
Vegetable Bean Soup (116)
Iced herbal tea

SNACK
Papaya

DINNER
Crab Quiche (77)
Carrot Pancakes (126)
Zesty Bean Salad (183)
Forbidden Food Treat: ice cream sandwich
Grapefruit Spritzer (234)

DAY 5 Stay-Slim I

BREAKFAST
Wheat cereal
Blueberries
Tangerine juice
Coffee or tea

SNACK
Apple

LUNCH
>Pasta Salad with Tuna (41)
>Pineapple
>Iced Espresso (236)

SNACK
>*Plum*

DINNER
>Shrimp Jambalaya (92)
>Nasturtium-Leaf Salad (171)
>Mushroom Salad (169)
>Frozen Whipped Berries (201)
>Apple juice

DAY 6 Stay-Slim I

BREAKFAST
>Apple Pancakes (1)
>Grapefruit juice
>Coffee or tea

SNACK
>*Orange*

LUNCH
>Pizza Sandwich (42)
>Skim milk

SNACK
>*Kiwi*

DINNER
>Tofu Miso Soup (115)
>Chinese-Style Chicken with Peanuts (76)
>Rice
>*Forbidden Food Treat:* cheesecake
>Herbal tea

DAY 7 Stay-Slim I

BREAKFAST
  Blueberry muffin
  Banana
  Orange juice
  Reduced calorie hot chocolate

SNACK
  Cucumber

LUNCH
  Vegetable soup
  Egg Salad Plate (32)
  Hard roll
  Frosty Spiced Tea (230)

SNACK
  Apricot

DINNER
  Turbot
  Madrid Potatoes (136)
  Stuffed mushrooms (145)
  Beet and Apple Salad (152)
  Applesauce Mousse (186)
  Grapefruit Sling (233)

DAY 8 Stay-Slim I

BREAKFAST
  Bran Muffin (5)
  Vitamin C Delight (20)
  Tomato juice
  Coffee or tea

SNACK
  Pear

LUNCH
> Chicken Salad (28)
> Whole wheat roll
> Apple
> Skim milk

SNACK
> *Peach*

DINNER
> Artichoke and Potato Soup (104)
> Stuffed Cabbage Rolls with Tomato Sauce (94)
> Sautéed Parsnips with Sesame Seeds (140)
> Brite Ice (192)
> Iced herbal tea

DAY 9 Stay-Slim I

BREAKFAST
> Low fat yogurt
> Raspberries
> Bagel
> Skim milk
> Coffee or tea

SNACK
> *Tangelo*

LUNCH
> Greek Salad (36)
> Hard roll
> Lemonade

SNACK
> *Honeydew melon*

DINNER
> Chicken Divan (72)
> Baked Stuffed Tomatoes (122)
> Potatoes au Gratin (138)
> Artichoke Salad (149)
> Lemon Chiffon Mousse (205)
> Lime flavored carbonated water

DAY 10 Stay-Slim I

BREAKFAST
Poached egg
Whole wheat toast
Orange juice
Coffee or tea

SNACK
Pear

LUNCH
Sea Island Salad (45)
Tangy Cottage Cheese (48)
Oatmeal toast
Iced Espresso (236)

SNACK
Nectarine

DINNER
Scallops au Gratin (90)
Artichokes in Mustard Sauce (119)
Noodles
Plum Slaw (173)
Baked Peaches (189)
Mint Lemonade (240)

DAY 11 Stay-Slim I

BREAKFAST
Blueberry muffin
Cantaloupe
Coffee or tea

SNACK
Papaya

LUNCH
>Asparagus Noodle Bake (22)
>Watercress, Romaine and Radish Salad (182)
>Apple cider

SNACK
>*Nectarine*

DINNER
>Flank steak
>Zucchini and Carrots Julienne (148)
>Mixed Green Salad with Radishes (168)
>Orange Sorbet
>Orange flavored carbonated water

DAY 12 Stay-Slim I

BREAKFAST
>Low calorie yogurt
>Bran Muffin (5)
>Pineapple
>Coffee or tea

SNACK
>*Plum*

LUNCH
>Cabbage and Lentil Soup (107)
>Zucchini Stuffed with Tuna and Cheese (60)
>Whole wheat roll
>Tomato juice

SNACK
>*Farmer's cheese*

DINNER
>Pasta Primavera (89)
>Green Beans with Sesame Seeds (132)
>Rice
>Asparagus Salad (151)
>Cherry Festival (194)
>Lemon flavored carbonated water

DAY 13 Stay-Slim I

BREAKFAST
Eggs Benedict with Hollandaise Sauce (9)
Grapefruit
Coffee or tea

SNACK
Pear

LUNCH
Turkey and Apple Roll-ups (55)
Tomato soup
Orange juice

SNACK
Apple

DINNER
Beef Curry (67)
Bulgar wheat
Spinach and Tofu with Tamari and Ginger (142)
Steamed Apples with Honey (218)
Iced herbal tea

DAY 14 Stay-Slim I

BREAKFAST
Bran cereal
Banana
Grapefruit
Coffee or tea

SNACK
Grapes

LUNCH
Zucchini and Shrimp Salad (59)
Hard roll
Cantaloupe
Vegetable juice

SNACK
> *Cucumber*

DINNER
> Veal Parmigiana (100)
> Linguine
> Romaine and Boston lettuce with Mustard
>   Shallot Vinaigrette (176)
> Rice Pudding (217)
> Orange flavored carbonated water

DAY 15 Stay-Slim I

BREAKFAST
> Corn cereal
> Blueberries
> Orange juice
> Coffee or tea

SNACK
> *Apple*

LUNCH
> Burrito Casserole (24)
> Cole Slaw (157)
> Apple cider

SNACK
> *Cherries*

DINNER
> Chicken Breasts with Vegetables in Cheese
>   Sauce (71)
> Herbed Brussels Sprouts (134)
> Rice Salad (175)
> Orange Rhubarb Parfait (209)
> Herbal tea

DAY 16 Stay-Slim I

BREAKFAST
Cranberry muffin
Morning Berry Mix (14)
Coffee or Tea

SNACK
Broccoli

LUNCH
Spinach and Mushroom Salad with Cheese (47)
Whole wheat roll
Skim milk

SNACK
Persimmon

DINNER
Vichyssoise (118)
Lamb chops
Stuffed Baked Zucchini (144)
Cucumber and Onion Salad (160)
Strawberry Chiffon Pie (219)
Carrot juice (225)

DAY 17 Stay-Slim I

BREAKFAST
French Toast (12)
Peach
Grapefruit juice
Coffee or tea

SNACK
Orange

LUNCH
Manhattan Clam Chowder (111)
Tuna-Vegetable Skillet (54)

Hard roll
Skim milk

SNACK
Pear

DINNER
Pork chop
Kohlrabi in Cheese Sauce (135)
Saffron Rice Timbales (139)
Apple Sorbet (185)
Orange Spritzer (241)

DAY 18 Stay-Slim I

BREAKFAST
Poached egg
Corn muffin
Tomato juice
Coffee or tea

SNACK
Banana

LUNCH
Vegetable Beef Soup (117)
Antipasto Hero Sandwich (21)
Spiced Coffee (244)

SNACK
Rice cake

DINNER
Swordfish steak
Fluffy Baked Potatoes (131)
Shrimp with Cold Cilantro Sauce (93)
Artichoke Vinaigrette (150)
Yogurt-Gelatin Delight (223)
Apple cider

DAY 19 Stay-Slim I

BREAKFAST
Asparagus Omelet (2)
Bacon
Peach
Coffee or tea

SNACK
Popcorn

LUNCH
Fruit Salad and Cottage Cheese Plate (34)
Oatmeal toast
Strawberry Spritzer (245)

SNACK
Tangerine

DINNER
Cold Broccoli Soup (108)
Beef Ragout (68)
Noodles
Braised Fennel (124)
Pears in Red Wine (214)
Herbal tea

DAY 20 Stay-Slim I

BREAKFAST
Wheat cereal
Nectarine
Orange juice
Coffee or tea

SNACK
Honeydew melon

LUNCH
Black Bean Soup (106)

Low fat yogurt
Grapefruit juice

SNACK
Apple

DINNER
Glazed Chicken Breasts (80)
Peas
Wild rice
Banana Flambé (190)
Lime flavored carbonated water

DAY 21 Stay-Slim I

BREAKFAST
Rice cereal
Bananas
Strawberries
Grapefruit
Coffee or tea

SNACK
Pear

LUNCH
Creamy Tomato Soup (110)
Cheese and Sprout Pitas (26)
Skim milk

SNACK
Carrots

DINNER
Tofu Miso Soup (115)
Indonesian Chicken (84)
Tofu in Mushroom Sauce (146)
Lemon Baked Apple (204)
Tropical Fizz (248)

DAY 1 Stay-Slim II

BREAKFAST
> Canadian bacon
> Bagel
> Coffee or tea

SNACK
> *Plum*

LUNCH
> Crab Salad (30)
> Papaya
> Pear juice

SNACK
> *Radishes*

DINNER
> Veal chop
> Cauliflower au Gratin (127)
> Zucchini Salad with Tomato Vinaigrette (184)
> Pears and Ginger (213)
> Grape Spritzer (232)

DAY 2 Stay-Slim II

BREAKFAST
> Low fat yogurt
> Wheat germ
> Nectarine
> Coffee or tea

SNACK
> *Grapes*

LUNCH
> Four Bean Salad (164)
> Hard roll

Celery Boats (156)
Herbal tea

SNACK
Tangerine

DINNER
Beef and Vegetable Stew (66)
Artichoke Vinaigrette (150)
Romaine and Boston Lettuce with Mustard Shallot
   Vinaigrette (176)
Carrot Cake (193)
Apple cider

DAY 3 Stay-Slim II

BREAKFAST
Low fat cottage cheese
Peach
English muffin
Coffee or tea

SNACK
Cucumber

LUNCH
Tuna and Vegetable Salad (52)
Whole wheat roll
Skim milk

SNACK
Neufchâtel

DINNER
Onion Soup (113)
Baked Fish in Tomato Sauce (63)
Country Vegetables (129)
Frozen Orange Yogurt (200)
Herbal tea

DAY 4 Stay-Slim II

BREAKFAST
English muffin
Papaya
Tangerine
Reduced calorie hot chocolate

SNACK
Sweet peppers

LUNCH
Barley Soup (105)
Grilled Tofu Sandwich (37)
Mint Lemonade (240)

SNACK
Celery

DINNER
Lamb chop
Tofu in Mushroom Sauce (146)
Baked Stuffed Tomatoes (122)
Mushroom Tossed Greens (170)
Glazed Apple Rings (202)
Skim milk

DAY 5 Stay-Slim II

BREAKFAST
Cheese Omelet (6)
Cantaloupe
Grapefruit juice
Coffee or tea

SNACK
Grapes

LUNCH
Vegetable Bean Soup (116)

Camembert cheese
Hot Spiced Apple Cider (235)

SNACK
Peach

DINNER
Chicken and Shrimp Kebabs (69)
Broccoli in Cheese Sauce (125)
Artichoke Salad (149)
Mixed Green Salad with Radishes (168)
Orange Custard (208)
Pineapple Mint Spritzer (243)

DAY 6 Stay-Slim II

BREAKFAST
Cottage Cheese Blintzes (8)
Mango
Coffee or tea

SNACK
Skim milk

LUNCH
Chicken soup
Tofu Sloppy Joe (49)
Iced coffee

SNACK
Melon

DINNER
Herbed Chicken Breast (83)
Stir-Fried Asparagus (143)
Spinach, Fennel and Pink Grapefruit Salad (179)
Persimmon Pudding (215)
Herbal tea

DAY 7 Stay-Slim II

BREAKFAST
Tofu Rancheros (19)
Bagel
Orange juice
Coffee or tea

SNACK
Peach

LUNCH
Warm Acapulco Salad (58)
Celery stalks
Skim milk

SNACK
Grapes

DINNER
Flounder with Coriander (79)
Tomatoes Provençal (147)
Cucumber Aspic (161)
Orange Sorbet (210)
Lime flavored carbonated water

13 WHY YOU'LL NEVER NEED ANOTHER DIET

If you're like most people, you've tried a new diet every Monday and Thursday. Now that you've decided to follow the Woman's Advantage Diet, you can end your search for a diet that's right for you.

Let me sum up the major *advantages* of the Woman's Advantage Diet:

It's scientifically and nutritionally sound.

The diet offers a wide variety of food during its four phases, so you won't be bored.

You'll lose weight gradually, continually and safely.

Best of all, you'll never be hungry while you diet.

The diet helps rid you of the burdens of PMS.

You can overcome those terrible cravings for all the wrong kinds of food once and for all.

You can get the most out of exercise.

Your family will enjoy—and not resent—the diet, too.

Saying Goodbye to Dieting Anxieties

I think that everyone who starts a new diet has anxious moments. There's the fear that "this will never work for me," combined with "and even if it does work, I'll never be able to keep it up." Much of this anxiety stems from memories and guilts about earlier diet failures.

You're about to embark on a new, very different dieting experience. I'd like you to forget about all those other diets that didn't work for you for one reason or another. Don't look back. Instead, look forward to how good you're going to look and feel on the Woman's Advantage Diet.

I'm suggesting that you follow a diet that works and that's easy to follow. Don't you owe it to yourself to try it?

14

SPECIAL RECIPES FOR THE WOMAN'S ADVANTAGE DIET

BREAKFASTS

1. Apple Pancakes
2. Asparagus Omelet
3. Baked Cinnamon Apples
4. Banana Nut Muffins
5. Bran Muffins
6. Cheese Omelet
7. Cinnamon French Toast
8. Cottage Cheese Blintzes
9. Eggs Benedict with Hollandaise Sauce
10. Eggs in a Nest
11. Egg White Omelet with Herbs
12. French Toast
13. Herbed Zucchini 'n' Eggs
14. Morning Berry Mix
15. New England Buckwheat Pancakes
16. Scrambled Eggs
17. Scrambled Eggs with Tomato and Basil
18. Shirred Eggs with Cheese
19. Tofu Rancheros
20. Vitamin C Delight

1—Apple Pancakes

2 servings

1   apple, cored, peeled, and diced
1   tablespoon vegetable oil
¼   teaspoon cinnamon
⅔   cup all-purpose flour
1   teaspoon baking powder
½   cup low fat milk
1   egg, beaten
½   teaspoon vanilla extract
1   teaspoon reduced calorie margarine

1. In a skillet, heat the oil over a low heat and sauté the apple, stirring frequently, until it is soft, about 5–7 minutes. Sprinkle the apple with cinnamon and stir to mix. Scrape the apple into a bowl and reserve.

2. In a bowl, sift together the flour and baking powder. Stir in the milk, egg and vanilla. Mix together with the apple until the ingredients are just blended.

3. In a large, nonstick skillet, heat the margarine on a low heat. Pour the batter, in large spoonfuls, into the skillet and cook for 1–2 minutes or until bottom of pancake is brown. Using a spatula, flip the pancake and cook the other side until brown. Repeat with the remaining batter.

2—Asparagus Omelet

2 servings

2   eggs
     Dash of hot pepper sauce, or Tabasco
     Salt and freshly ground black pepper, to taste
1   teaspoon reduced calorie margarine
6   asparagus tips, cooked
1   teaspoon fresh dill, minced, or ¼ teaspoon dried

1. In a bowl, beat the eggs with the hot pepper sauce, salt and pepper.

2. In a nonstick omelet pan, heat the margarine. Add the egg mixture and cook, tipping the pan until the eggs set.

3. Slide the omelet onto a plate. Place the asparagus tips on top of the omelet, fold the omelet in half, garnish with the dill and serve.

3—Baked Cinnamon Apple

2 servings

2   baking apples
1   teaspoon light brown sugar
½   teaspoon ground cinnamon
⅛   teaspoon nutmeg
½   teaspoon reduced calorie margarine

1. Preheat the oven to 375 degrees.

2. Core the apples and place them on a baking pan or pie plate.

3. In a small bowl, mix the sugar, cinnamon and nutmeg. Spoon the mixture into the center of the apples. Dot the tops of the apples with the margarine.

4. Bake the apples for 20–30 minutes, or until they can be pierced easily with a fork. Serve warm or cold.

4—Banana Nut Muffin

12 muffins

1   medium ripe banana
1¼   cups all purpose flour
1½   cups chopped walnuts
1½   teaspoons double acting baking powder
½   cup sugar
2   tablespoons reduced calorie margarine, melted
2   eggs
1   teaspoon grated lemon rind

1. Preheat the oven to 400 degrees. Place 12 paper liners in muffin tin.

2. Mash the banana in a large bowl until smooth. Add the remaining ingredients and mix until thoroughly blended.

3. Divide the batter evenly among the muffin cups. Bake for 20–25 minutes, or until a toothpick comes out clean when inserted into the center of a muffin.

5—Bran Muffin

¾ cup raw bran
1 cup buttermilk
1 egg
⅓ cup honey
¼ cup vegetable oil
½ cup raisins
½ cup shredded carrots
½ cup all purpose flour
½ cup whole wheat flour
1 teaspoon baking soda
1 teaspoon grated nutmeg

1. Preheat the oven to 425 degrees.

2. In a bowl, combine the bran, buttermilk, egg, honey, oil, raisins and carrots. Let the mixture stand for 10 minutes.

3. In another bowl, combine the dry ingredients. Make a hole in the center of the dry ingredients and pour in the buttermilk-bran mixture. Stir just until the ingredients are mixed. (The batter should be lumpy.)

4. Line the muffin tins with paper liners, or spray with a vegetable cooking spray, and fill the cups two-thirds full with batter. Bake the muffins for 15–20 minutes, or until a toothpick comes out clean when inserted into the center of a muffin.

6—Cheese Omelet

2 eggs
1 teaspooon club soda
1 teaspoon reduced calorie margarine
1 ounce low fat American, grated, or other low fat cheese

1. In a bowl, combine the egg yolks, whites and club soda, and beat until thoroughly blended.

2. In a nonstick skillet, melt the margarine over low heat.

3. Increase the heat to medium and add the egg mixture. Cook, tilting the skillet from side to side until the eggs set.

4. Slide the omelet from the skillet onto a plate. Add the cheese and fold the omelet over. Serve immediately.

7—Cinnamon French Toast

2 servings

2   egg whites
½   cup low fat milk
¼   teaspoon cinnamon
¼   teaspoon vanilla extract
1   teaspoon reduced calorie margarine
2   slices reduced calorie white bread

1. In a medium bowl, beat together the egg whites, milk, cinnamon and vanilla. Pour the mixture into a flat pan.

2. In a frying pan, melt the margarine over a medium heat. Dip the bread in the egg mixture and sauté in pan, about 1 minute a side, or until brown.

8—Cottage Cheese Blintzes

2 servings

1   egg yolk
½   cup low fat cottage cheese
½   cup skim milk
½   teaspoon vanilla
⅓   cup flour
3   egg whites

1. In a mixing bowl, beat the egg yolk until it is thick, then add the cottage cheese and beat until smooth. Mix in skim milk and vanilla, then the flour.

2. In another bowl, beat the egg whites until peaks form. Gently fold the egg whites into the batter.

3. Brush a skillet lightly with oil. Drop the batter in spoonfuls into the skillet and cook over a medium heat, about 1 minute a side, until brown.

9—Eggs Benedict with Hollandaise Sauce   *2 servings*

¼ cup liquid egg substitute
1 tablespoon lemon juice
4 tablespoons reduced calorie margarine, melted
2 thin slices boiled ham
2 English muffin halves, lightly toasted
2 eggs, poached

1. In a blender, combine the egg substitute and lemon juice. Blend at moderate speed for 1 minute. Add the melted margarine and blend for an additional 30 seconds, or until sauce is creamy and thick.

2. Pour the sauce into the top of a double boiler and warm over a low heat.

3. Place one slice of ham on each muffin half. Top each with a poached egg. Spoon the warm Hollandaise sauce over each egg and serve immediately.

10—Eggs in a Nest   *2 servings*

2 slices reduced calorie white bread, lightly toasted
2 eggs, separated
  Salt and freshly ground black pepper, to taste

1. Preheat the oven to 325 degrees.

2. Place the toast on a cookie sheet.

3. Beat the egg whites until they are stiff.

4. Using a large spoon, create a border of egg white on each slice of toast. Place one egg yolk in the center of each slice of toast. Season with salt and pepper.

5. Bake the eggs for 8–10 minutes, or until the eggs have set.

11—Egg White Omelet with Herbs

2 servings

4   egg whites
⅛   teaspoon salt
⅛   teaspoon freshly ground black pepper
1   teaspoon reduced calorie margarine
¼   teaspoon chervil
1   tablespoon fresh parsley, chopped

1. In a bowl, whisk together the egg whites, salt and pepper.

2. In an omelet pan or nonstick skillet, melt the margarine over a low heat. Add the egg white to the pan and cook. As the egg whites begin to set, lift the edges with a spatula to let uncooked portion run underneath.

3. When the egg whites are set, turn the omelet onto a plate. Sprinkle chervil and parsley over the top, gently fold the omelet in half, cut it into 2 portions and serve.

12—French Toast

2 servings

2   egg whites
½   cup low fat milk
¼   teaspoon vanilla extract
¼   teaspoon nutmeg
2   slices whole wheat or cracked wheat bread
1   teaspoon reduced calorie margarine

1. In a bowl, combine the egg whites, milk, vanilla and nutmeg and beat until all the ingredients are thoroughly blended.

2. Pour the egg mixture into a pie plate or other shallow dish and add the bread slices. Coat the bread evenly with the egg mixture.

3. In a nonstick skillet, heat the margarine over a low heat. Increase the heat to medium, add the bread slices to the skillet and cook 1–2 minutes on each side, until the bread is light brown.

13—Herbed Zucchini 'n' Eggs

2 servings

1   teaspoon reduced calorie margarine
1   medium zucchini, thinly sliced
¾   cup chopped onion
1   teaspoon chopped parsley
¼   teaspoon oregano
½   teaspoon dried basil, or 1½ teaspoons fresh basil, minced
2   egg yolks
4   egg whites
1   tablespoon seltzer

1. Preheat the oven to 350 degrees.

2. In a skillet, heat the margarine over a medium heat, add the zucchini, onion, parsley, oregano and basil, and cook, stirring, for 10 minutes. Spoon the zucchini into a baking pan and reserve.

3. In a bowl, whisk together the egg yolks, egg whites and seltzer. Pour the egg mixture over the zucchini. Bake the mixture for 20–25 minutes, until the egg is set.

14—Morning Berry Mix

2 servings

½   cup strawberries, halved
½   cup blueberries
1   teaspoon honey
1   teaspoon lemon juice
    Fresh mint sprigs

1. In a bowl, toss the strawberries and blueberries together.

2. Mix the honey and lemon juice well. Spoon the mixture over the berries, stir to coat the fruit, garnish with mint sprigs and serve.

15—New England Buckwheat Pancakes   *2 servings*

½   cup buckwheat flour
½   teaspoon double acting baking powder
1   tablespoon sugar
1   egg yolk
3   tablespoons reduced calorie margarine, melted
¾   cup buttermilk
1   egg white
1   tablespoon reduced calorie margarine

1. In a bowl, combine the buckwheat flour, baking powder, sugar, egg yolk, margarine and buttermilk, and mix until just combined. In another bowl, beat the egg white until it is stiff. Gently fold the egg white into the batter.

2. In a nonstick skillet, heat a small amount of margarine. Pour a quarter cup of batter into the skillet, and cook the pancake until it is brown on one side. Turn and brown on the other side.

3. Repeat until all the batter is used. Serve with fresh sliced strawberries or peaches.

16—Scrambled Eggs   *2 servings*

1   teaspoon reduced calorie margarine
    Egg substitute equivalent to 4 eggs
2   ounces low fat cheese, such as Jarlsberg, grated

1. In a skillet, heat the margarine over a medium heat. Add the egg mixture and cook, scrambling with a fork until the egg is almost set.

2. Stir in the cheese and continue cooking for 30 seconds, or until the cheese has melted.

17—Scrambled Eggs with Tomato and Basil   *2 servings*

2   eggs
1   tablespoon seltzer
1   teaspoon reduced calorie margarine
½   tomato, peeled, seeded and diced
2   teaspoons chopped fresh basil, or ¼ teaspoon dried

1. In a bowl, beat together the eggs and seltzer. Reserve.
2. In a nonstick skillet, melt the margarine and sauté the tomato and basil for 1 minute, stirring.
3. Pour the eggs into the skillet and cook, stirring, until the eggs are set.

18—Shirred Eggs with Cheese   *2 servings*

1   teaspoon reduced calorie margarine
2   eggs
2   tablespoons grated low fat cheese, such as American

1. Preheat the oven to 350 degrees.
2. Spread the margarine on the inside of 2 custard cups, small ramekins, or other small ovenproof dishes.
3. Break 1 egg carefully into each cup. Sprinkle the cheese over the top and bake for 6–10 minutes, until the egg white has set.

19—Tofu Rancheros   *2 servings*

1   teaspoon vegetable oil
½   onion, diced
½   green pepper, seeded and diced
1   cup cooked diced carrots
1   cup cooked corn kernels
1   teaspoon sesame oil
⅓   cup scallions, chopped
½   pound extra firm tofu, diced
         Pinch of cumin, cayenne or chili powder
¼–½   cup salsa or taco sauce
1   tablespoon miso
1   tablespoon cornstarch dissolved in 1 cup water

1. In a skillet, heat the oil over a low heat. Add the onion and green pepper and cook, stirring, for 1 minute. Then add the carrots and corn and cook for 2 minutes, or until the vegetables are warm.
2. Add the sesame oil, scallions, tofu, cumin, salsa and miso to the skillet, and cook, stirring, for 1 minute. Stir in the cornstarch mixture and continue cooking until the sauce is thick and all the ingredients are hot, about 2 minutes. Serve immediately.

20—Vitamin C Delight

2 servings

½   cup orange juice
1   cup pineapple chunks
¼   teaspoon ground cinnamon
½   cantaloupe, sliced
½   grapefruit, separated into segments

1. In a blender, puree the orange juice, pineapple and cinnamon until smooth. Spoon the puree into a bowl and freeze for 2 hours.

2. Remove the mixture from the freezer, break up ice, and puree until smooth but not melted.

3. Arrange the cantaloupe slices and grapefruit segments in 2 dessert bowls. Add the puree to the fruit, chill for 30 minutes, then serve.

LUNCHES

21. Antipasto Hero Sandwiches
22. Asparagus Noodle Bake
23. Boston Brown Bread
24. Burrito Casserole
25. Caesar's Pasta
26. Cheese and Sprout Pitas
27. Chicken and Tomato Sandwiches
28. Chicken Salad
29. Chicken Salad Pitas
30. Crab Salad
31. Cucumber Sandwiches
32. Egg Salad Plate
33. French-Toasted Ham and Cheese
34. Fruit Salad and Cottage Cheese Plate
35. Fruit Salad Delight
36. Greek Salad
37. Grilled Tofu Sandwiches
38. Ham and Tomato Pitas
39. Open Face Dijon Turkey Sandwiches
40. Orzo and Shrimp Salad
41. Pasta Salad with Tuna
42. Pizza Sandwiches
43. Rigatoni and Mushroom Salad
44. Salmon Salad
45. Sea Island Salad
46. Shrimp Salad
47. Spinach and Mushroom Salad with Cheese
48. Tangy Cottage Cheese
49. Tofu Sloppy Joe
50. Tomato and Cheese Layers

51. Tuna and Bean Salad
52. Tuna and Vegetable Salad
53. Tuna Salad
54. Tuna-Vegetable Skillet
55. Turkey and Apple Roll-Ups
56. Turkey Salad
57. Vegetarian Pizza
58. Warm Acapulco Salad
59. Zucchini and Shrimp Salad
60. Zucchini Stuffed with Tuna and Cheese

21—Antipasto Hero Sandwiches
2 servings

1	cup romaine or green leaf lettuce, chopped
1	tomato, peeled, seeded and diced
½	green pepper, seeded and chopped
2	Nicoise or other imported black olives, chopped
1	tablespoon capers
1	tablespoon olive oil
1	tablespoon balsamic or red wine vinegar
½	small clove garlic, minced
¼	teaspoon oregano
2	small Italian rolls
2	teaspoons grated Parmesan cheese

1. In a bowl, toss together the lettuce, tomato, green pepper, olives and capers.

2. Whisk together the oil, vinegar, garlic and oregano until well blended. Pour the dressing over the vegetables and toss until well coated.

3. Cut the rolls in half lengthwise and hollow them out partially. Spoon the vegetables into each bread hollow, top with cheese and serve.

22—Asparagus Noodle Bake
2 servings

4	ounces medium wide egg noodles
1	teaspoon vegetable oil
1	tablespoon finely chopped onion
½	pound fresh asparagus, trimmed and cut into ½ inch pieces
1	cup low fat milk
2	ounces low fat cheese, such as American or Monterey Jack, grated
¼	teaspoon dry mustard
1	teaspoon chopped fresh dill, or ¼ teaspoon dried
½	teaspoon freshly ground black pepper
1	egg

1. In a large pot of boiling water, cook the noodles until they are cooked through but still slightly firm. Drain the noodles and rinse them under cold water. Reserve.

2. Preheat the oven to 350 degrees. Lightly grease a small baking dish.

3. In a saucepan, heat the oil over a medium heat. Add the onion and sauté, stirring frequently, for 2–3 minutes, until the onions are translucent.

4. Add the asparagus and 3 tablespoons of water to the sauce-pan. Bring the liquid to a boil, then reduce the heat and simmer until the asparagus is tender, about 4–5 minutes.

5. Add ¾ cup of the milk, 1½ ounces of the cheese, the mustard, dill and pepper. Heat the mixture, stirring frequently, until the milk is hot and the cheese melts. Remove the pan from the heat.

6. In a small bowl, beat together the remaining ¼ cup milk and the egg until smooth, then stir the mixture into the asparagus.

7. To assemble the casserole, spread the noodles over the bottom of the baking dish. Pour the asparagus mixture over the noodles. Sprinkle the top of the casserole with the remaining cheese and bake, uncovered, for 30–40 minutes, until the top is nicely browned and the custard is set. Allow the casserole to cool for 10 minutes before serving.

23—Boston Brown Bread   *4 servings*

2	tablespoons molasses
1	tablespoon reduced calorie margarine
1	egg
¾	cup low fat milk, or buttermilk
½	teaspoon vanilla extract
1¼	cup all purpose flour
1	teaspoon baking soda
½	cup chopped walnuts
⅓	cup raisins
1	teaspoon reduced calorie margarine

1. Preheat the oven to 350 degrees.

2. In a bowl, cream together the molasses and tablespoon of margarine, until well blended. Add the egg, milk and vanilla and beat well.

3. Sift together the flour and baking soda. Add the dry ingredients to the batter and mix thoroughly. Stir in the nuts and raisins.

4. Spread the teaspoon of margarine over the inside of a loaf pan.

5. Pour the batter into the prepared pan and bake for 45–50 minutes, or until a toothpick inserted in the center comes out clean. Let the bread cool for 10 minutes, then remove from the pan and slice.

24—Burrito Casserole

1	teaspoon vegetable oil
⅓	pound lean ground beef
½	onion, chopped
½	red pepper, seeded and chopped
1	clove garlic, minced
¼	cup corn
½	cup cooked kidney beans
1½	cups tomato sauce
1	teaspoon chili powder, or to taste
	Pinch cayenne pepper, optional
2	flour tortillas
2	ounces low fat cheese, such as Monterey Jack, grated

1. Preheat the oven to 350 degrees.

2. In a skillet, heat the oil over a medium heat and brown the beef, breaking up the lumps with a fork. Scrape the meat into a large bowl and reserve.

3. Add the onion, red pepper and garlic to the skillet and sauté over a low heat, stirring, until the vegetables are soft, about 3–4 minutes. Add the corn and kidney beans to the skillet and cook just to heat. Scrape the mixture into the bowl with the beef.

4. In a saucepan, combine the tomato sauce, chili powder and cayenne and cook over a low heat for 5 minutes. Pour half the sauce into the beef mixture and mix well.

5. Place half the beef mixture in a line down the center of each tortilla. Gently roll up the tortillas and place them in a baking dish. Pour the remaining sauce over the tortillas, sprinkle the cheese over the tops and bake for 20–25 minutes, or until the cheese has melted.

25—Caesar's Pasta   *2 servings*

1   clove garlic, halved
½   egg yolk
2   ounces vermicelli
1   bunch arugula
3   radishes, thinly sliced
1   tablespoon olive oil
1   tablespoon lemon juice
½   teaspoon salt
¼   teaspoon freshly ground pepper
½   cup herb flavored croutons
2   tablespoons grated Parmesan cheese

1. Rub a wooden salad bowl with the garlic clove halves, then discard the clove.

2. Add the egg yolk to the bowl and stir lightly with a fork.

3. Cook the vermicelli until it is al dente, or firm. Drain and rinse the vermicelli, and add to the salad bowl. Toss with the egg yolk. Then add the lettuce and radishes and toss to mix.

4. In a small bowl, whisk the olive oil, lemon juice, salt and pepper, and pour over the lettuce. Toss until the salad is evenly coated with the dressing. Top with the croutons and cheese, toss lightly and serve.

26—Cheese and Sprout Pitas   *2 servings*

1   cucumber, peeled and diced
1   tomato, chopped
1   scallion, chopped
2   teaspoons olive oil
1   teaspoon red wine or balsamic vinegar
2   small pita breads
2   ounces low fat cheese, such as American or Monterey Jack
1   cup alfalfa sprouts

1. Preheat the oven to 325 degrees.

2. Place the cucumber, tomato, scallion, oil and vinegar in a bowl, and mix thoroughly.

3. Carefully open the pitas and place a slice of cheese into each bread pocket. Bake the pitas for 5 to 7 minutes, until the cheese has melted.

4. Remove the pitas from the oven. Spoon the vegetable mixture evenly into the pitas and add sprouts. Serve while warm.

27—Chicken and Tomato Sandwiches   *2 servings*

1   tablespoon reduced calorie mayonnaise
1   tablespoon low fat yogurt
¼   teaspoon Dijon mustard
¼   teaspoon tarragon
2   slices reduced calorie white bread
4   ounces white meat chicken, sliced and skinless
2   thin slices tomato
2   tablespoons alfalfa sprouts
     Watercress sprigs

1. In a small bowl, whisk together the mayonnaise, yogurt, mustard and tarragon. Spread the mixture over the bread.

2. Arrange the chicken, tomato and alfalfa sprouts over the bread, garnish with watercress and serve.

28—Chicken Salad   *2 servings*

½   pound chicken breast, boiled and skinned
1   scallion, diced
¼   red pepper, seeded and diced
1   cup small broccoli flowerets
2   tablespoons low fat yogurt
1   tablespoon reduced calorie mayonnaise
½   teaspoon Dijon mustard
¼   teaspoon tarragon or dill
     Lettuce leaves
     Watercress sprigs

1. Cut the chicken into small pieces and place them in a bowl. Mix in the scallion, red pepper and broccoli.

2. In a small bowl, whisk together the yogurt, mayonnaise, mustard and tarragon. Spoon the dressing over the chicken, toss to coat well, place on a bed of lettuce, garnish with watercress, and serve.

29—Chicken Salad Pitas   *2 servings*

1   cup cooked chicken, cubed
½   apple, peeled and chopped
1   stalk celery, chopped
1   scallion, diced
2   tablespoons reduced calorie mayonnaise
2   tablespoons low fat yogurt
1   teaspoon Dijon mustard
1   teaspoon chopped fresh coriander or dill, or ¼ teaspoon dried
2   small pita breads

1. In a bowl, combine the chicken, apple, celery and scallion.

2. In another bowl, mix the mayonnaise, yogurt, mustard and coriander until thoroughly blended. Add the dressing to the chicken mixture and toss until well coated.

3. Carefully open each pita. Spoon the chicken salad into each and serve.

30—Crab Salad   *2 servings*

¾   cup diced celery
2   teaspoons lemon juice
1   teaspoon Worcestershire sauce
½   cup reduced calorie mayonnaise
1   cup lump crabmeat, (about ½ pound)
4   large lettuce leaves
2   tomatoes, quartered
1   hard boiled egg, quartered

1. In a large bowl, combine the celery, lemon juice, Worcestershire sauce and mayonnaise and mix thoroughly. Fold the crabmeat into the mayonnaise mixture.

2. Place the lettuce leaves on 2 plates. Spoon the crabmeat onto the lettuce, garnish with tomato and egg quarters and serve.

31—Cucumber Sandwiches
2 servings

2   teaspoons reduced calorie mayonnaise
1   teaspoon chopped fresh dill, or ¼ teaspoon dried
2   small pita breads
1   cucumber, peeled and sliced

1. In a small bowl, combine the mayonnaise and dill, mixing thoroughly.

2. Carefully open the pitas to form bread pockets. Spread the mayonnaise mixture inside the pitas.

3. Place the cucumber slices inside, cut the pitas in half and serve.

32—Egg Salad Plate
2 servings

4   eggs, hard boiled
4–5   leaves red or green leaf lettuce
¼   red pepper, seeded and cut into ¼-inch strips
¼   green pepper, seeded and cut into ¼-inch strips
1   tomato, quartered
2   tablespoons olive oil
1   tablespoon tarragon or white wine vinegar
¼   teaspoon Dijon mustard
2   teaspoons minced scallions
      Freshly ground black pepper, to taste

1. Peel the eggs and cut them into quarters.

2. Arrange the lettuce on a serving platter. Place the eggs in a line in the center. Place the red pepper strips along one side of the platter, green pepper along the other, and tomato wedges at each end.

3. In a small bowl, whisk together the oil, vinegar, mustard and scallions. Season to taste with pepper and spoon the dressing over the eggs.

33—French-Toasted Ham and Cheese

2 servings

2   tablespoons orange marmalade
½   tablespoon dry mustard
4   thin slices rye bread
2   ounces thinly sliced cooked ham
2   ounces thinly sliced low fat cheese, such as provolone
½   cup skim milk
½   egg

1. Preheat the oven to 450 degrees.

2. In a bowl, blend the marmalade and mustard. Spread the mixture over 2 slices of bread, top with the ham and cheese and the last 2 slices of bread.

3. Beat together the milk and egg and pour the mixture into a shallow pan. Dip the sandwiches into the batter, then turn and coat the other side. Place the sandwiches on a nonstick cookie sheet.

4. Bake the sandwiches until they are golden brown on both sides, about 7–10 minutes a side. Cut each sandwich in half and serve hot.

34—Fruit Salad and Cottage Cheese Plate

2 servings

1   small bunch chicory
¾   cup low fat cottage cheese
¼   honeydew melon, sliced
½   cup cantaloupe melon balls
1   banana, cut into quarters
½   cup strawberries
½   cup seedless grapes
1   navel orange, peeled and separated into segments
½   cup pineapple chunks
½   cup blueberries
     Mint sprigs

1. Separate chicory into leaves and place the leaves on 2 plates.

2. Using an ice cream scoop, place a spoonful of cottage cheese in the center of the lettuce. Arrange the fruit around the cottage cheese, top with blueberries, garnish with mint and serve.

35—Fruit Salad Delight

4 servings

1 banana, sliced
½ cup pineapple chunks
1 cup orange segments
½ cup green or red grapes
½ honeydew melon, cut into chunks
1 apple, peeled and cut into chunks
½ cup low fat yogurt
½ cup tofu
2 tablespoons orange or pineapple juice
1 tablespoon honey
   Romaine lettuce leaves
   Fresh mint sprigs, optional

1. In a salad bowl, mix the fruit.

2. Combine the yogurt, tofu, orange juice and honey in a blender, and puree until smooth.

3. Pour the dressing over the fruit and refrigerate for one hour before serving. Place on a bed of lettuce, garnish with mint and serve.

36—Greek Salad

2 servings

1 tomato, chopped
½ head romaine or red-leaf lettuce, cut into bite-size pieces
¼ cup finely chopped Bermuda onion
1 stalk celery, sliced
1 tablespoon olive oil
1 tablespoon lemon juice
½ teaspoon fresh ground black pepper
1 tablespoon fresh basil, minced or ½ teaspoon dried
1 tablespoon minced fresh parsley
1 ounce feta cheese, crumbled
½ cup ripe, imported black olives, pitted

1. In a large salad bowl, mix the vegetables.

2. In a small bowl, combine the oil, lemon juice, pepper, basil and parsley. Mix thoroughly and pour over the vegetables. Toss the salad well.

3. Allow the salad to marinate for 30 minutes. Before serving, toss in the feta cheese and olives.

37—Grilled Tofu Sandwiches
2 servings

1	tablespoon reduced calorie mayonnaise
1	teaspoon sesame oil
2	slices reduced calorie white bread
4	ounces tofu, cut into 4 slices
2	teaspoons soy sauce
1	tomato, thinly sliced
2	ounces low fat cheese, such as American or Monterey Jack, grated

1. Preheat the broiler.

2. Whisk together the mayonnaise and sesame oil. Spread each slice of bread with the mixture.

3. Top the bread with the tofu. Sprinkle the soy sauce over the tofu, top with tomato slices, then with cheese.

4. Broil the sandwiches until the cheese melts, about 3 minutes, and serve.

38—Ham and Tomato Pitas
2 servings

½	cup shredded red or green leaf lettuce
½	cup diced cucumber
1	small tomato, diced
¼	cup diced red pepper
¼	pound lean boiled ham, chopped
1	tablespoon olive oil
1	tablespoon red wine vinegar
1	teaspoon capers
¼	teaspoon oregano
	Freshly ground black pepper, to taste
2	small pitas

1. In a bowl, place the lettuce, cucumber, tomato, red pepper and ham and mix thoroughly.

2. In a small bowl, whisk together the oil, vinegar, capers and oregano. Season to taste with pepper. Spoon the dressing over the ham mixture and toss well to combine.

3. Carefully open each pita. Divide the ham mixture into the pita pockets and serve.

39—Open Face Dijon Turkey Sandwiches   *2 servings*

½   teaspoon Dijon mustard
1   teaspoon reduced calorie mayonnaise
2   slices reduced calorie rye bread
6   ounces sliced breast of turkey (skin removed)
4   slices tomato
4   leaves romaine lettuce
8   sprigs watercress

1. In a small bowl, combine the mustard and mayonnaise, and mix until thoroughly blended.

2. Spread the mustard mixture over the bread.

3. Layer the turkey, tomato, lettuce on the bread. Garnish with watercress sprigs.

40—Orzo and Shrimp Salad   *2 servings*

½   cup orzo
½   pound shrimp, cooked and shelled
¼   cup diced green pepper
3   stalks celery with leaves, finely chopped
3   tablespoons minced fresh parsley
3   tablespoons minced scallions
1   tablespoon olive oil
1   tablespoon lemon juice
¼   teaspoon Dijon mustard
¼   teaspoon salt
¼   teaspoon freshly ground white pepper
½   teaspoon oregano or dill

1. Cook orzo until it is al dente, or firm. Drain and refrigerate for 30 minutes.

2. Put the shrimp, green pepper, celery, parsley and scallions in a large bowl and mix thoroughly. Add orzo.

3. In a small bowl, combine the olive oil, lemon juice, mustard, salt, pepper and oregano. Mix thoroughly and spoon over the orzo and shrimp mixture. Toss to coat the salad with the dressing.

41—Pasta Salad with Tuna   *2 servings*

2   tablespoons olive oil
1   clove garlic, finely minced
½   ounce pine nuts
1   cup roughly chopped tomatoes
4   ounces fettucine, or fusilli
1   3½-ounce can tuna (packed in water)
¼   red pepper, cut into thin strips
½   cup imported black olives
2   tablespoons chopped fresh parsley
2   tablespoons red wine vinegar
     Freshly ground pepper, to taste

1. In a skillet, heat the olive oil, add the garlic and pine nuts and sauté over a low heat, while stirring until the garlic is translucent and pine nuts are golden, about 2–3 minutes. Add the tomatoes and cook just-to-heat. Turn the mixture into a large serving bowl and cool at room temperature.

2. Cook fettuccine until it is al dente, or just firm. Drain well and rinse under cold running water. Add the pasta to the tomato mixture and toss gently. Add the tuna, pepper strips, black olives, parsley and vinegar. Toss gently and season to taste with pepper.

42—Pizza Sandwiches   *2 servings*

1   tablespoon olive oil
1   clove garlic
½   cup tomato sauce
1   tablespoon tomato paste
1   tablespoon diced sun-dried tomatoes, optional
1   tablespoon chopped fresh basil, or ½ teaspoon dried
½   teaspoon oregano
¼   cup low fat ricotta cheese
2   English muffins, separated into halves and lightly toasted
¼   onion, thinly sliced
¼   green pepper, seeded and thinly sliced into rings
¼   cup thinly sliced mushrooms
1   tablespoon grated Romano cheese

1. Preheat the oven to 425 degrees.

2. In a saucepan, heat the olive oil over a low heat and sauté the garlic for 2 minutes. Remove the garlic and discard.

3. Add the tomato sauce, tomato paste, sun-dried tomato and seasonings. Simmer the sauce 10–15 minutes, stirring occasionally.

4. Remove the sauce from the heat and stir in the ricotta cheese, mixing until thoroughly combined.

5. Place the English muffin halves on a flat baking pan or cookie sheet. Spoon the sauce over the muffins, top with the onion rings, green pepper rings, mushrooms and Romano cheese.

6. Bake the pizzas for 20 minutes, or until the sauce is bubbly and the vegetables are tender.

43—Rigatoni and Mushroom Salad

2 servings

4	ounces rigatoni
½	pound mushrooms, diced
3	scallions, diced
2	tablespoons olive oil
2	tablespoons red wine or tarragon vinegar
	Salt and freshly ground black pepper, to taste
2	tablespoons minced fresh parsley
1½	tablespoons chopped fresh basil, or ½ teaspoon dried
2	tablespoons grated Romano cheese

1. Cook pasta until it is al dente, or firm. Drain and cool under running water. Put the rigatoni into a large bowl. Add the mushrooms and scallions.

2. In a small bowl, combine the oil, vinegar, salt, pepper, parsley and basil. Mix thoroughly and spoon over the rigatoni.

3. Cover the salad and chill for 2 hours. Garnish with Romano cheese and serve.

44—Salmon Salad

2 servings

½   pound cooked salmon, skinned and boned
2   teaspoons lemon juice
½   cup finely chopped celery
¼   cup diced green pepper
2   scallions, diced
2   tablespoons low fat yogurt
1   tablespoon reduced calorie mayonnaise
½   teaspoon Dijon mustard
1   tablespoon chopped fresh dill, or ½ teaspoon dried
      Freshly ground black pepper, to taste
4   leaves red or green leaf lettuce
1   tablespoon capers

1. Break the salmon into chunks and place it in a bowl. Add the lemon juice, celery, green pepper and scallions and toss to mix.

2. In a bowl, whisk together the yogurt, mayonnaise, mustard and dill. Season to taste with pepper, and spoon the dressing over the salmon mixture. Toss until well combined.

3. Arrange the lettuce on a serving platter. Spoon the salmon salad onto the lettuce and garnish with capers.

45—Sea Island Salad

2 servings

½   cup cooked crabmeat
½   cup cooked shrimp
¼   cup finely chopped onion
½   cup chopped celery
⅓   cup sliced water chestnuts
¼   cup fresh pineapple chunks
1   tablespoon walnut oil
1   tablespoon vegetable oil
      Juice of ½ lemon
      Lettuce leaves
1   tablespoon chopped cashew nuts

1. Combine all ingredients, except the lettuce and cashew nuts, in a bowl. Toss lightly and refrigerate for at least 2 hours.

2. Arrange the lettuce leaves on 2 individual plates and spoon the seafood salad onto the lettuce. Garnish with cashews and serve.

46—Shrimp Salad   *2 servings*

½   pound shrimp, cooked
2   scallions, diced
⅓   cup sliced water chestnuts
2   tablespoons olive oil
1½   tablespoons lemon juice
¼   teaspoon Dijon mustard
2   teaspoons chopped fresh dill, or ¼ teaspoon dried
4–5   leaves romaine lettuce
1   tomato, sliced
2   mushrooms, sliced
      Parsley sprigs

1. In a bowl, toss together the shrimp, scallions and water chestnuts. Reserve.

2. In a small bowl, whisk together the oil, lemon juice, mustard and dill. Spoon the dressing over the shrimp and toss well.

3. Arrange the lettuce on serving plates. Divide the shrimp on the lettuce, and lay the tomato and mushroom slices around the salad.

4. Garnish with parsley.

47—Spinach and Mushroom Salad with Cheese   *2 servings*

½   pound fresh spinach, washed and well drained
¼   pound mushrooms, sliced
4   scallions, chopped
2   tablespoons olive oil
1½   tablespoons balsamic or red wine vinegar
½   clove garlic, minced
      Freshly ground black pepper, to taste
1   carrot, shredded
2   ounces low fat mozzarella cheese, grated

1. Remove tough stems from spinach leaves. Tear the spinach leaves into bite-size pieces and place them in salad bowl. Add the mushrooms and scallions.

2. In a small bowl, whisk together the oil, vinegar, garlic and pepper. Drizzle the dressing over the spinach and toss until all the ingredients are thoroughly mixed.

3. Garnish the salad with the carrots and cheese.

48—Tangy Cottage Cheese   *2 servings*

1½	cups low fat cottage cheese
1	teaspoon turmeric
½	teaspoon cinnamon
2	scallions, diced
1	tablespoon finely chopped cashews
½	head red or green leaf lettuce
½	red pepper, seeded and cut into ¼-inch strips
½	yellow pepper, seeded and cut into ¼-inch strips

1. In a bowl, mix the cottage cheese with the turmeric, cinnamon, scallions and cashews.

2. Arrange the lettuce on a serving plate. Place the cottage cheese in the center and the peppers around the cottage cheese.

49—Tofu Sloppy Joes   *2 servings*

1	teaspoon vegetable oil
½	onion, finely chopped
½	pound firm tofu, crumbled
1	clove garlic, minced
¼	teaspoon oregano
½	teaspoon basil
¾	cup tomato sauce
2	English muffins, split and lightly toasted
1	tablespoon grated Parmesan cheese

1. Preheat the oven to 350 degrees.

2. In a nonstick skillet, heat the oil over a medium heat. Add the onion and tofu and cook, stirring until both are brown, about 5 minutes.

3. Add the garlic, oregano and basil to the tofu and cook, stirring, for 2 minutes. Add the tomato sauce and continue cooking for 2–3 minutes, until all the ingredients are thoroughly combined.

4. Place the English muffin halves on a cookie sheet. Spoon the sauce over the muffin halves. Sprinkle each with cheese and bake for 10–15 minutes, or until the cheese melts and the sauce is bubbly.

50—Tomato and Cheese Layers
2 servings

2 tomatoes
2 ounces low fat mozzarella cheese
1 tablespoon olive oil
2 tablespoons champagne vinegar
1½ tablespoons chopped fresh basil, or ½ teaspoon dried
Salt and freshly ground black pepper, to taste

1. Slice the tomatoes and cheese and lay the slices on a platter, alternating the tomatoes and the cheese.
2. In a small bowl combine the oil, vinegar, basil, salt and pepper and mix well. Spoon the dressing over the tomatoes and cheese and serve.

51—Tuna and Bean Salad
2 servings

2 tablespoons red wine vinegar
2 tablespoons olive oil
½ clove garlic, minced
⅛ teaspoon salt
½ teaspoon pepper
1 cup chickpeas, cooked
1 3½-ounce can tuna (packed in water)
½ red pepper, seeded and diced
¼ cup green beans, cooked and diced
¼ cup Nicoise or other imported black olives
½ cup minced fresh parsley
½ head bibb lettuce, separated into leaves

1. In a large bowl, combine the vinegar, oil, garlic, salt and pepper, and mix thoroughly.
2. Add the chickpeas, tuna, red pepper, green beans, olives and parsley to the dressing and toss to combine.
3. Arrange the lettuce leaves on a platter. Spoon the tuna-bean mixture onto the lettuce.

52—Tuna and Vegetable Salad   *2 servings*

¼	pound rigatoni or fusilla
1	3½-ounce can tuna (packed in water)
¼	pound green beans, cooked and diced
3	tablespoons capers, drained
½	red pepper, seeded and diced
1	cup chopped spinach
1	tablespoon olive oil
1	tablespoon lemon juice
¼	teaspoon garlic, minced
2	tablespoons finely chopped chives, or parsley
¼	teaspoon salt
½	teaspoon oregano

1. Cook the rigatoni until al dente, or firm. Drain and let cool.

2. In a salad bowl, mix the tuna, green beans, capers, red pepper and spinach. Toss the salad well, then add the rigatoni and toss just to blend.

3. In a small bowl, combine the oil, lemon juice, garlic, chives, salt and oregano. Mix the dressing thoroughly, spoon over salad and serve.

53—Tuna Salad   *2 servings*

1	3½-ounce can tuna (packed in water)
⅓	red pepper, seeded and diced
2	scallions, diced
2	tablespoons reduced calorie mayonnaise
1	tablespoon low fat yogurt
½	teaspoon Worcestershire sauce
1	teaspoon lemon juice
	Lettuce
1	tablespoon chopped fresh parsley

1. In a small bowl, place the tuna and break it up well with a fork. Add the red pepper and scallion and mix.

2. In another bowl, mix the mayonnaise, yogurt, Worcestershire sauce and lemon juice. Pour the dressing over the tuna and toss. Place on a bed of lettuce, garnish with parsley and serve.

54—Tuna-Vegetable Skillet

2 servings

1	tablespoon olive oil
¼	onion, chopped
¼	red pepper, seeded and diced
1	small clove garlic, minced
½	zucchini, diced
1	tomato, chopped
2–3	Nicoise or other imported black olives, pitted and chopped
½	cup water
1	3½-ounce can tuna (packed in water)
1	cup brown rice, cooked
½	cup chickpeas, cooked
1	tablespoon lemon juice
1	teaspoon chopped fresh rosemary leaves, or a scant ¼ teaspoon dried
2	tablespoons chopped fresh parsley

1. In a skillet, heat the oil over a medium heat and sauté the onion, red pepper and garlic, stirring, until the vegetables are tender, about 3 minutes. Add the zucchini and tomato, and sauté another minute. Stir in the olives and water.

2. Break the tuna up well with a fork, and add it to the skillet. Then add the rice, chickpeas, lemon juice and rosemary, and cook over a low heat for 5 minutes. Garnish with parsley and serve.

55—Turkey and Apple Roll-Ups

2 servings

½	apple, peeled, cored and finely chopped
2	tablespoons finely chopped walnuts
¼	cup low fat yogurt
2	teaspoons lemon juice
½	teaspoon curry powder, or to taste
⅛	teaspoon ginger
4	thin slices breast of turkey
2	Boston lettuce leaves
2	small white, or whole wheat, baguettes

1. In a bowl, combine the apple, walnuts, yogurt, lemon juice, curry powder and ginger, and mix thoroughly.

2. Using 2 turkey slices for each portion, spoon the apple mixture onto the turkey slices and roll them up.

3. Line each baguette with a lettuce leave and 2 turkey roll-ups.

56—Turkey Salad

2 servings

2	ounces turkey breast, cut into 1-inch pieces
½	cucumber, peeled and diced
½	red pepper, seeded and diced
1	stalk celery, diced
¼	bunch broccoli, cut into small flowerets
1½	tablespoons olive oil
1½	tablespoons tarragon vinegar
½	teaspoon Dijon mustard
	Pinch tarragon
	Salt and freshly ground pepper, to taste
4–6	leaves romaine lettuce
1	tomato, thinly sliced

1. In a bowl, toss together the turkey, cucumber, red pepper, celery and broccoli.

2. Whisk the oil, vinegar, mustard, tarragon, salt and pepper until mixed, and pour over the turkey. Toss until well blended.

3. Arrange the lettuce and tomato slices on plates, top with turkey salad and serve.

57—Vegetarian Pizza

4 servings

½	package active dry yeast
⅓	cup warm water, about 110 degrees
½	teaspoon sugar
2	teaspoons olive oil
½	cup enriched all purpose flour
¼	cup whole wheat flour
1	tablespoon cornmeal
1	cup tomato sauce
1	tablespoon tomato paste
½	clove garlic, minced
1–2	sun-dried tomatoes, diced
1	teaspoon chopped fresh rosemary, or a scant ¼ teaspoon dried
2	teaspoons chopped fresh basil, or ½ teaspoon dried
4	ounces low fat mozzarella, shredded, or 3 ounces low fat and 1 ounce smoked mozzarella, shredded
3	scallions, diced
½	red pepper, seeded and thinly sliced into rings
½	yellow pepper, seeded and thinly sliced into rings
1	tablespoon olive oil

1. In a bowl, combine the yeast and sugar in the warm water. Add the 2 teaspoons of olive oil, stir lightly, then let stand for 5 minutes.

2. Stir in the flours and cornmeal, mixing with a wooden spoon until the ingredients are combined. Then, turn it out onto a lightly floured board and knead until it is smooth and elastic, about 3–4 minutes.

3. Place the dough in an oiled bowl, cover and let sit in a draft-free place until it has doubled in bulk, about 45 minutes.

4. Preheat the oven to 425 degrees.

5. In a saucepan, combine the tomato sauce, tomato paste, garlic, sun-dried tomatoes, rosemary and basil, and let the sauce simmer for 15–20 minutes. Remove the pan from the heat and reserve.

6. When the dough is ready, punch it down and roll it into a 12-inch round on a lightly floured board. Place the dough on a lightly oiled cookie sheet. Bake the dough for 5 minutes, then remove the sheet from the oven.

7. Spread the tomato sauce over the dough and sprinkle the cheese evenly over the top. Next, sprinkle on the scallions, red peppers and yellow peppers. Finally, drizzle with the tablespoon of oil.

8. Return the pizza to the oven and bake for 15–20 minutes, or until the cheese has melted and the edges of the dough are light brown.

58—Warm Acapulco Salad

2 servings

½   pound lean ground beef
½   cup canned whole tomatoes
¼   green pepper, chopped
½   cup cooked corn
⅓   onion, chopped
1   teaspoon chili powder
    Freshly ground black pepper, to taste
¼   teaspoon ground cumin
    Pinch coriander
½   head lettuce, separated into leaves
1   tomato, sliced
¼   cup chopped black olives
½   cup low fat cheese, such as Monterey Jack, shredded

1. In a nonstick skillet, brown the beef over a low heat, stirring to break the meat up evenly.

2. Dice the tomatoes and add them with their liquid. Stir in the green pepper, corn, onion and seasonings and cook, stirring frequently, until the liquid evaporates and the mixture is thick, approximately 15 minutes.

3. Place the lettuce leaves on a platter and top with the meat mixture. Garnish with tomato slices and olives, and top with shredded cheese. Serve while warm.

59—Zucchini and Shrimp Salad

2 servings

1   zucchini, sliced
2   scallions, chopped
1   tomato, diced
⅓   pound shrimp, cooked
2   tablespoons red wine vinegar
½   clove garlic, minced
1½   tablespoons chopped fresh basil, or ½ teaspoon dried
1   teaspoon Dijon mustard
2   tablespoons olive oil
1   cup sliced escarole

1. Steam the zucchini until it is just tender, then cool under cold running water. Mix the zucchini together with the scallions, tomato and shrimp in a bowl.

2. In a small bowl, combine the vinegar, garlic, basil and mustard. Whisk in the oil, and spoon the dressing over the zucchini-shrimp mixture, tossing the salad well.

3. Serve the salad on a bed of escarole.

60—Zucchini Stuffed with Tuna and Cheese   *2 servings*

2	small zucchini
1	teaspoon olive oil
¼	onion, chopped
1	clove garlic, minced
1	cup tomato sauce
1	tablespoon chopped fresh parsley
1	tablespoon chopped fresh basil, or ¼ teaspoon dried
1	3½-ounce can tuna (packed in water)
2	tablespoons grated Parmesan cheese

1. Preheat the oven to 350 degrees.

2. Cut the zucchini in half lengthwise. Using a melon ball cutter, scoop out the inside of the zucchini. Reserve the zucchini shells and pulp.

3. In a skillet, heat the oil, add the onion and garlic and cook, stirring, for 2–3 minutes until the onion is tender. Add the zucchini pulp, tomato sauce, parsley and basil to the skillet, and simmer for 10 minutes. Add the tuna and mix well.

4. Spoon the tuna mixture into the zucchini shells. Place the stuffed zucchini in a baking pan, pour the tomato sauce around the zucchini shells and top them with grated cheese. Bake, uncovered, for 20–25 minutes, until the tops begin to brown.

DINNERS

90. Scallops au Gratin
91. Shrimp Creole
92. Shrimp Jambalaya
93. Shrimp with Cold Cilantro Sauce
94. Stuffed Cabbage Rolls with Tomato Sauce
95. Sukiyaki
96. Sweet and Sour Vegetables
97. Tofu Burgers
98. Tofu Chow Mein
99. Tofu Parmesan
100. Veal Parmigiana
101. Vegetarian Beans in Spicy Tomato Sauce
102. Vegetarian Lasagna
103. Ziti with Grated Parmesan

61—Almond Chicken

4 servings

1   teaspoon reduced calorie margarine
¼   cup slivered almonds
1   teaspoon vegetable oil
4   split chicken breasts, skinned and boned
2   scallions, diced
¼   cup dry white wine
¾   cup chicken broth, defatted
1   teaspoon lemon juice
2   tablespoons chopped fresh parsley
     Freshly ground black pepper, to taste

1. In a skillet, melt the margarine over a low heat and sauté the almonds, stirring occasionally, until they are lightly browned. Remove the almonds and reserve.

2. Add the oil to the skillet, and sauté the chicken until it is cooked through and tender, about 6–8 minutes a side. Remove the chicken and keep warm.

3. Add the scallions to the skillet and sauté, stirring, for 1 minute. Add the wine, chicken broth, lemon juice and parsley. Bring the liquid to a boil, then reduce the heat and simmer until the liquid is reduced by half. Season to taste with pepper.

4. Arrange the chicken on serving plates and spoon a little sauce over each. Garnish with the almonds and serve.

62—Angel Hair with Tomato-Basil Sauce

4 servings

2   tablespoons olive oil
1   clove garlic, minced
5–6 plum tomatoes, diced
¼   cup chopped fresh basil
2   tablespoons capers
     Freshly ground black pepper, to taste
8   ounces capellini, or angel hair pasta

1. In a saucepan, heat the oil and sauté the garlic until it is soft, about 1 minute. Add the tomato and basil, and cook until the tomato is just heated, about 1 minute. Remove the pan from the heat and keep warm. Stir in the capers and season to taste with pepper.

2. In a large pot of boiling water, cook the capellini until it is just al dente, or firm to the bite. Drain and rinse under hot running water.

3. Pour the sauce into a serving bowl, add the capellini and toss lightly. Serve immediately.

63—Baked Fish in Tomato Sauce *4 servings*

1	pound scrod or other thick whitefish, trimmed, cut into 4 serving pieces
1	tablespoon fresh lemon juice
	Salt and freshly ground black pepper
½	cup flat leaf or Italian fresh parsley
1	slice reduced calorie white bread, crusts trimmed
1	shallot, peeled, quartered
2	teaspoons olive oil
1	onion, chopped
5	tomatoes, peeled, seeded and chopped
¼	cup dry white wine
½	teaspoon crumbled dried rosemary
3	tablespoons chopped chives

1. Preheat the oven to 400 degrees.

2. Place fish in a large, nonstick baking dish. Drizzle the lemon juice over the fish, and season lightly with salt and pepper. Reserve.

3. In a blender or food processor, combine the parsley, bread and shallot, and blend until finely chopped. Reserve.

4. In a large skillet, heat the oil over a medium heat and sauté the onion for 3–4 minutes, until it is translucent. Add the tomatoes, wine and rosemary to the onions. Cook, while stirring, for 15 minutes, or until the mixture is reduced by half. Spoon the mixture over the fish, covering the pieces completely.

5. Cover the dish loosely with parchment paper or aluminum foil and bake for 5 minutes. Reduce the heat to 375 degrees, uncover the dish and scrape the sauce to the sides of the fish.

6. Spoon parsley and bread crumb mixture evenly over the fish and bake, uncovered, for 8–10 minutes, until the fish flakes easily with a fork.

7. Place the dish under the broiler for 2 minutes to brown the crumb topping. Garnish with chopped chives, and serve with the sauce spooned around the fish.

64—Baked Ziti with Meat Sauce   *4 servings*

1   tablespoon olive oil
1   onion, diced
½   pound lean ground beef
2   cups canned whole tomatoes, chopped
½   teaspoon oregano
       Pinch rosemary
¼   teaspoon red pepper flakes
8   ounces ziti noodles
¼   pound low fat mozzarella cheese, shredded
4   tablespoons grated Parmesan cheese

1. Preheat oven to 350 degrees.

2. In a large skillet, heat the olive oil over a medium heat. Add the onion, and cook until it is translucent, about 3 minutes.

3. Add the meat to the onion and cook until brown, stirring occasionally to break up the meat.

4. Add the tomatoes and seasonings to the skillet, cover, and simmer for 45 minutes.

5. Cook ziti noodles al dente, or firm. Drain and rinse under cold running water.

4. Pour the sauce into a baking dish. Add the cooked ziti and the mozzarella cheese, and stir to combine.

7. Bake the ziti for 20–25 minutes, until the sauce is bubbly and the cheese is melted. Serve with the Parmesan cheese.

65—Barbecued Chicken

4 servings

1	clove garlic, minced
1	cup chopped onions
1¼	cups tomato juice
1	tablespoon tomato paste
2	tablespoons soy sauce
1	tablespoon Worcestershire sauce
1	tablespoon Dijon mustard
2	tablespoons red wine or balsamic vinegar
1	teaspoon ginger
1	tablespoon lemon juice
2	whole chicken breasts, skinned and split

1. In a saucepan, combine the garlic, onion, tomato juice, tomato paste, soy sauce, Worcestershire sauce, mustard, vinegar, ginger and lemon juice. Stir the ingredients to blend, then cook, at a simmer, for 10 minutes. Remove the sauce from the heat and let it cool.

2. Place the chicken in a pan and pour the marinade over the chicken, turning the pieces so that they are covered with marinade. Refrigerate the chicken for 8 hours, or overnight.

3. Preheat the broiler, or use a barbecue grill.

4. Broil, or barbecue, the chicken about 20 minutes to a side, or until the chicken is thoroughly cooked and tender.

66—Beef and Vegetable Stew

4 servings

2	teaspoons olive oil
1	onion, chopped
2	cloves garlic, minced
¾	pound stew beef, cubed and trimmed of fat
½	cup canned whole tomatoes, chopped and undrained
1	cup beef broth, defatted
2	tablespoons tomato paste
2	carrots, diced
1	celery stalk, diced
1	bay leaf
1	teaspoon basil
½	cup red wine
½	pound peas

1. In a Dutch oven, over a low heat, heat the oil. Add the onion and garlic and cook until the onion is wilted, about 3 minutes.

2. Add the beef and sauté the meat until it is brown on all sides, about 5–7 minutes.

3. Add the remaining ingredients, except the peas, and bring to a boil. Reduce the heat to a simmer and cook the stew, covered, for 1½–2 hours, until the meat is tender. Just before serving, add the peas and cook another 10 minutes.

67—Beef Curry   *4 servings*

1	tablespoon vegetable oil
¾	pound top round, cubed and trimmed of fat
2	onions, thinly sliced
1	clove garlic, minced
2	tablespoons reduced calorie margarine
2	tablespoons enriched flour
1¾	cups chicken broth, defatted
¼	cup dry white wine
1	teaspoon curry powder, or to taste
½	teaspoon cinnamon
1	pound spinach

1. Heat the oil in a skillet and brown the beef over a low heat, stirring. Remove the beef and reserve.

2. Add the onions and garlic to the skillet and sauté, stirring frequently, until the onions are soft, about 5–7 minutes. Remove the skillet from the heat.

3. In a saucepan, melt the margarine over a medium heat. Stir in the flour and cook, stirring, for 1 minute. Pour in the chicken broth and continue to cook, stirring, until the sauce has thickened, about 2–3 minutes. Stir in the wine, curry and cinnamon.

4. Chop the spinach coarsely and add it to the sauce. Stir in the beef and onions, bring the sauce to a simmer and cook, covered, for 35–45 minutes, or until the beef is tender.

68—Beef Ragout
4 servings

1	tablespoon olive oil
1	pound top round, cubed
2	tablespoons all purpose flour
2	tablespoons tomato paste
2	cups beef broth, defatted
2	onions, sliced
½	cup sliced mushrooms
2	carrots, peeled and sliced
1	bay leaf
1	tablespoon chopped fresh parsley
1	teaspoon chopped fresh basil, or ½ teaspoon dried
½	teaspoon thyme
½	teaspoon freshly ground black pepper

1. In a Dutch oven, heat the oil over a medium heat. Add the beef, brown on all sides, then remove and reserve.

2. Add the flour to the Dutch oven, stir and cook for 1 minute. Then add the tomato paste. Slowly stir in the beef broth and cook until the ingredients are thoroughly blended, about 5 minutes.

3. Add the vegetables and seasonings to the Dutch oven and bring the sauce to a simmer.

4. Return the beef to the pot, cover and simmer for 1–2 hours, or until the beef is tender.

69—Chicken and Shrimp Kebabs
4 servings

12	large shrimp, peeled and deveined
1	whole chicken breast, about ½ pound, skinned, boned and cut into 12 pieces
2	green peppers, seeded and quartered
2	onions, quartered
12	mushrooms, stems trimmed
3	tablespoons soy sauce
3	tablespoons dry sherry
1	teaspoon sesame oil
1	teaspoon grated gingerroot
1	clove garlic, minced

1. Mix the shrimp, chicken, and vegetables in a large bowl.

2. In a small bowl, combine the remaining ingredients, mix thoroughly and pour over the shrimp-chicken mixture. Toss to coat all the pieces with marinade, then refrigerate for 1 hour, or longer.

3. Preheat the broiler.

4. Thread the shrimp, chicken, and vegetables alternately, on four skewers. Broil, turning the skewers every 3 minutes, until the chicken is thoroughly cooked, about 12–15 minutes.

70—Chicken and Spinach Manicotti   *4 servings*

1	teaspoon olive oil
¼	onion, finely chopped
1	clove garlic, minced
2	cups canned crushed tomatoes
½	teaspoon basil
¼	teaspoon oregano
8	manicotti shells
1¼	cups finely chopped chicken, cooked
¾	cup chopped spinach, cooked
1	egg, beaten
	Pinch nutmeg
2	tablespoons grated Romano cheese
	Salt and freshly ground black pepper, to taste

1. In a saucepan, heat the oil and sauté the onion and garlic over a low heat, stirring, until the onion is soft, about 3 minutes. Add the tomatoes, basil and oregano, and simmer for 10 minutes. Remove the saucepan from the heat and reserve.

2. Preheat the oven to 350 degrees.

3. In a large pot of boiling water, cook the manicotti until al dente, or firm to the bite. Drain, rinse under cold water and reserve.

4. In a bowl, mix together the chicken, spinach, egg, nutmeg and cheese. Season to taste with salt and pepper.

5. Fill the manicotti shells with the chicken mixture. Then lay them in a baking dish and cover with sauce. Bake for 20–25 minutes, or until the sauce is bubbly.

71—Chicken Breasts with Vegetables in Cheese Sauce

4 servings

1   teaspoon vegetable oil
1   scallion, diced
2   cups chopped spinach leaves
1   cup chopped mushrooms
    Salt and freshly ground black pepper, to taste
    Pinch nutmeg
4   split chicken breasts
1   tablespoon reduced calorie margarine
1   tablespoon all purpose flour
1   cup low fat milk
2   ounces low fat cheese, such as American or Monterey Jack, shredded

1. Preheat the oven to 350 degrees.

2. In a small skillet, heat the oil and sauté the scallion, spinach and mushrooms over a low heat, stirring, until the vegetables are tender, about 3–5 minutes. Season to taste with salt, pepper and nutmeg, and reserve.

3. Make a slit lengthwise in the chicken breasts just under the skin, and stuff the breasts with the vegetable filling.

4. Place the chicken in a baking dish and bake, covered, for 30–40 minutes.

5. While the chicken is cooking, make the cheese sauce: In a saucepan, melt the margarine over a low heat. Add the flour and cook, stirring, for 1 minute. Then pour in the milk and continue cooking, while stirring, until the sauce thickens, about 3 minutes. Add the cheese and cook just until the cheese melts. Remove the sauce from the heat and keep warm.

6. When the chicken is almost done, remove it from the oven. Carefully peel off the skins and discard. Pour the cheese sauce over the chicken, return the dish to the oven and bake another 5–7 minutes, or until the chicken is tender.

72—Chicken Divan

2½   tablespoons reduced calorie margarine
2   tablespoons all purpose flour
1½   cups chicken broth, defatted
1   tablespoon dry sherry
¼   pound mushrooms, sliced
1   teaspoon lemon juice
½   pound asparagus, steamed
4   split chicken breasts, boned and poached
2   tablespoons chopped fresh parsley
2   tablespoons bread crumbs
2   tablespoons grated Parmesan cheese

   1. Preheat the oven to 375 degrees.

   2. In a saucepan, heat 2 tablespoons of the margarine over a medium heat. Add the flour and cook, whisking constantly, for 1 minute. Add the chicken broth and cook, stirring, until the sauce thickens, about 2–3 minutes. Stir in the sherry, remove the sauce from the heat and keep warm.

   3. In a small skillet, melt the remaining ½ tablespoon margarine, and sauté the mushrooms until they are tender, about 3–4 minutes. Sprinkle the lemon juice over the mushrooms.

   4. To assemble: Lay the asparagus spears over the bottom of a baking dish. Place the chicken over the asparagus, then sprinkle the mushrooms over the chicken. Spoon the sauce over all.

   5. In a small bowl, stir together the parsley, bread crumbs and cheese, and sprinkle the topping over the chicken.

   6. Bake the casserole for 20–25 minutes, or until the sauce is bubbly and the top begins to brown.

73—Chicken Florentine   *4 servings*

2   whole chicken breasts, skin removed, split
     Salt and freshly ground white pepper, to taste
1   cup chicken broth, defatted
¼   cup dry white wine
½   cup sliced mushrooms
½   pound spinach, cooked, drained and chopped
     Pinch nutmeg
½   tablespoon lemon juice

1. Season the chicken breasts lightly with salt and pepper and reserve.

2. In a large skillet, combine the chicken broth and wine, and bring to a simmer over a medium heat. Add the mushrooms and simmer for 5 minutes or until the mushrooms are tender.

3. Place the chicken breasts in the skillet, cover and simmer 15–20 minutes, or until the chicken is completely cooked and tender.

4. Preheat the oven to 350 degrees.

5. Spoon the spinach into a baking dish. Sprinkle the nutmeg and lemon juice over the spinach.

6. Place the chicken pieces with the mushrooms on top of the spinach and bake for 10–15 minutes, until all the ingredients are warm.

74—Chicken Ratatouille   *4 servings*

2	tablespoons olive oil
1	onion, thinly sliced
2	cloves garlic, minced
2	whole chicken breasts, skinned
1	tablespoon all purpose flour
1	cup canned whole tomatoes, undrained
½	teaspoon oregano
1	teaspoon basil
¼	teaspoon dill
½	teaspoon freshly ground black pepper
1	small eggplant, about ½ pound, cubed
1	zucchini, sliced
½	green pepper, seeded and cut into ½-inch strips
½	red pepper, seeded and cut into ½-inch strips
2	tablespoons chopped fresh parsley

1. In a large nonstick skillet, heat 1 tablespoon of the oil and sauté the onions and garlic until the onion is translucent. Scrape the onion into a Dutch oven or casserole dish.

2. Heat the remaining oil in the skillet and add the chicken. Sauté, turning, until the chicken pieces have browned. Add the chicken to the onion and garlic.

3. Add the flour to the skillet, and cook, stirring, for 1–2 minutes, until the mixture is slightly browned.

4. Add the tomatoes and seasoning to skillet, chop up the tomatoes with a spoon and cook, stirring, until the mixture has thickened, about 10–15 minutes. Reserve.

5. Add the eggplant, zucchini, green and red peppers to the chicken. Pour the sauce from the skillet over the casserole.

6. Cover and cook the chicken over a low heat for 30–40 minutes, until the chicken and vegetables are tender. Garnish with the parsley and serve.

75—Chinese Pepper Steak   *4 servings*

2   tablespoons soy sauce
2   tablespoons dry sherry wine
1   tablespoon fresh ginger, chopped
1   clove garlic, minced
1   pound lean top round, thinly sliced
½   cup beef broth, defatted
1   tablespoon cornstarch
1   tablespoon peanut oil
2   scallions, chopped
1   onion, thinly sliced
1   green pepper, seeded and sliced
½   cup sliced mushrooms

1. In a small bowl, combine the soy sauce, sherry, ginger and garlic. Pour the mixture over the beef and let it marinate for 2 hours.

2. Combine the beef broth and cornstarch, mix thoroughly and reserve.

3. In a wok or large skillet, heat the oil over a medium heat, add the vegetables and cook, stirring, for 2–3 minutes, until the vegetables are just tender. Remove the vegetables and reserve.

4. Add the beef to the wok and sauté, stirring for 5 minutes.

5. Return the vegetables to the wok. Pour in the beef broth mixture and cook, stirring, until the sauce thickens, about 5 minutes.

76—Chinese Style Chicken with Peanuts   *4 servings*

1   large whole chicken breast, about 1 pound
2   tablespoons soy sauce
1   teaspoon sesame oil
2   tablespoons dry sherry
1   teaspoon grated fresh gingerroot
1   clove garlic, minced
1   tablespoon peanut oil
¼   cup shelled, unsalted peanuts
¼   pound mushrooms, sliced
2   scallions, chopped
1   red or yellow pepper, seeded and cut into ¼-inch strips
1   cup sliced water chestnuts
½   cup snow peas

1. Remove the skin and the bone from the chicken and cut the meat into 1-inch cubes.

2. In a bowl, combine the soy sauce, sesame oil, sherry, ginger and garlic, and mix thoroughly.

3. Add the chicken to the soy marinade, tossing until the chicken is completely coated. Refrigerate the chicken for 1–2 hours.

4. In a skillet or wok, heat the oil over a high heat. Add the peanuts to the skillet and cook, stirring, for 1 minute. Remove the peanuts and reserve.

5. Add the chicken to the skillet and sauté, stirring, for about 2 minutes, until the chicken is completely white. Pour in the marinade, add the vegetables and continue cooking, while stirring constantly, for 4–5 minutes, or until the chicken is cooked through and the vegetables begin to feel tender.

6. Spoon the chicken-vegetable mixture onto a serving platter and garnish with the peanuts.

77—Crab Quiche

4 servings

¾	cup sifted all purpose flour
¼	teaspoon salt
¼	cup reduced calorie margarine, at room temperature.
2–3	tablespoons ice water
2	eggs, beaten
1	cup skim milk
¼	teaspoon dry mustard
¼	teaspoon Worcestershire sauce
3	ounces crab meat
3	scallions, diced
1	tablespoon chopped fresh parsley

1. Sift the flour and salt into a mixing bowl. Then, using a fork or a pastry blender, cut in the margarine quickly until the pastry begins to stick together. Sprinkle on the ice water and mix, quickly. Shape the dough into a ball; wrap in waxed paper, and chill for 1 hour.

2. Preheat the oven to 375 degrees.

3. On a floured board, roll out the dough into a thin 10-inch circle. Lay the dough carefully into a small 8-inch quiche pan and flute the edges with your fingers.

4. In a bowl, beat the eggs. Stir in the remaining ingredients until well combined and pour the batter into the quiche pan.

5. Bake the quiche for 35–45 minutes, until the quiche is set and bubbly.

78—Fillet of Flounder Amandine   *4 servings*

1   tablespoon reduced calorie margarine
2   tablespoons slivered almonds
1   tablespoon vegetable oil
4   flounder fillets, about 1 pound
     Salt and freshly ground white pepper, to taste
¼   cup white wine
2   tablespoons lemon juice
2   tablespoons chopped fresh parsley

1. In a large skillet, melt the margarine over a medium heat. Add the almonds and sauté, stirring, until they are lightly browned. Remove the almonds and reserve.

2. Heat the oil in the skillet. Season the flounder lightly with salt and pepper. Lay the flounder into the skillet and cook over a medium heat, about 1–2 minutes a side, or until the fish flakes easily with a fork. Gently remove the flounder and keep warm.

3. Add the wine and lemon juice to the pan, let the liquid come to a boil and reduce by half. Stir in the parsley.

4. Arrange the fillets on serving plates, spoon a little of the wine-lemon mixture over each fillet, and garnish with the almonds.

79—Flounder with Coriander   *4 servings*

1	teaspoon reduced calorie margarine
2	teaspoons finely chopped shallots
½	zucchini, cut in julienne strips
1	carrot, cut in julienne strips
1	small leek, cut in julienne strips
4	flounder fillets, about 1½ pounds
	Salt and freshly ground black pepper, to taste
¼	cup dry white wine
3	tablespoons lemon juice
¼	cup finely chopped coriander leaves

1. Preheat the oven to 375 degrees. Grease a baking dish with the margarine, and sprinkle the shallots over the bottom.

2. In a saucepan, lightly steam the zucchini, carrots and leeks until they are just tender, about 1 minute.

3. Divide the vegetables evenly over the centers of the flounder fillets. Roll the fillets up, and place them in the baking dish. Season lightly with salt and pepper.

4. Drizzle the fish with the wine and lemon juice, and bake, covered, for 20–25 minutes, or until the fish flakes easily with a fork.

5. Gently remove the fish from the baking dish and keep warm. Add the coriander to the pan, bring the liquid to a boil over a medium heat, then reduce the heat and simmer, while stirring, for a minute.

6. Arrange the fish on serving plates, spoon a little sauce over each fillet and serve.

80—Glazed Chicken Breasts   *4 servings*

2   whole chicken breasts, split and skinned
1   tablespoon vegetable oil
     Salt and freshly ground white pepper, to taste
1   cup reduced calorie currant jelly
¾   cup water
1   teaspoon ground allspice
2   tablespoons brandy
1   tablespoon lemon juice
2   tablespoons chopped fresh parsley

1. Preheat the oven to 450 degrees.

2. Place the chicken breasts in a baking dish, brush with oil and season with salt and pepper. Reserve.

3. In a saucepan, combine the jelly, water, allspice, brandy and lemon juice, and cook slowly over a low heat stirring constantly, until the sauce thickens.

4. Pour the sauce over the chicken breasts and bake, uncovered, for 10 minutes.

5. Reduce the heat to 350 degrees and bake for another 30 minutes, basting frequently until the chicken is tender. (If the sauce cooks down and gets too thick, thin it out with a little water or chicken broth.) Garnish with the parsley and serve.

81—Grilled Beef Kebabs
4 servings

½   pound top round steak, cut into 1-inch cubes, and trimmed of fat
¼   cup soy sauce
¼   cup dry sherry
1   clove garlic, minced
2   teaspoons grated gingerroot
2   tablespoons vegetable oil
8   2-inch cubes fresh pineapple
2   green peppers cut into quarters
12   cherry tomatoes

1. Place the meat in a bowl.

2. In another bowl, mix the soy sauce, sherry, garlic, gingerroot and oil and pour the sauce over the meat.

3. Cover the meat and refrigerate it for at least 8 hours, or overnight.

4. Preheat the broiler.

5. Drain the meat, reserving the marinade. On 4 skewers, thread the meat alternately with the green pepper, cherry tomatoes and pineapple.

6. Broil the kebabs for 4–5 minutes on each side, basting each side with the marinade.

82—Hearty Baked Macaroni   *4 servings*

8	ounces elbow macaroni
1	tablespoon vegetable oil
1	clove garlic, minced
2	scallions, chopped
½	pound mushrooms, sliced
2	cups tomato puree
1	teaspoon basil
¼	teaspoon oregano
	Salt and freshly ground pepper, to taste
1	cup low fat cottage cheese
¼	ounces low fat mozzarella cheese, grated
2	tablespoons grated Parmesan cheese

1. Preheat oven to 350 degrees.

2. Cook elbow macaroni until it is al dente, or firm. Drain and reserve.

3. In a large skillet, heat the oil over a medium heat, and sauté the garlic and scallions, stirring, until the scallions are wilted, about 3 minutes.

4. Add the mushrooms and cook until they are soft, about 5 minutes.

5. Add the tomato puree and seasonings, stir and simmer for another 10 minutes.

6. Spoon one-third of the sauce over the bottom of a baking dish. Add half the macaroni, and top with half the cottage cheese. Repeat the layering.

7. Sprinkle the mozzarella cheese and the Parmesan over the top and bake for 20–30 minutes, until the cheese begins to brown.

83—Herbed Chicken Breasts   *4 servings*

1   teaspoon vegetable oil
½   green pepper, diced
3   scallions, diced
6   mushrooms, diced
4   tablespoons chicken bouillon
½   cup cooked brown or wild rice, or a combination
1   tablespoon chopped fresh basil, or ½ teaspoon dried
        Salt and freshly ground pepper, to taste
4   split chicken breasts, boned, with skin

1. Preheat oven to 350 degrees.

2. In a skillet, heat the oil over a medium heat. Add the green pepper, scallions and mushrooms and sauté until the vegetables are tender, about 3 minutes. Add the broth and cook another 3–4 minutes. Combine the vegetables with the rice, basil, salt and pepper.

3. Cut a pocket in each chicken breast by pressing down on the skin side with one hand while slicing parallel with the counter top almost, but not all the way, to the back of the breast. Open the pocket and stuff it with 2 tablespoons of the rice-pepper mixture.

4. Place the chicken breasts in a nonstick baking pan, skin side up, and roast the chicken for 35–40 minutes, until the chicken is tender. Broil an additional 5 minutes to brown the skin.

84—Indonesian Chicken
4 servings

1	teaspoon olive oil
1	onion, chopped
1	clove garlic, minced
2	whole chicken breasts, skins removed and split
1	cup tomato sauce
1	cup crushed tomatoes
1	teaspoon turmeric
½	teaspoon ground cinnamon
½	teaspoon cardamon
½	teaspoon cumin
1	teaspoon lemon juice

1. Preheat the oven to 350 degrees.

2. In a large nonstick skillet heat the oil over a medium heat and sauté the onion and garlic for 3 minutes, stirring, or until the onion is tender.

3. Add the chicken and cook for 15 minutes, browning the chicken on both sides. Transfer the chicken to a covered baking dish.

4. Pour the sauce, tomatoes and seasonings into the baking dish, then cover and bake for 30 minutes. Remove the cover and bake for an additional 10 minutes. Serve the chicken with the sauce spooned on top.

85—Lamb Chops Diablo   *4 servings*

1   clove garlic, minced
2   tablespoons lemon juice
1   teaspoon oregano
½   teaspoon basil
1   tablespoon Dijon mustard
1   tablespoon olive oil
1   tablespoon honey
4   loin lamb chops

1. Preheat the broiler.

2. In a bowl, combine all the ingredients, except the lamb chops, and mix well.

3. Place the chops on a rack in a broiling pan. Spread half of the lemon juice mixture over the chops. Broil the chops for 3–5 minutes, then turn and spread the remaining mixture over the chops. Continue broiling another 3–5 minutes, or until the chops are as well done as you prefer.

86—Lamb Curry   *4 servings*

1   tablespoon vegetable oil
¾   pound lean lamb, cut into 1-inch cubes and trimmed of fat
1   onion, chopped
1   apple, peeled and chopped
1   stalk celery, chopped
2   tablespoons reduced calorie margarine
2   tablespoons enriched flour
1¾   cups chicken broth, defatted
¼   cup dry white wine
1   teaspoon curry powder, or to taste
½   teaspoon cinnamon
⅛   teaspoon allspice
¼   cup white raisins
2   cups cooked white, or brown, rice

1. In a large saucepan, heat the oil over a medium heat and saute the lamb, stirring until it is brown on all sides. Remove the lamb and reserve.

2. Add the onion, apple and celery to the saucepan, and saute until the vegetables are soft, about 5 minutes. Remove the saucepan from the heat and reserve.

3. In another saucepan, melt the margarine over a medium heat. Add the flour and cook, while stirring, for 1 minute. Pour in the chicken broth and continue cooking, while stirring, until the sauce thickens, about 2–3 minutes. Add the wine, curry powder, cinnamon and allspice.

4. Pour the curry sauce into the saucepan with the vegetables. Add the lamb, bring the sauce to a simmer and cook, covered, for 35–45 minutes, or until the lamb is tender. Just before serving, stir in the raisins. Serve over the rice.

87—Lemon Chicken

4 servings

1	teaspoon vegetable oil
1	clove garlic, minced
¾	cup chicken broth, defatted
¼	cup dry white wine
2	tablespoons lemon juice
1	teaspoon grated lemon peel
4	split chicken breasts, skinned
2	tablespoons chopped fresh parsley

1. Preheat the oven to 350 degrees.

2. In a saucepan, heat the oil and sauté the garlic over a low heat, stirring, for 1 minute. Add the chicken broth, wine, lemon juice and peel, bring the liquid to a boil, then let it reduce slightly, about 2–3 minutes.

3. Lay the chicken in a baking pan, then spoon the lemon mixture evenly over each piece. Cover the pan and bake for 30 minutes. Remove the cover and bake another 10 minutes, or until the chicken is cooked through. Garnish with the parsley and serve.

88—Moussaka

6 servings

2   medium eggplants, about 1½ pounds
1   tablespoon olive oil
2   onions, chopped
2   cloves garlic, peeled and crushed
4   medium size tomatoes, peeled, cored and coarsely chopped
½   teaspoon thyme
2   tablespoons minced fresh mint or 1 teaspoon mint flakes, optional
2   tablespoons minced fresh parsley
1   8-ounce can tomato sauce
    Salt and freshly ground black pepper, to taste
1   pound low fat cottage cheese
2   egg whites
¼   teaspoon leaf rosemary, crumbled
½   teaspoon mace
    Freshly ground black pepper, to taste
¼   cup olive oil
½   cup grated Parmesan cheese

1. Slice the eggplants into ½-inch slices. Place the slices between layers of paper towel, weight down with a plate and let stand 1 hour.

2. In a large saucepan, heat the tablespoon of oil and sauté the onions and garlic until the onions are translucent, about 5 minutes. Add the tomatoes, thyme, mint and parsley. Cook, uncovered, stirring occasionally, until the tomatoes begin to release their juices. Cover, lower the heat and simmer for one hour, stirring occasionally. Stir in the tomato sauce and simmer, uncovered, for 15 minutes. Season, to taste, with salt and pepper.

3. While tomato sauce simmers, prepare the cheese filling. Mix together the remaining ingredients except the oil and Parmesan cheese.

4. Preheat the oven to 375 degrees.

5. Preheat the broiler. Brush both sides of each eggplant slightly with olive oil, then broil quickly on each side to brown.

6. To assemble the moussaka, spoon half the tomato sauce over the bottom of a 13-by-9-by-2-inch baking pan. Arrange half the eggplant slices on top, then cover with the cheese filling. Arrange the remaining eggplant slices on top. Spread the eggplant with the remaining tomato sauce, and sprinkle with the Parmesan cheese.

7. Bake the moussaka, uncovered, for 45–50 minutes, until bubbling and browned. Remove from the oven and let stand 15 minutes before serving.

89—Pasta Primavera   *4 servings*

2   tablespoons olive oil
2   cloves garlic, minced
2   scallions, diced
¼   red pepper, seeded and cut into ¼-inch strips
¼   yellow pepper, seeded and cut into ¼-inch strips
2   cups broccoli flowerets
½   zucchini, sliced
2 . tablespoons chopped fresh basil, or 1 teaspoon dried
1   pound fettuccine
     Freshly ground pepper, to taste

1. In a large saucepan, heat the oil over a medium heat and sauté the garlic and scallions until tender, about 1 minute. Add the peppers, broccoli and zucchini, and continue to sauté, stirring constantly, until the vegetables are just tender, about 3–5 minutes. Stir in the basil, remove the pan from the heat and reserve.

2. In a large pot of boiling water, cook the fettuccine until it is al dente, or just firm to the bite. Drain and rinse under hot running water.

3. Put the vegetables in a serving bowl, then the fettuccine. Toss lightly to combine, season to taste with pepper and serve.

90—Scallops au Gratin
4 servings

2	tablespoons reduced calorie margarine
1½	pounds bay scallops
¼	cup dry white wine
	Salt and freshly ground white pepper, to taste
1	tablespoon all purpose flour
¾	cup low fat milk
¼	cup grated low fat cheese, such as Fontina or Jarlsberg
¼	cup bread crumbs
1	tablespoon grated Parmesan cheese

1. Preheat the oven to 350 degrees.

2. In a large skillet, heat 1 tablespoon of the margarine over a medium heat, add the scallops and cook for 2–3 minutes, turning the scallops as they cook. Remove the scallops from the heat and add the wine, salt and pepper. Spoon the scallops into a nonstick baking pan and reserve.

3. Heat the remaining margarine in a saucepan. Add the flour and cook over a low heat, stirring, for 1 minute. Gradually stir in the milk and cook for 3–4 minutes, or until sauce begins to thicken.

4. Add the cheese, and continue cooking until the cheese melts. Remove the sauce from the heat and pour it over the scallops. Top the casserole with bread crumbs and Parmesan cheese, and bake for 15–20 minutes, or until the sauce is bubbling and all the ingredients are hot.

91—Shrimp Creole

2   tablespoons olive oil
½   cup chopped onions
¼   cup chopped celery
¼   cup chopped green or red pepper
1   clove garlic, minced
2   cups stewed tomatoes
1   tablespoon tomato paste
¼   teaspoon thyme
1   tablespoon chopped fresh parsley
½   bay leaf
1   pound shrimp, shelled and deveined
2   cups cooked rice, either white or wild rice, or a combination

1. In a large skillet, heat the oil over a low heat. Add the onion, celery, pepper and garlic, and sauté, while stirring, until the vegetables are tender, about 5 minutes.

2. Add the tomatoes, tomato paste and seasonings, cover, and simmer for 30 minutes.

3. Add the shrimp to the vegetables and cook, uncovered, for 5 minutes, or until the shrimp turn pink. Remove the bay leaf.

4. Spoon the rice onto a serving platter and top with the shrimp and sauce.

92—Shrimp Jambalaya   *4 servings*

2	tablespoons reduced calorie margarine
½	cup chopped onion
½	cup chopped green pepper
1	clove garlic, minced
2	tablespoons all purpose flour
1½	cups stewed tomatoes
½	cup water
2	bay leaves
½	teaspoon thyme
½	teaspoon basil
¼	teaspoon salt
⅛	teaspoon cayenne pepper
	Dash black pepper
¾	cup quick cooking rice
1	pound medium shrimp, shelled and deveined

1. In a saucepan melt the margarine and sauté the onion, green pepper, and garlic over a medium heat until the vegetables are tender, about 3–4 minutes.

2. Stir the flour into the vegetables, then add tomatoes, water, bay leaves, thyme, basil, salt, cayenne and pepper.

3. Stir the uncooked rice and shrimp into the saucepan, bring the liquid to a boil, then reduce the heat and cook, stirring frequently, for 10–15 minutes or till rice and shrimp are done. Remove the bay leaves and serve the jambalaya in bowls.

93—Shrimp with Cold Cilantro Sauce
4 servings

¼   cup cilantro
1   tablespoon olive oil
1   small clove garlic
1   teaspoon lemon juice
2   tablespoons low fat yogurt
2   tablespoons reduced calorie mayonnaise
1   teaspoon lime juice
   Salt to taste
   Bibb lettuce leaves
1   pound cooked, cleaned shrimp
1   avocado, sliced
   Lime slices
   Cilantro leaves

1. In a food processor, puree the cilantro, oil, garlic and lemon juice.

2. Combine the cilantro pesto, yogurt, mayonnaise and lime juice in a small bowl. Add salt to taste and reserve.

3. Place the lettuce on a serving platter and arrange the shrimp and avocado over the lettuce.

4. Spoon the sauce over the shrimp. Garnish with lime slices and cilantro leaves.

94—Stuffed Cabbage Rolls with Tomato Sauce   *4 servings*

1   head savoy cabbage, about 2 pounds
1   teaspoon vegetable oil
1   clove garlic, minced
¼   onion, chopped
¼   green pepper, seeded and diced
½   pound lean ground beef
3   cups cooked rice
1   egg, beaten
¼   teaspoon thyme
⅛   teaspoon sage
     Salt and freshly ground black pepper, to taste
2   cups tomato sauce
1   tablespoon beef broth, defatted
1   teaspoon dried basil

1. Separate 8 large, outer cabbage leaves and parboil them for about 5 minutes, or until they begin to feel tender. Drain the leaves and cool.

2. In a nonstick skillet, heat the oil and sauté the garlic, onion and green pepper, stirring, over a medium heat until the vegetables are soft, about 2–3 minutes. Remove the vegetables and reserve.

3. Add the ground beef to the skillet and sauté, breaking up the chunks with a fork, until the meat is cooked. Remove the meat and drain.

4. In a bowl, combine the vegetables, beef, rice, egg, thyme and sage, and mix thoroughly. Season to taste with salt and pepper.

5. Spoon 3–4 tablespoons of the meat mixture onto the center of a cabbage leaf. Roll the leaf and tuck in the ends. Repeat with each cabbage leaf.

6. Combine the tomato sauce, beef broth and basil and pour the sauce into a casserole or Dutch oven. Place the stuffed cabbage leaves on top of the sauce. Bring the sauce to a simmer over a low heat, then cover the casserole and cook for about 1 hour, or until the cabbage is very tender.

95—Sukiyaki *4 servings*

2   tablespoons peanut oil
¾   pound beef tenderloin, thinly sliced
4   scallions, chopped
1   cup cooked bamboo shoots
1   cup sliced mushrooms
1   cup bean sprouts
2   cups spinach leaves, left whole, tough stems removed
2   teaspoons cornstarch
1   tablespoon grated gingerroot
1   clove garlic, minced
½   cup water
⅓   cup soy sauce
2   cups cooked rice

1. In a large skillet or wok, heat 1 tablespoon of the oil over a medium heat. Add the meat and cook, stirring, for 2 minutes. Remove the meat from the skillet and reserve.

2. Add the remaining oil to the skillet, heat, then add the vegetables and sauté, stirring, until the vegetables are just tender, about 2 minutes.

3. In a small bowl, mix the cornstarch, gingerroot, garlic and water. Stir in the soy sauce, mix thoroughly and add to the vegetables in the skillet. Cook the vegetables for an additional minute. The vegetables should remain crisp.

4. Add the meat to the skillet and stir just to heat and thoroughly mix the ingredients. Serve the sukiyaki over the rice.

96—Sweet and Sour Vegetables
4 servings

2	teaspoons cornstarch
¾	cup water
1	cup pineapple juice
2	tablespoons lemon juice
1	tablespoon honey
2	tablespoons soy sauce
1	tablespoon grated gingerroot
2	tablespoons peanut or vegetable oil
1	onion, chopped
1	carrot, thinly sliced
1½	cups broccoli flowerets
1	red pepper, chopped
¾	pound tofu, cut into cubes
1	cup pineapple chunks
2	cups cooked white rice

1. In a small bowl, whisk together the cornstarch and ½ cup of the water. Reserve.

2. In another bowl, combine the pineapple juice, lemon juice, the remaining water, the honey, soy sauce and gingerroot. Mix thoroughly and reserve.

3. In a large skillet or wok, heat the oil over a medium heat, add the onion, carrot, broccoli and red pepper, and sauté for 5 minutes.

4. Add the tofu to the skillet and sauté, stirring, for 5 more minutes.

5. Reduce the heat and add the pineapple chunks. Cook, stirring, for 1 minute. Then add the pineapple juice to the skillet and cook, stirring for 1 minute.

6. Pour in the cornstarch mixture and cook, stirring until all ingredients are hot and the sauce thickens, about 5 minutes. Serve over the rice.

97—Tofu Burgers

1	teaspoon vegetable oil
½	cup minced onion
½	cup minced red pepper
¼	cup minced celery
½	clove garlic, minced
1	pound tofu, crumbled
1	tablespoon whole wheat flour
1	tablespoon soy sauce
1	egg, beaten
⅓	cup grated low fat cheese, such as American or Monterey Jack
¼	cup tomato sauce or Worcestershire sauce

1. Preheat the oven to 350 degrees.

2. In a skillet, over a medium heat, heat the vegetable oil and sauté the onion, red pepper, celery and garlic until the vegetables are tender, about 3 minutes.

3. In a bowl, combine the vegetables with the tofu, flour, soy sauce, egg and cheese. Shape the mixture into patties.

4. Place the patties on a nonstick baking pan and cook for 30 minutes. Serve with tomato or Worcestershire sauce.

98—Tofu Chow Mein

4 servings

1 tablespoon peanut oil
1 cup chopped onions
½ cup chopped celery
1 cup chopped red or yellow pepper
1 cup sliced mushrooms
2 cups shredded bok choy, or savoy cabbage
1 cup soy bean sprouts
1 cup sliced water chestnuts
1 pound tofu, cut into small cubes
1 tablespoon cornstarch
1 cup water
1 tablespoon miso, dissolved in ¼ cup water
2 tablespoons dry sherry
2 cups cooked brown rice

1. In a large skillet or wok, heat the oil over a high heat. Add the onions and celery and sauté, stirring, for 2 minutes.

2. Add the red pepper, mushrooms and bok choy to the wok and continue to sauté, stirring constantly, for 3–4 minutes, or until the vegetables just begin to feel tender.

3. Add the bean sprouts, water chestnuts and tofu, and cook another minute. Remove the vegetables from the wok and reserve.

4. Dissolve the cornstarch in the water and pour the mixture into the wok. Cook, stirring, about 1 minute, or until the sauce thickens. Add the miso and sherry and cook another minute.

5. Return the vegetables to the wok and toss to coat with the sauce. Arrange the rice on a serving plate. Spoon the chow mein over the rice and serve.

99—Tofu Parmesan

2   tablespoons olive oil
1   pound firm tofu, cut into ½-inch slices
½   onion, chopped
1   clove garlic, minced
2   cups canned crushed tomatoes
½   teaspoon oregano
⅛   teaspoon rosemary
¼   pound low fat mozzarella cheese, grated
1   tablespoon grated Parmesan

1. Preheat the oven to 350 degrees.

2. In a skillet, heat 1 tablespoon of the oil over a medium heat, and saute the tofu until it is light brown, about 1–2 minutes a side. Remove from the heat and drain on paper towels.

3. In a saucepan, heat the remaining oil and sauté the onion and garlic, stirring, until the onion is translucent, about 2–3 minutes. Add the tomatoes and seasonings and simmer for 10–15 minutes.

4. Lay the tofu in a baking dish. Spoon the sauce over the tofu, then sprinkle the cheeses over the top. Bake the tofu, uncovered, for 20–25 minutes, or until the cheese begins to brown.

100—Veal Parmigiana   *4 servings*

1   tablespoon olive oil
1   onion, chopped
1   clove garlic, minced
1   pound veal scallopini, cut into small pieces
1   cup tomato sauce
½   teaspoon basil
¼   teaspoon oregano
2   teaspoons chopped fresh parsley
¼   cup grated low fat mozzarella cheese
2   tablespoons grated Parmesan cheese

1. Preheat the oven to 350 degrees.

2. In a large skillet, heat the oil over a medium heat, and sauté the onion and garlic, stirring, for 2 minutes.

3. Add the veal to the skillet and sear each piece quickly on both sides. Then, place the veal in a baking dish. Spoon the garlic and onion over the veal.

4. Combine the tomato sauce, basil, oregano and parsley, and pour the sauce over the veal. Top the veal first with the mozzarella, then with the Parmesan cheese.

5. Bake the veal for 15 minutes, or until cheese has melted and sauce is hot.

101—Vegetarian Beans in Spicy Tomato Sauce   *4 servings*

8   ounces navy or pinto beans
5   cups water
2   cups tomato sauce
1   onion, chopped
2   teaspoons molasses
2   tablespoons brown sugar
1   teaspoon Dijon mustard
1   teaspoon cider vinegar
1   teaspoon Worcestershire sauce

1. Soak the beans in water for at least 2 hours. Drain them and add to a large saucepan with 5 cups of water. Bring the water to a boil, reduce the heat and simmer, covered, for 45 minutes, or until the beans are tender. Drain and reserve.

2. Preheat the oven to 250 degrees.

3. In a saucepan, combine the tomato sauce, onion, molasses, brown sugar, mustard, vinegar and Worcestershire sauce and simmer over a low heat for 10–15 minutes.

4. Place the beans and sauce in a casserole and mix well. Cover the casserole and bake, stirring occasionally, for 6–8 hours. Let the beans sit for at least 30 minutes before serving.

102—Vegetarian Lasagna

4 servings

1	tablespoon olive oil
½	onion, chopped
1	clove garlic, minced
½	red pepper, seeded and diced
2	cups canned crushed tomatoes
2	tablespoons chopped fresh basil, or 1 teaspoon dried
2	sun-dried tomatoes, diced
½	pound spinach, cooked, well drained and chopped
1	cup low fat ricotta cheese
1	small clove garlic, minced
1	egg, beaten
	Freshly ground black pepper, to taste
½	pound lasagna
3	tablespoons grated Parmesan

1. In a saucepan, heat the oil over a medium heat and sauté the onion, garlic and red pepper, stirring occasionally, until the vegetables are tender, about 3 minutes. Stir in the tomatoes, basil and sun-dried tomatoes and simmer for 15 minutes. Remove the sauce from the heat.

2. In a bowl, combine the spinach, ricotta, the small garlic clove and egg. Season to taste with pepper. Reserve.

3. In a large pot of boiling water, cook the lasagna until it is al dente, or just firm to the bite. Drain and rinse under cold running water until it is cool enough to handle.

4. Preheat the oven to 350 degrees.

5. To assemble: Spread a little tomato sauce over the bottom of a loaf pan or baking dish. Make a layer of lasagna, cover the lasagna with half the ricotta filling, then top with a little sauce. Repeat the layering, then sprinkle the top with the Parmesan.

6. Bake the lasagna for 35–45 minutes, until the top begins to brown. Let the lasagna sit for 10 minutes before serving.

103—Ziti with Grated Parmesan   *4 servings*

½   pound ziti
1   tablespoon olive oil
1   clove garlic, minced
1   onion, coarsely chopped
1   Italian, or cubanel pepper, seeded and chopped
3   tomatoes, coarsely chopped
1   tablespoon chopped fresh basil, or ½ teaspoon dried
½   teaspoon rosemary
2   tablespoons Italian chopped fresh parsley
    Salt and freshly ground black pepper, to taste
4   tablespoons Parmesan cheese

1. Cook ziti until it is al dente, or firm. Drain and reserve.

2. In a large skillet, heat the olive oil over medium heat. Add the garlic, and cook, stirring, for 1 minute. Add the onion and pepper, and sauté until the vegetables are tender.

3. Add the tomatoes and seasonings to the skillet. Cover and simmer for 1 hour.

4. Scrape the sauce into a serving dish, add the ziti, and toss to blend well. Sprinkle the Parmesan cheese over the top and serve.

SOUPS

104—Artichoke and Potato Soup *4 servings*

3   artichoke hearts, chopped
1   potato, peeled and chopped
½   leek, chopped
5   cups chicken broth, defatted
     Freshly ground white pepper, to taste
     Chopped parsley

1. Place the artichokes, potato, leek and chicken broth in a large saucepan. Bring the liquid to a boil, then reduce the heat and simmer, covered, for 30 minutes, or until the vegetables are tender.

2. Puree the soup in a blender until smooth. Return the soup to the saucepan, season to taste with pepper and reheat. Garnish with parsley and serve.

105—Barley Soup *4 servings*

2   tablespoons vegetable oil
2   carrots, peeled and diced
1   celery stalk, diced
1   onion, diced
½   pound mushrooms, diced
4   cups beef broth, defatted
¼   cup barley
¼   teaspoon oregano
1   teaspoon basil
     Salt and freshly ground black pepper, to taste
¼   pound broccoli, cut into small flowerets

1. In a large saucepan, heat the oil over a medium heat and sauté the carrots, celery, onion and mushrooms for 10 minutes.

2. Stir in the remaining ingredients, except the broccoli, and bring the soup to a boil. Reduce the heat, and simmer, covered, until the barley is tender, about 45 minutes.

3. Allow the soup to cool, then refrigerate for 8 hours, or overnight.

4. Return the soup to a saucepan and bring to simmer. Add the broccoli and cook until the broccoli is tender, about 10 minutes.

106—Black Bean Soup   *4 servings*

1	cup black beans
4	cups water
1	sprig parsley
1	whole clove
¼	teaspoon thyme
1	bay leaf
1	tablespoon vegetable oil
½	onion, chopped
½	green pepper, seeded and chopped
1	stalk celery, diced
1	clove garlic, minced
2	ounces tomato sauce
2	tablespoons dry sherry

1. Soak the beans overnight in water. Discard any beans that float to the top, then drain the beans.

2. In a large saucepan, combine the beans, the water, parsley, clove, thyme and bay leaf. Bring the liquid to a boil, reduce the heat and cook until the beans are tender, about 1 hour.

3. In a skillet, heat the oil and sauté the onion, green pepper, celery and garlic until the vegetables are tender. Add the vegetables to the beans along with the tomato sauce and cook until the soup has thickened.

4. Stir in the sherry and serve.

107—Cabbage and Lentil Soup   *6 servings*

1½	cups shredded savoy cabbage
2	carrots, thinly sliced
½	cup diced onion
1	stalk celery, diced
½	cup diced leek
½	cup finely chopped potato
½	cup lentils, rinsed
1	clove garlic, minced
6	cups vegetable broth
2	Italian plum tomatoes, diced
½	teaspoon thyme
¼	teaspoon marjoram
	Salt and freshly ground black pepper, to taste

1. In a large soup pot, combine the cabbage, carrots, onion, celery, leek, potato, lentils, garlic and broth. Bring the liquid to a boil, then reduce the heat and simmer, covered, for 1 hour, or until the lentils are tender.

2. Add the tomatoes, thyme and marjoram to the soup and simmer another 10 minutes. Season to taste with salt and pepper.

108—Cold Broccoli Soup
4 servings

1   tablespoon vegetable oil
½   onion, chopped
1   clove garlic, minced
¾   pound broccoli flowerets
4   cups chicken broth, defatted
2   teaspoons lemon juice
      Salt and freshly ground black pepper, to taste
½   cup low fat yogurt

1. In a saucepan, heat the oil and sauté the onion and garlic, stirring, until the onion is soft, about 2 minutes.

2. Add the broccoli. Pour in the chicken broth, bring the liquid to a boil, then reduce the heat and simmer, covered, for 30 minutes, until the broccoli is very tender.

3. Puree the soup in a blender or food processor until smooth.

4. Return the soup to the saucepan. Stir in the lemon juice and season to taste with salt and pepper.

5. Chill the soup for at least 2 hours. Just before serving, stir in the yogurt.

109—Creamy Asparagus Soup

4 servings

1	pound asparagus, trimmed and chopped
½	potato, peeled and chopped
¼	cup chopped onion
¼	cup chopped celery
5	cups chicken broth, defatted
2	teaspoons lemon juice
	Freshly ground white pepper, to taste

1. Place the asparagus, potato, onion, celery and chicken broth in a saucepan. Bring the liquid to a boil, then reduce the heat and simmer, covered, for 30 minutes.

2. Puree the soup in a blender or food processor until smooth. Return the soup to the saucepan, stir in the lemon juice, and season to taste with pepper.

110—Creamy Tomato Soup

4 servings

1	tablespoon vegetable oil
½	cup chopped onion
½	cup chopped celery
¼	cup chopped leek
¼	cup chopped green pepper
1	clove garlic, minced
1	tablespoon chopped fresh basil, or ½ teaspoon dried
1	cup tomato juice
1	cup chicken broth, defatted
2	cups crushed tomatoes
	Freshly ground black pepper, to taste
2	tablespoons low fat yogurt
2	tablespoons diced yellow pepper

1. In a saucepan, heat the oil over a low heat. Add the onion, celery, leek, green pepper and garlic. Sauté, stirring, until the vegetables are soft, about 5–7 minutes.

2. Add the basil, tomato juice, chicken broth and crushed tomatoes. Bring the liquid to a boil, then reduce the heat and simmer for 30 minutes.

3. Puree the soup in a blender or food processor until smooth. Return the soup to the saucepan, season to taste with pepper and reheat. Stir in yogurt, garnish with yellow pepper and serve.

111—Manhattan Clam Chowder   *4 servings*

1	teaspoon vegetable oil
½	onion, finely chopped
½	cup finely minced celery
2	tablespoons finely minced green pepper
1	clove garlic, minced
1	cup diced potatoes
2	cups hot water
3	tomatoes, peeled, seeded and diced
¾	pint clams, minced, or 1½ cups canned minced clams
1	teaspoon salt
¼	teaspoon black pepper
1	bay leaf
½	teaspoon thyme, crumbled
	Dash of cayenne
1	teaspoon minced parsley
3 to 4	soda crackers, coarsely crumbled

1. In a large soup pot, heat the oil over a medium heat. Add the onion, celery, green pepper and garlic to the pot and sauté for 5 minutes, or until the vegetables are tender.

2. Add the potato and water. Bring the liquid to a simmer and cook for 20–25 minutes, until the potato is tender.

3. Add the tomatoes, clams, salt, pepper, bay leaf, thyme and cayenne, and let the chowder simmer another 15 minutes. Remove the bay leaf, garnish with the parsley and soda crackers, and serve.

112—Minestrone

6 servings

2	tablespoons olive oil
1	garlic clove, minced
½	cup chopped onion
⅓	cup chopped celery
1	carrot, peeled and diced
½	cup chopped tomatoes
¾	cup chopped green cabbage
1	cup shredded spinach leaves
5	cups water
2	ounces fusilla pasta
½	cup cooked garbanzo beans
2	tablespoons chopped fresh basil leaves, or 1 teaspoon dried

1. In a large saucepan, heat the oil over a medium heat and sauté the garlic, onion, celery and carrot until the vegetables are soft and translucent.

2. Add the tomatoes to the vegetables, cook for 5 minutes.

3. Stir in the cabbage and spinach. Add the water, cover the saucepan and simmer the soup for 30 minutes.

4. In another saucepan, cook the fusilla until it is al dente, or firm. Drain and add to the soup.

5. Add the garbanzo beans and basil to the saucepan and simmer an additional 5–7 minutes, or until the beans are hot.

113—Onion Soup

4 servings

1	tablespoon vegetable oil
1	large onion, thinly sliced
1	tablespoon all purpose flour
4	cups beef broth, defatted
1	bay leaf
1	tablespoon dry sherry

1. In a saucepan, heat the oil over a medium heat.

2. Add the onion slices and cook, stirring frequently until the onion is very translucent and golden brown, approximately 15–20 minutes.

3. Sprinkle the flour over the onion and continue cooking, stirring, for 2 minutes.

4. Add the beef broth and bay leaf and stir well. Let the soup simmer, covered, for at least 30 minutes. Just before serving, remove the bay leaf and stir in the sherry.

114—Seafood Chowder   *4 servings*

2	teaspoons reduced calorie margarine
1	cup finely chopped onions
¼	cup chopped green pepper
½	cup finely chopped leeks, white part only
2	tablespoons all purpose flour
2	cups chicken broth, defatted
1½	cups diced potatoes
¾	pound sea scallops, diced
	Salt and freshly ground black pepper, to taste
2	tablespoons chopped fresh parsley

1. In a large saucepan, heat the margarine over a low heat. Add the onions, green pepper and leeks to the saucepan and cook, stirring, until the vegetables are tender, about 5 minutes.

2. Sprinkle the flour over the vegetables and cook, stirring, for 2 minutes.

3. Pour the chicken broth into the saucepan. Bring the liquid to a simmer for 5 minutes.

4. Add the potatoes, cover, and simmer for 30 minutes, or until the potatoes are tender.

5. Add the scallops and cook, covered, for 5 minutes.

6. Season to taste with salt and pepper. Garnish with the parsley and serve.

115—Tofu Miso Soup   *4 servings*

1	tablespoon vegetable oil
1	carrot, thinly sliced
1½	cups chopped onions
4	cups water
2	2-inch pieces wakame seaweed
1	tablespoon miso, dissolved in 3 tablespoons water
⅓	pound tofu
2	tablespoons minced fresh parsley

1. In a saucepan, heat the oil over a medium heat and sauté the carrots and onions for 5 minutes, or until the vegetables are tender.

2. Add the water and wakame seaweed to the saucepan. Bring the liquid to a boil, reduce the heat and simmer for 15 minutes.

3. Add the miso and tofu and simmer for 1 minute.

4. Pour the soup into bowls, garnish with the parsley and serve.

116—Vegetable Bean Soup   *4 servings*

2	ounces dried red or white kidney beans, rinsed
4	cups chicken broth, defatted
1	cup canned crushed tomatoes
½	cup diced onions
½	cup diced carrots
¼	cup diced celery
¼	cup diced white turnip
1	clove garlic, minced
1	cup shredded spinach
¼	cup dry white table wine
	Salt and freshly ground pepper, to taste
2	tablespoons chopped fresh parsley

1. In large bowl, let the beans soak in water overnight. Drain the beans and discard the water.

2. In a large saucepan, combine the beans with the chicken broth. Add the tomatoes, onions, carrots, celery, turnip, and garlic. Bring the liquid to a simmer and cook, stirring occasionally, until the beans are tender, about 1 hour.

3. Add remaining ingredients, except the parsley, and simmer 30 minutes longer. Garnish with the parsley and serve.

117—Vegetable Beef Soup

4 servings

1   teaspoon vegetable oil
¼   pound lean beef, cut into small cubes
½   onion, chopped
½   potato, diced
1   stalk celery, sliced
1   carrot, sliced
½   small white turnip, diced
2   tablespoons chopped parsley
1   teaspoon chopped fresh dill weed, or ¼ teaspoon dried
       Pinch cayenne pepper
¼   teaspoon thyme
2   cups beef broth, defatted
1   cup water
½   cup canned crushed tomatoes
       Salt and freshly ground black pepper, to taste

1. In a skillet, heat the oil over a medium heat and brown the meat. Transfer the meat to a large soup pot and reserve.

2. Sauté the onion in the skillet until translucent, approximately 3 minutes. Remove the onion and add to the soup pot.

3. Add the remaining ingredients to the soup pot. Bring the liquid to a simmer and cook, covered, for 1 hour. Season to taste with salt and pepper.

118—Vichyssoise

4 servings

2   medium leeks, white part only, well washed and chopped
1   medium potato, peeled and chopped
3   cups chicken broth, defatted
1   cup whole milk
       Salt and freshly ground white pepper, to taste
       Chopped chives

1. In a saucepan, combine the leeks, potato and chicken broth. Bring the liquid to a simmer. Cover, and cook over a medium heat. Cook until the potato is tender, about 20–25 minutes. Let the soup cool.

2. Puree the vegetables and broth in a blender, or food processor, until smooth. Refrigerate the mixture for at least 1 hour.

3. Add the milk to the soup, stir to combine and season to taste with salt and pepper. Refrigerate until ready to serve. Garnish with chives and serve.

VEGETABLES AND GRAINS

119—Artichokes in Mustard Sauce
4 servings

4 artichokes
3 tablespoons olive oil
1 tablespoon lemon juice
1 teaspoon Dijon mustard
   Freshly ground black pepper, to taste

1. Cut off the stems and steam the artichokes in a saucepan until tender. Remove and drain.

2. In a small bowl, combine the oil, lemon juice and mustard, and mix thoroughly. Season with pepper, to taste.

3. Divide the sauce into four small bowls and serve as a dipping sauce with the warm artichokes.

120—Baked Carrots
4 servings

8 carrots, peeled
1 teaspoon ground cinnamon
1 tablespoon reduced calorie margarine
2 tablespoons minced fresh parsley

1. Preheat the oven to 350 degrees.

2. Slice the carrots in half, lengthwise, and place on aluminum foil.

3. Sprinkle the carrots with cinnamon and dot them with the margarine.

4. Wrap the foil around the carrots and bake for 1 hour. Garnish lightly with parsley and serve.

121—Baked Potato
4 servings

4 baking potatoes, scrubbed and dried
2 teaspoons vegetable oil
1 tablespoon chopped fresh dill, or ½ teaspoon dried
1 teaspoon black pepper

1. Preheat the oven to 375 degrees.

2. Cut the potatoes in half lengthwise and place them face up on a baking sheet. Brush each potato half with oil.

3. Sprinkle the dill and black pepper evenly over each potato and bake for ¾ hour, until the tops are browned.

122—Baked Stuffed Tomatoes
4 servings

4   large firm tomatoes
1   tablespoon olive oil
⅓   cup chopped onion
½   clove garlic, minced
1   cup grated zucchini
1   tablespoon chopped fresh dill, or ½ teaspoon dried
¼   cup low fat ricotta cheese
½   egg beaten
1   tablespoon pine nuts, chopped
1   tablespoon Parmesan cheese
2   tablespoons chopped fresh parsley

    1. Preheat the oven to 350 degrees.

    2. Slice the tops off the tomatoes. Using a small spoon, scoop out the pulp, leaving the shells intact. Turn the shells upside down onto paper towels to drain. Chop the pulp and reserve.

    3. In a skillet, heat the oil over a medium heat and sauté the onion and garlic, stirring, until the onion is soft, about 2 minutes. Add the zucchini and cook another minute.

    4. Add the dill, ricotta, egg, reserved tomato pulp and pine nuts to the pan, stir to mix the ingredients well, then remove the pan from the heat.

    5. Place the tomato shells in a baking dish. Spoon the filling into the shells, and sprinkle the tops with the Parmesan cheese. Bake, uncovered, for 25–30 minutes, until the tops begin to brown. Garnish with the parsley and serve.

123—Braised Endive
4 servings

6   Belgian endives
1   tablespoon reduced calorie margarine
¼   cup finely diced onion
1½   cups chicken broth, defatted
¼   cup dry white wine
        Salt and freshly ground black pepper, to taste

    1. Preheat the oven to 350 degrees.

    2. Core the endives by removing a ½-inch-deep cone of flesh from the bottoms. Split the endives in half lengthwise and arrange them, cut side up, in a baking dish.

3. In a saucepan, melt the margarine over a low heat, and sauté the onion, stirring, until soft, about 2 minutes. Add the broth and wine to the saucepan and simmer for 3–4 minutes. Season to taste with salt and pepper.

4. Pour the broth mixture over the endives and bake, covered, for 30–40 minutes, until the endives are tender.

124—Braised Fennel
4 servings

2   medium fennel bulbs
2   tablespoons reduced calorie margarine
½   cup chicken bouillon
    Salt and freshly ground black pepper, to taste
2   tablespoons Parmesan cheese

1. Preheat the oven to 350 degrees.

2. Wash and trim the fennel bulbs. Discard any tough, brown outer layers. Cut each bulb in half lengthwise, then cut each half into four wedges about 1 inch wide.

3. Use 1 tablespoon of the margarine to grease a baking dish. Arrange the fennel wedges, cut side down, in a single layer in the dish.

4. Pour the chicken broth over the fennel, season with salt and pepper, and sprinkle the tops with Parmesan cheese. Dot the fennel with the remaining margarine and bake, uncovered, for 30–40 minutes, until the fennel is tender.

125—Broccoli in Cheese Sauce
4 servings

1   bunch broccoli, separated into flowerets, and steamed
2   tablespoons reduced calorie margarine
2   tablespoons all purpose flour
1   cup low fat milk
4   tablespoons grated low fat cheese, such as American or Monterey Jack

1. Place the broccoli on a serving platter and keep warm.

2. In a saucepan, heat the margarine over a medium heat. Stir in the flour and cook, stirring for 1 minute.

3. Gradually add the milk and cook while stirring, until the sauce thickens. Stir in the cheese and let it melt.

4. Pour the sauce over the broccoli and serve.

126—Carrot Pancakes
4 servings

3   cups grated carrots
¼   cup chopped onion
2   tablespoons chopped fresh parsley
2   eggs, beaten
4   teaspoons olive oil

1. Combine the carrots, onion, parsley and eggs in a bowl and mix thoroughly.

2. In a small nonstick skillet, heat half a teaspoon of the oil over a medium heat. Pour ¼ cup batter into the pan, and cook the pancake until brown on one side, about 3 minutes. Using a spatula, flip the pancake and cook on the other side until brown, about 1–2 minutes.

3. Repeat, using a small amount of oil for each pancake, until all the batter is used. Makes about 8 pancakes.

127—Cauliflower au Gratin
4 servings

1   head cauliflower, cut into flowerets and steamed
2   tablespoons reduced calorie margarine
2   tablespoons all purpose flour
1   cup low fat milk
2   tablespoons grated low fat cheese, such as American or Monterey Jack
     Pinch cayenne pepper
2   tablespoons bread crumbs

1. Preheat the oven to 350 degrees.

2. Place the cauliflower in a baking dish.

3. In a saucepan, heat the margarine over a medium heat. Stir in the flour and cook, stirring, for 1 minute.

4. Gradually add the milk and cook, while stirring, until the sauce thickens, about 3–4 minutes. Stir in the cheese and cayenne and cook, stirring until the cheese melts.

5. Pour the sauce over the cauliflower. Sprinkle the cauliflower with bread crumbs and bake for 20 minutes, or until the top begins to brown.

128—Corn-Stuffed Tomatoes with Basil   *4 servings*

4   large tomatoes
1   tablespoon vegetable oil
¼   cup chopped onion
⅓   cup chopped green pepper
1   cup cooked corn kernels
¼   cup bread crumbs
1   tablespoon chopped fresh basil, or ½ teaspoon dried
2   tablespoons chopped fresh parsley

1. Preheat the oven to 350 degrees.

2. Cut the tops off the tomatoes. With a small spoon, carefully scoop out the pulp, leaving the tomato shells intact. Turn the shells upside down onto paper towels and let them drain. Place the tomato pulp in a strainer and let it drain. Chop and reserve ¼ cup pulp. (The rest may be frozen for soups or sauces.)

3. In a skillet, heat the oil over a medium heat, and sauté the onion and green pepper, stirring, until the vegetables are soft, about 2 minutes.

4. Add the reserved pulp, corn, bread crumbs and basil, and cook, stirring, for another minute.

5. Place the tomato shells in a baking dish. Spoon the corn mixture into the shells, and bake, uncovered, for 20 minutes. Garnish with parsley and serve.

129—Country Vegetables

4 servings

1   tablespoon olive oil
1   cup shredded savoy cabbage
1   cup shredded red cabbage
¼   teaspoon thyme
⅛   teaspoon tarragon
½   cup chicken bouillon
2   cups peas
1   cup diced carrots
    Salt and freshly ground black pepper, to taste

1. In a large saucepan, melt the olive oil over a low heat.

2. Add the cabbages, thyme and tarragon to the saucepan and cook, stirring, for 5 minutes, or until cabbages are tender.

3. Add the chicken broth, peas and carrots to the saucepan. Bring the liquid to a boil, then reduce the heat and simmer, covered, until the peas and carrots are tender, about 5–7 minutes. Season, to taste, with salt and pepper.

130—Endive with Cheese Sauce

4 servings

8   small Belgian endives
1   tablespoon reduced calorie margarine
1   tablespoon all purpose flour
1   cup low fat milk
3   ounces grated low fat cheese, such as American or Monterey Jack
    Freshly ground white pepper, to taste

1. Place the endives in a large skillet and add enough water to cover them. Bring the water to a boil, then reduce the heat and simmer, covered, until the endives are tender, about 10 minutes. Drain the endives and reserve.

2. Preheat the broiler.

3. In a saucepan, melt the margarine over a medium heat. Stir in the flour and cook, stirring, for 1 minute. Pour in the milk and continue to cook until the sauce thickens, about 2 minutes. Add the cheese and cook just until the cheese melts.

4. Place the endives in a baking dish, pour the sauce over them and broil just until the cheese sauce begins to brown, about 2 minutes. Sprinkle with pepper to taste and serve.

131—Fluffy Baked Potato   *4 servings*

2   baking potatoes
4   tablespoons Neufchâtel cheese
2   teaspoons chopped chives

1. Preheat the oven to 350 degrees.

2. Bake the potatoes for 1 hour.

3. Then, cut the potatoes in half lengthwise, scoop out the insides and mash. Return the mashed potatoes to their shells.

4. Beat the Neufchatel lightly. Top the potatoes with the cheese, reheat until the cheese melts, then sprinkle with the chives and serve.

132—Green Beans with Sesame Seeds   *4 servings*

2   tablespoons sesame seeds
2   teaspoons vegetable oil
1   onion, finely chopped
1   garlic clove, minced
1   pound green beans, trimmed and cut in half
1   cup water
½   teaspoon lemon juice
⅛   teaspoon salt
⅛   teaspoon black pepper, preferably freshly ground

1. Spread the sesame seeds in a nonstick skillet and cook, stirring, over a high heat until the seeds are lightly browned, about 3–4 minutes. Remove the seeds and reserve.

2. In a skillet, heat the oil over a medium heat. Add the onions and garlic, and sauté, stirring, for 2–3 minutes, until the onion is tender.

3. Add the beans, water, lemon juice, salt and pepper. Cover the skillet and simmer for 10 minutes, or until beans are almost tender.

4. Remove the lid and continue cooking until the beans are tender and all the excess liquid has evaporated. Spoon the beans into a serving dish and garnish with the sesame seeds.

133—Grilled Mushrooms

4 servings

½   pound mushrooms
2   tablespoons olive oil
2   tablespoons lemon juice
2   tablespoons chopped scallions
1   teaspoon freshly ground black pepper

1. Wash or brush clean the mushrooms and dry thoroughly.

2. In a small bowl, combine the remaining ingredients and blend thoroughly. Pour the mixture over the mushrooms and marinate for at least 2 hours.

3. Preheat the broiler.

4. Place the mushrooms on a baking sheet and broil for 2–3 minutes, until brown.

134—Herbed Brussels Sprouts

4 servings

1   tablespoon reduced calorie margarine
1   tablespoon all purpose flour
1   cup chicken broth, defatted
½   teaspoon tarragon leaves
1   teaspoon Dijon mustard
1   tablespoon lemon juice
1   pound Brussels sprouts, steamed

1. In a saucepan, heat the margarine over a medium-high heat, add the flour and cook, stirring, for 1 minute.

2. Add broth, tarragon and mustard to the saucepan and cook, stirring, for 2–3 minutes, until the sauce thickens. Add the lemon juice, lower the heat and simmer 1 minute more.

3. Place the Brussels sprouts on a serving dish, top with the sauce and serve.

135—Kohlrabi in Cheese Sauce

4 servings

1	teaspoon reduced calorie margarine
5	medium-sized kohlrabi, trimmed, peeled, and cut into ¼-inch slices
1¼	cups chicken broth, defatted
	Reserved kohlrabi cooking liquid
2	tablespoons reduced calorie margarine
2	tablespoons all purpose flour
½	cup low fat milk
½	teaspoon Dijon mustard
	Pinch nutmeg
⅓	teaspoon freshly ground white pepper
2	ounces grated low fat cheese, such as American or Monterey Jack

1. Preheat the oven to 375 degrees. Spread the teaspoon of margarine on the bottom and sides of an ovenproof casserole dish.

2. Combine the kohlrabies and broth in a saucepan and bring the liquid to a boil over a medium high heat. Cook the kohlrabi slices until they are tender, about 15–20 minutes.

3. Remove the kohlrabi slices from the pan, reserving the cooking liquid, and place the kohlrabi in the casserole dish.

4. Heat the margarine in a saucepan over a low heat. Add the flour and cook, stirring, for 1–2 minutes. Gradually add ½ cup of the cooking liquid and the milk and cook, stirring, for 2 minutes, or until the sauce thickens. Stir in the mustard and nutmeg.

5. Pour the sauce over the kohlrabi slices. Top with the grated cheese and bake for 25–30 minutes, or until the sauce is bubbly and the kohlrabies are tender. Sprinkle with sauce to taste and serve.

136—Madrid Potatoes

4 servings

2	baking potatoes
¼	teaspoon paprika
¼	teaspoon garlic salt
2	tablespoons vegetable oil

1. Preheat the oven to 375 degrees.

2. Peel and wash the potatoes and cut them into thin strips. Put the potatoes in a broiling pan and toss with the paprika, garlic salt and oil.

3. Spread the potatoes in a single layer on a cookie sheet and bake, turning occasionally, for 30 minutes, or until the potates are golden brown.

137—Oven French Fries

4 servings

2   baking potatoes
2   teaspoons vegetable oil

1. Preheat the oven to 425 degrees. Slice the potatoes into thin strips and toss with the oil in a bowl.

2. Place the potatoes on a cookie sheet. Bake for 10 minutes, turn, and bake 15 minutes longer, or until the potatoes are golden brown.

138—Potatoes au Gratin

4 servings

2   potatoes, peeled and boiled
2   tablespoons reduced calorie margarine
2   tablespoons all purpose flour
1   cup low fat milk
1   onion, chopped
¼   teaspoon grated nutmeg
1   cup grated low fat cheese, such as American or Monterey Jack

1. Preheat oven to 350 degrees.

2. Slice potatoes into ¼-inch rounds and reserve.

3. In a saucepan, melt the margarine. Add the flour to the margarine and cook the mixture over medium heat, stirring, for 3 minutes, or until the flour mixture is lightly browned.

4. Add the milk slowly to the saucepan, stirring, and cook for 2–3 minutes until the sauce has thickened.

5. Add the onion and nutmeg to the sauce and continue to cook for 2–3 more minutes.

6. Place the potatoes in a baking dish and cover with the sauce. Top with the grated cheese and bake for 20–30 minutes, or until the potatoes are tender and the sauce begins to brown.

139—Saffron Rice Timbales

4 servings

1½   tablespoons reduced calorie margarine
⅓   cup minced onion
⅛   teaspoon crumbled saffron threads
½   teaspoon cinnamon
⅔   cup long grain rice
1¼   cups chicken broth, defatted

1. In a saucepan, heat the margarine over medium heat until melted. Add the onion and cook over a low heat for 2 minutes. Add the saffron, cinnamon and rice and cook, stirring, for 1 minute, or until the rice becomes translucent.

2. Pour in the broth, bring the liquid to a simmer, cover, and cook for 18–20 minutes, or until all the liquid is absorbed. Remove the pan from the heat.

3. Let the rice stand, covered, for 5 minutes. Pack the rice into 4 ½-cup timbale molds or custard cups, and invert the timbales onto heated plates.

140—Sautéed Parsnips with Sesame Seeds

4 servings

1   tablespoon sesame seeds
2   teaspoons vegetable oil
1   pound parsnips, peeled and thinly sliced
5   scallions, chopped
1   clove garlic, minced
½   pound snow peas
   Freshly ground black pepper, to taste

1. In a nonstick skillet, sauté the seeds over low heat for 3 minutes, until golden brown. Remove the seeds from the skillet and reserve.

2. Heat the oil in the skillet and add parsnips, scallions and garlic. Sauté the vegetables for 5–7 minutes, or until tender.

3. Add snow peas and sauté for 1 minute. Season, to taste, with pepper, garnish with the sesame seeds and serve.

141—Sesame Asparagus

4 servings

1½   tablespoons sesame seeds
1½   teaspoons reduced calorie margarine
1   tablespoon lemon juice
      Salt and freshly ground white pepper, to taste
1   pound fresh asparagus spears, steamed

1. In a nonstick skillet, brown the sesame seeds while stirring lightly, about 2 minutes. Reserve.

2. In a small saucepan, heat the margarine over a medium heat. Add the lemon juice, salt and pepper, and stir to combine.

3. Arrange the asparagus on a serving platter, spoon the lemon butter sauce on top and garnish with the toasted sesame seeds.

142—Spinach and Tofu with Tamari and Ginger

4 servings

½   cup water
1   pound fresh spinach, chopped, stems removed
1   pound extra firm tofu, cubed
2   tablespoons soy sauce, or tamari
½   teaspoon grated gingerroot
4   tablespoons chopped fresh parsley

1. In a saucepan, bring water and spinach to a boil and cook the spinach for 1 minute.

2. Add all the other ingredients, except the parsley, to the saucepan and simmer over a medium heat for 5 minutes.

3. Garnish with the parsley and serve.

143—Stir-Fried Asparagus

4 servings

2   pounds asparagus, trimmed and cut into diagonal, 1-inch slices
1½   tablespoons peanut oil, or 1 tablespoon peanut oil and ½ tablespoon sesame oil
½   clove garlic, minced
1   teaspoon grated gingerroot
⅛   teaspoon freshly ground black pepper
2   teaspoons lemon juice
2   tablespoons soy sauce

1. In a saucepan, steam the asparagus until just tender, about 3–4 minutes, then cool under cold running water.

2. In a large skillet, heat the oil over a high heat and add the asparagus, garlic, gingerroot, pepper, lemon juice and soy sauce. Sauté the asparagus, stirring, for 2 minutes, or until it is heated and tender.

144—Stuffed Baked Zucchini

4 servings

4   medium zucchini
    Salt and freshly ground pepper, to taste
¼   cup chopped fresh mint leaves
½   cup chopped fresh parsley
2   small cloves garlic, pressed
1   cup bread crumbs
2–3 tablespoons water
1   tablespoon olive oil

1. Preheat the oven to 350 degrees.

2. Cut the zucchini in half lengthwise. Using a melon ball cutter, scoop out the seeds. Place the zucchini halves cut-side up in a single layer in a nonstick baking dish, season with salt and pepper and reserve.

3. Combine the mint, parsley, garlic, bread and water in a bowl and mix until the ingredients are just moistened. Spoon the bread mixture into the zucchini and drizzle the olive oil over the tops.

4. Bake the zucchini for 30 minutes, or until they are tender and the stuffing brown.

145—Stuffed Mushrooms

4 servings

12 large mushrooms
1   teaspoon olive oil
1   cup chopped spinach
4   scallions, chopped
2   tablespoons bread crumbs
1   tablespoon chopped fresh basil
1   tablespoon chopped fresh parsley
2   tablespoons grated Parmesan cheese

1. Preheat the oven to 350 degrees.

2. Separate the stems from mushroom caps. Reserve the caps. Chop stems finely.

3. In a skillet, heat the oil over a low heat and sauté the mushroom stems for 2 minutes.

4. Add the spinach, scallions, bread crumbs, basil, parsley, and cheese to the skillet and cook, stirring, for 2 minutes.

5. Remove the skillet from the heat. Stuff the mushroom caps with the spinach mixture. Place the mushroom caps on a baking sheet and bake for 15–20 minutes, until the tops begin to brown.

146—Tofu in Mushroom Sauce

4 servings

1   egg
2   tablespoons whole wheat flour
1   tablespoon water
½   pound extra firm tofu, sliced
2   tablespoons peanut oil
¼   pound mushrooms, sliced
1   tablespoon miso, dissolved in 1 cup water
2   teaspoons soy sauce, or to taste
2   tablespoons cornstarch or arrowroot, dissolved in ¼ cup water

1. In a bowl, combine the egg, flour and water and mix until the batter is smooth. Dip the tofu slices in the batter and coat on all sides.

2. In a large skillet, heat the oil over a medium heat. Add the tofu and brown for 2 minutes, set aside. Remove the tofu and reserve.

3. Add mushrooms and the miso to the skillet and cook for 3 minutes over a medium heat. Add soy sauce and cornstarch and cook to heat through. Lay the tofu into the mushroom sauce and continue cooking for 3 minutes, or until the sauce is thick.

147—Tomatoes Provençal
4 servings

4   medium firm ripe tomatoes
¼   teaspoon salt
½   teaspoon freshly ground black pepper
1   teaspoon finely chopped fresh basil, or ¼ teaspoon dried
⅛   teaspoon oregano
½   teaspoon garlic powder
1   tablespoon Parmesan cheese
1   tablespoon reduced calorie margarine

1. Preheat the oven to 350 degrees.

2. Cut off the tops of the tomatoes about one quarter of the way down from the top. Place the tomatoes, topside up, in a baking dish.

3. In a bowl, mix the salt, pepper, basil, oregano, garlic powder and Parmesan cheese. Stir until the seasonings are well mixed.

4. Sprinkle the seasonings over the tops of the tomatoes, dot each with a little margarine and bake for 30–40 minutes, until the tomatoes are tender.

148—Zucchini and Carrots Julienne
4 servings

1   teaspoon reduced calorie margarine
¼   cup diced onion
2   zucchini, shredded
3   carrots, peeled and shredded
1   tablespoon water
3   tablespoons chopped fresh parsley
    Freshly ground black pepper, to taste

1. In a saucepan, melt the margarine over a low heat and sauté the onion, stirring, until it is tender, about 2 minutes.

2. Add the zucchini, carrots and water to the saucepan, cover and steam until the vegetables are just tender, about 2–3 minutes. Toss in the parsley and pepper to taste.

SALADS

178. Sliced Tomatoes and Red Onions
179. Spinach, Fennel and Pink Grapefruit Salad
180. Tomato-Mozzarella Salad
181. Watercress and Bibb Salad
182. Watercress, Romaine and Radish Salad
183. Zesty Bean Salad
184. Zucchini Salad with Tomato Vinaigrette

149—Artichoke Salad

4 servings

4   artichoke hearts, cubed
6   Nicoise or other imported black olives, pitted and chopped
½   head romaine lettuce, cut into serving pieces
2   tablespoons olive oil
1   tablespoon lemon juice
½   clove garlic, minced
1   tablespoon grated Parmesan
       Freshly ground black pepper, to taste

1. Place the artichokes, olives and lettuce in a salad bowl.

2. In a small bowl, whisk together the oil, lemon juice, garlic and Parmesan. Season to taste with pepper.

3. Pour the dressing over the salad, toss lightly and serve.

150—Artichokes Vinaigrette

4 servings

4   artichokes, steamed and cooled
1   clove garlic, minced
       Juice of 1 lemon
3   tablespoons olive oil
2   tablespoons red wine vinegar
1   teaspoon Dijon mustard

1. Place the artichokes on a serving platter

2. In a small mixing bowl, whisk together the remaining ingredients. Pour the dressing into a serving bowl and pass, as a dipping sauce, with the artichokes.

151—Asparagus Salad   *4 servings*

2   tablespoons red wine vinegar
½   teaspoon ground pepper
3   tablespoons olive oil
1   tablespoon chopped fresh dill, or ½ teaspoon dried
3   tablespoons finely minced green pepper
½   teaspoon dried chives
1½   pounds asparagus

1. In a small bowl, combine all the ingredients, except the asparagus. Mix until thoroughly blended.

2. Break off the tough asparagus ends and trim. Steam the asparagus until just tender. Cool under cold tap water and arrange the spears on a serving plate.

3. Spoon the dressing over asparagus and marinate for 1 hour, at room temperature, before serving.

152—Beet and Apple Salad   *4 servings*

5   small beets
1   medium tart apple
2   hard cooked eggs, peeled and halved
1   scallion, minced
1   tablespoon vegetable oil
1   tablespoon red wine vinegar
¼   teaspoon salt
        Pinch freshly ground black pepper
3   tablespoons finely chopped walnuts
2   tablespoons chopped fresh parsley

1. Trim the tops of the beets. Place the beets in a saucepan, add water to cover, and cook over a medium heat, covered, for 25–30 minutes, until the beets are tender. Drain and rinse the beets under cold water.

2. When the beets are cool enough to handle, cut them into ½-inch cubes. Peel, core and cut the apple into ½-inch cubes. Mix the beets and apple together in a salad bowl.

3. Finely chop one egg and add it to the beets and apple. Chop the remaining egg yolk and discard the white.

4. In a small bowl, combine the chopped egg yolk, the scallion, oil, vinegar, salt and pepper and mix until thoroughly blended.

5. Pour the dressing over the beet mixture and toss to combine. Garnish with the walnuts and parsley and serve.

153—Broccoli Blue Cheese Salad

4 servings

1   clove garlic, minced
2   tablespoons olive oil
1   tablespoon red wine vinegar
1   tablespoon low fat yogurt
1   tablespoon reduced calorie mayonnaise
1   tablespoon Danish blue cheese, crumbled
    Salt and freshly ground black pepper, to taste
1   tablespoon capers
½   pound broccoli
¼   small red onion, thinly sliced
½   red or green pepper, seeded and cut into ¼-inch strips
    Lettuce
1   hard boiled egg, chopped

1. In a bowl, whisk together the garlic, oil, vinegar, yogurt, mayonnaise and blue cheese. Season to taste with salt and pepper, add the capers and reserve.

2. Mix the vegetables together in a bowl. Pour in the dressing and toss well to combine the ingredients.

3. Arrange lettuce leaves on a serving plate. Place the broccoli salad in a mound on the lettuce and garnish with egg.

154—Broccoli Vinaigrette

4 servings

1   pound broccoli, separated into flowerets
½   head romaine lettuce, separated into leaves
2   tablespoons olive oil
2   tablespoons red wine vinegar
¼   teaspoon ground white pepper
½   clove garlic, minced
¼   teaspoon Dijon mustard
2   tablespoons chopped fresh parsley

1. Steam the broccoli until just tender, then cool under cold running water.

2. Arrange the lettuce leaves on individual plates and top with broccoli.

3. In a small bowl, combine the oil, vinegar, pepper, garlic and mustard, and mix thoroughly.

4. Pour the dressing over the broccoli. Chill until you're ready to serve, then garnish with the parsley.

155—Cauliflower Salad   *4 servings*

1   large head cauliflower, separated into flowerets
1   head red leaf lettuce, separated into leaves
2   tomatoes, quartered
1   green pepper, cut into strips
4   tablespoons low fat yogurt
2   tablespoons olive oil
1   tablespoon lemon juice
¼   teaspoon dry mustard
2   tablespoons chopped fresh parsley

1. Steam the cauliflower until just tender, about 5 minutes, then drain and refrigerate until thoroughly cooled.

2. Arrange the lettuce leaves on a serving platter. Place the cauliflower in the center of the lettuce and arrange the tomatoes and green peppers around the sides.

3. In a small bowl, combine the yogurt, oil, lemon juice and mustard, mix thoroughly, and spoon the dressing over the vegetables. Garnish with the parsley and serve.

156—Celery Boats   *4 servings*

8   stalks celery
2   ounces low fat cream cheese
1   teaspoon horseradish, optional
1   tablespoon chives

1. Cut celery into 4-inch pieces.

2. In a bowl, combine the cream cheese, horseradish and chives and mix thoroughly. Fill the celery stalks with the cheese mixture and chill for at least 30 minutes before serving.

157—Coleslaw

4 servings

2   cups shredded cabbage
2   carrots, peeled and shredded
1   small Bermuda onion, thinly sliced
½   cup plain low fat yogurt
2   teaspoons vegetable oil
1   teaspoon horseradish
2   teaspoons caraway seeds
⅛   teaspoon salt
    Dash cayenne pepper

1. In a bowl, toss together the cabbage, carrots and onion.

2. In a small bowl, combine the yogurt, oil, horseradish, caraway seeds, salt and cayenne pepper, and mix thoroughly. Spoon the dressing over the cabbage mixture and toss until well mixed.

158—Coleslaw Bowl

4 servings

1   small head green cabbage
1   tablespoon cider vinegar
1   tablespoon lemon juice
½   teaspoon black pepper
1   tablespoon chopped fresh dill, or ½ teaspoon dried
¼   teaspoon celery seeds
¼   cup low fat yogurt
½   cup reduced calorie mayonnaise
    Paprika
    Parsley sprigs

1. Scoop out the center of the cabbage, leaving a shell. Refrigerate the shell. Shred the scooped-out cabbage; place in ice water and let stand for 30 minutes.

2. Drain the shredded cabbage thoroughly, then toss with the vinegar, lemon juice, pepper, dill weed and celery seeds. Let stand 1 hour, then drain thoroughly and place in a bowl.

3. In a small bowl, mix the yogurt and mayonnaise. Pour the dressing over the cabbage and toss until the cabbage is evenly coated. Spoon the mixture into the cabbage shell. Sprinkle the coleslaw with paprika and garnish with parsley sprigs.

159—Crispy Spinach Salad   *4 servings*

1   pound fresh spinach, well washed, stems removed
½   pound mushrooms, sliced
2   carrots, peeled and shredded
8   scallions, thinly sliced
2   tablespoons olive oil
2   tablespoons red wine or balsamic vinegar
½   clove garlic, minced
½   teaspoon Dijon mustard
      Freshly ground black pepper, to taste
2   ounces low fat mozzarella cheese, shredded

1. In a large salad bowl, combine the spinach, mushrooms, carrots and scallions.

2. In a small bowl, whisk together the oil, vinegar, garlic, mustard and pepper. Spoon the dressing over the salad and toss.

3. Garnish the salad with the cheese and serve.

160—Cucumber and Onion Salad   *4 servings*

2   cucumbers, peeled and thinly sliced
1   small Bermuda onion, thinly sliced
10   black olives, pitted
2   tablespoons olive oil
2   tablespoons tarragon or red wine vinegar
¼   clove garlic, minced
2   tablespoons chopped fresh parsley

1. In a bowl, mix the cucumbers, onions and olives.

2. In a small bowl, whisk together the oil, vinegar and garlic.

3. Spoon the dressing over the cucumber mixture and toss until all ingredients are thoroughly combined. Garnish with the parsley and serve.

161—Cucumber Aspic   *4 servings*

2   cucumbers, peeled, seeded and quartered
1   tablespoon lemon juice
1   tablespoon chopped onion
2   cups boiling water
1   package reduced calorie lemon gelatin
¾   cup low fat yogurt
2   tablespoons lemon juice
1   tablespoon chopped fresh dill, or ½ teaspoon dried
     Lettuce

1. In a blender, puree the cucumber, lemon juice and onion until smooth. Reserve.

2. Pour the boiling water into a bowl and add the gelatin very slowly, while whisking, until all the gelatin is dissolved.

3. Add the cucumber puree to the gelatin and mix thoroughly. Pour the mixture into a mold or bowl and refrigerate for 2 hours, or until the aspic is firm.

4. In a bowl, mix the yogurt, lemon juice and dill until well blended, then chill.

5. When ready to serve the aspic, invert it onto a bed of lettuce and serve with the yogurt-dill dressing.

162—Cucumber Rounds   *4 servings*

2   cucumbers
2   tablespoons reduced calorie mayonnaise
2   tablespoons low fat yogurt
1   tablespoon chopped fresh dill weed, or ½ teaspoon dried
     Pinch cayenne

1. Score the cucumbers with a fork and slice thinly.

2. Combine the mayonnaise, yogurt, dill weed and cayenne in a small serving bowl and mix until thoroughly blended.

3. Arrange the cucumbers around a plate and place the mayonnaise-yogurt mixture in the center. Chill before serving.

163—Dandelion Greens Salad

4 servings

1   cup dandelion greens
1   head romaine lettuce, shredded
2   tomatoes, sliced
1   small Spanish onion, thinly sliced
1   cucumber, peeled and thinly sliced
2   tablespoons olive oil
2   tablespoons tarragon or red wine vinegar
½   clove garlic, minced
¼   teaspoon tarragon
     Salt and freshly ground black pepper, to taste

1. In a salad bowl, combine the dandelion greens, lettuce, tomatoes, onion, and cucumber.

2. In a small bowl, whisk together the oil, vinegar, garlic, tarragon, salt and pepper. Pour the dressing over the salad, toss to combine and serve.

164—Four Bean Salad

4 servings

½   cup cooked kidney beans
½   cup cooked lima beans
½   cup cooked and diced wax beans
1   cup cooked and diced green beans
2   tablespoons wine vinegar
3   tablespoons olive oil
1   teaspoon Dijon mustard
½   teaspoon salt
¼   teaspoon freshly ground black pepper
½   clove garlic, minced
1   head red leaf lettuce, separated into leaves

1. In a bowl, combine the beans.

2. Combine vinegar, oil, mustard, salt, pepper and garlic. Mix to blend thoroughly. Spoon the dressing over the beans and toss well.

3. Place lettuce leaves on a serving platter and spoon the beans onto the center of the platter.

165—Green Salad with Asparagus Tips
4 servings

1	pound asparagus
1	head bibb lettuce
½	head romaine lettuce
2	tablespoons olive oil
2	tablespoons red wine vinegar
½	teaspoon Dijon mustard
½	teaspoon dried dill weed
	Salt and freshly ground black pepper to taste

1. Break off the tough ends of the asparagus and trim, then steam the tips until just tender. Cool under cold running water.

2. Break the lettuce into bite-size pieces and place them into a large salad bowl. Add the asparagus and toss.

3. In a small bowl, whisk together the oil, vinegar, mustard, dill, salt and pepper. Pour the dressing over the salad, toss thoroughly and serve.

166—Hearts of Palm, Radish and Bibb Lettuce Salad
4 servings

2	heads bibb lettuce, separated into leaves
1	can hearts of palm, sliced into ½ inch pieces
6	radishes, thinly sliced
2	cups watercress sprigs
½	teaspoon Dijon mustard
2	tablespoons wine vinegar
1	tablespoon walnut oil
1	tablespoon olive oil
1	hard cooked egg yolk, finely chopped

1. Lay the lettuce leaves on a serving platter. Arrange the hearts of palm and radishes over the lettuce. Garnish vegetables with watercress.

2. In a bowl, whisk together the mustard, vinegar, walnut oil and olive oil. Spoon the dressing over the salad. Garnish with the egg yolk and serve.

167—Herbed Tomato and Crouton Salad *4 servings*

¼   cup olive oil
1   garlic clove, minced
2   cups ½-inch cubes French or Italian bread
1½ tablespoons red wine vinegar
1   tablespoon Dijon mustard
    Salt and freshly ground black pepper, to taste
4   ripe tomatoes, chopped
2   tablespoons chopped fresh basil, or 1 teaspoon dried
½   cup finely chopped scallions
½   cup fresh parsley, minced

1. In a small bowl, combine the oil and garlic. Let the mixture stand for 30 minutes, then strain the oil and discard the garlic. Reserve the oil.

2. Preheat the oven to 350 degrees.

3. Place the bread cubes in one layer on a baking sheet and bake for 15–20 minutes, turning the cubes once, to toast the bread.

4. Remove the bread from the oven, and spoon half of the garlic-flavored oil over the croutons. Toss the croutons, then let them cool.

5. In a small bowl, combine the vinegar, mustard, salt and pepper with the remaining oil. Mix the dressing thoroughly.

6. In a salad bowl, combine the remaining ingredients with the croutons, add the dressing and toss well. Serve the salad at room temperature.

168—Mixed Green Salad with Radishes *4 servings*

1   hard boiled egg
1   head romaine lettuce, separated into leaves
12 radishes, sliced
4   tomatoes, sliced
2   tablespoons olive oil
2   tablespoons wine vinegar
½   clove garlic, minced
½   teaspoon Dijon mustard
½   teaspoon dried basil or tarragon
2   tablespoons chopped fresh parsley

1. Separate the egg yolk from the white. Chop the yolk and white separately and reserve.

2. Arrange the lettuce on a platter and garnish with radishes and a few tomato slices. Sprinkle the chopped egg white around the edge of the platter and spoon the yolk over the rest of the tomato slices in the center.

3 In a small bowl, combine the oil, vinegar, garlic, mustard and the basil or tarragon. Mix thoroughly, then spoon the dressing over the salad. Garnish with the parsley and serve.

169—Mushroom Salad
4 servings

½   pound mushrooms, sliced
2   tablespoons olive oil
2   tablespoons lemon juice
½   clove garlic, minced
¼   teaspoon ground white pepper
4–5 romaine, or green leaf, lettuce leaves

1. Place the mushrooms in a bowl.

2. Combine the oil, lemon juice, garlic and pepper in a small bowl and mix thoroughly. Pour the dressing over the mushrooms, toss and let marinate for 30 minutes. Serve the mushrooms on a bed of lettuce leaves.

170—Mushroom Tossed Greens
4 servings

½   head romaine lettuce, coarsely chopped
½   head red leaf lettuce, coarsely chopped
¼   pound mushrooms, thinly sliced
2   tablespoons olive oil
2   tablespoons red wine or tarragon vinegar
½   clove garlic, minced
¼   teaspoon oregano

1. Combine the lettuce and mushrooms in a large salad bowl.

2. In a small bowl, mix the oil, vinegar, garlic and oregano until thoroughly blended and pour over the lettuce-mushroom mixture. Toss the salad lightly and serve.

171—Nasturtium-Leaf Salad   *4 servings*

2	tablespoons red wine vinegar
2	tablespoons olive oil
½	teaspoon Dijon mustard
1½	heads chicory lettuce, separated into leaves
1	head Boston lettuce, separated into leaves
16	small nasturtium leaves, 1-inch in diameter
1	Bermuda onion, thinly sliced
1	cup raw fresh peas

1. In a bowl, combine the vinegar, oil, and mustard and mix until thoroughly blended.

2. In a salad bowl, toss together the lettuce leaves, nasturtium leaves, onion slices and peas. Spoon the dressing over the salad, toss and serve.

172—Okra Salad   *4 servings*

½	pound okra, sliced
¼	cup thinly sliced onion
2	tablespoons olive oil
1	tablespoon lemon juice
½	clove garlic, minced
	Salt and freshly ground pepper, to taste

1. Steam the okra until just tender, then cool under cold running water. Drain well.

2. Place the okra on a serving platter, and spread the onion over okra. In a small bowl, mix the oil, lemon juice, garlic, salt and pepper thoroughly. Pour the dressing over the okra and serve.

173—Plum Slaw

4 servings

1½ cups shredded cabbage
¾ cup shredded carrots
½ cup shredded apple
2 plums, sliced into julienne strips
¼ cup thinly sliced Bermuda onion
½ cup low fat yogurt
2 teaspoons vegetable oil
1 teaspoon horseradish
⅛ teaspoon salt
Dash pepper

1. In a large bowl, combine the cabbage, carrot, apple, plum and onion.

2. In another bowl, blend the yogurt, oil, horseradish, salt and pepper. Pour the dressing over the cabbage mixture, toss until well coated, then refrigerate for several hours before serving.

174—Raphael's Salad

4 servings

½ head red leaf lettuce, shredded
½ head green cabbage, shredded
2 sweet Italian peppers, seeded and thinly sliced
2 carrots, peeled and grated
4 celery stalks, thinly sliced
2 tablespoons olive oil
2 tablespoons tarragon or wine vinegar
½ clove garlic, minced
¼ teaspoon oregano
Salt and freshly ground black pepper, to taste

1. In a salad bowl, combine the lettuce, cabbage, peppers, carrots and celery. Toss to mix.

2. In a small bowl, whisk together the oil, vinegar, garlic, oregano, salt and pepper until thoroughly blended.

3. Spoon the dressing over the salad, toss and serve.

175—Rice Salad

4 servings

1   shallot, finely minced
1½   tablespoons red wine vinegar
3   tablespoons vegetable oil
3   tablespoons minced fresh parsley
¼   teaspoon salt
       Freshly ground black pepper to taste
1   green bell pepper, roasted, peeled, seeded and cut into strips
1   red bell pepper, roasted, peeled, seeded and cut into strips
2   cups cooked rice
½   cup cooked corn
1   avocado
       Juice of ½ lemon

1. In a small bowl, whisk together the shallot, vinegar, oil, parsley, salt and pepper. Reserve.

2. Combine the peppers, rice and corn in another bowl. Spoon the dressing over the rice mixture, cover and refrigerate until ready to serve.

3. Just before serving, peel and pit the avocado and cut it into ¼-inch slices. Drizzle the lemon juice over the avocado to keep it from turning brown. Spoon the rice salad onto a platter and arrange the avocado slices around the edge.

176—Romaine and Boston Lettuce Salad with Mustard Shallot Vinaigrette

4 servings

2   tablespoons minced shallots
1   teaspoon Dijon mustard
2   tablespoons white wine vinegar
       Salt and freshly ground black pepper, to taste
2   tablespoons olive oil
4   cups torn romaine leaves
4   cups torn Boston lettuce leaves

1. In a small bowl, combine the shallots, mustard, vinegar, salt and pepper. Add the oil gradually, while whisking until the dressing is thoroughly blended and thick.

2. Place the lettuce in a salad bowl. Add the dressing, and toss to combine and serve.

177—Salad with Parsley Dressing

4 servings

5   cups watercress sprigs
5   cups shredded bibb lettuce
1   red pepper, seeded and thinly sliced
1   yellow pepper, seeded and thinly sliced
1   cup chopped fresh parsley
2   tablespoons olive oil
2   tablespoons red wine vinegar
½   clove garlic
    Salt and freshly ground black pepper, to taste

1. In a salad bowl, toss together the watercress, bibb lettuce and peppers.

2. In a blender or food processor, puree the parsley with the oil, vinegar, and garlic. Pour the dressing over the lettuce mixture and toss. Season, to taste, with salt and pepper.

178—Sliced Tomatoes and Red Onions

4 servings

2   tomatoes, thinly sliced
1   medium red onion, thinly sliced
2   tablespoons champagne vinegar
2   tablespoons olive oil
½   clove garlic, minced
2   tablespoons chopped fresh basil

1. Alternate the tomato and onion slices in a circle on a platter.

2. In a small bowl, whisk together the vinegar, oil and garlic, and drizzle the dressing over the tomatoes and onions. Garnish with basil and serve.

179—Spinach, Fennel and Pink Grapefruit Salad   *4 servings*

4   cups small spinach leaves
2   pink grapefruit, cut into segments
2   small fennel bulbs, thinly sliced crosswise
1   tablespoon red wine vinegar
2   tablespoons pink grapefruit juice
½   teaspoon Dijon mustard
3   tablespoons olive oil
     Salt and freshly ground black pepper, to taste

1. Arrange the spinach leaves on 4 salad plates. Place the grapefruit segments around the spinach. Lay the fennel on top of the spinach.

2. In a small bowl, whisk together the vinegar, grapefruit juice and mustard. Add the oil, while whisking, and mix until the dressing is thick. Season, to taste, with salt and pepper.

3. Spoon some dressing over each salad and serve.

180—Tomato-Mozzarella Salad   *4 servings*

3   tomatoes, thinly sliced
1   cucumber, peeled and thinly sliced
¼   pound low fat mozzarella cheese, thinly sliced
2   tablespoons red wine vinegar
2   tablespoons olive oil
     Salt and freshly ground black pepper, to taste
½   cup fresh basil leaves

1. Arrange the tomato, cucumber and mozzarella slices on a serving platter.

2. In a bowl, mix the vinegar, oil, salt and pepper until thoroughly blended. Spoon the dressing over the salad, garnish with basil and serve.

181—Watercress and Bibb Salad
4 servings

1   bunch watercress
1   medium to large head bibb lettuce
1   red bell pepper, seeded and julienned
½   cup lightly packed fresh parsley leaves
3   tablespoons olive oil
1   tablespoon balsamic vinegar
½   clove garlic, minced
    Salt and freshly ground black pepper, to taste

1. Remove the coarse stems of the watercress and discard. Separate the bibb lettuce leaves and tear into bite-size pieces. Wash the watercress and lettuce and spin dry. Place the mixture into a salad bowl. Add the red pepper.

2. In a blender, puree the parsley with the oil, vinegar and garlic. Add salt and pepper to taste, pour the dressing over the watercress mixture and toss the salad until well coated.

182—Watercress, Romaine, and Radish Salad
4 servings

2   tablespoons olive oil
1   tablespoon lemon juice
1   tablespoon Dijon mustard
    Salt and freshly ground black pepper, to taste
2   bunches of watercress, coarse stems discarded
1   small head of romaine lettuce, leaves torn into bite-size pieces
8   radishes, sliced

1. In a small bowl, combine the oil, lemon juice, mustard, salt and pepper and mix until all the ingredients are thoroughly blended.

2. In a salad bowl, toss together the watercress, romaine lettuce and the radishes. Add the dressing, toss until thoroughly coated and serve.

183—Zesty Bean Salad

4 servings

1	cup cooked chickpeas
½	cup sliced pimento stuffed olives
½	cup chopped red onion
1	stalk celery, thinly sliced
¼	cup chopped fresh parsley
2	tablespoons red wine vinegar
1	teaspoon Dijon mustard
	Pinch cayenne pepper
1	small clove garlic, minced
2	tablespoons olive oil
	Romaine lettuce leaves
	Cherry tomatoes, for garnish

1. Toss together the chickpeas, olives, onions, celery and parsley in a bowl.

2. In another bowl, whisk together the vinegar, mustard, cayenne pepper and garlic. Add the oil gradually, while whisking, until the dressing is thick. Pour the dressing over the chickpeas, cover and refrigerate for 1–2 hours.

3. Line a salad bowl with lettuce leaves, spoon in the chickpeas, garnish with cherry tomatoes and serve.

184—Zucchini Salad with Tomato Vinaigrette *4 servings*

2   zucchini, grated
1   carrot, grated
1   shallot, minced
2   tablespoons olive oil
1   tablespoon balsamic or red wine vinegar
1   tablespoon chopped fresh basil, or ½ teaspoon dried
¼   tomato, diced
       Freshly ground black pepper, to taste
       Red or green leaf lettuce

1. Mix the zucchini and carrot together. Reserve.

2. In a small bowl, whisk together shallot, oil, vinegar and basil. Stir in the tomato until just mixed. Season to taste with pepper.

3. Arrange the lettuce on a serving platter, and place the zucchini-carrot mixture in a mound in the center. Drizzle the dressing over the vegetables and let the salad sit for 10 minutes before serving.

DESSERTS

215. Persimmon Pudding
216. Pineapple-Lemon Dessert-in-a-Glass
217. Rice Pudding
218. Steamed Apples with Honey
219. Strawberry Chiffon Pie
220. Tangerine Whip
221. Tangerine Sorbet
222. Tofu Lemon Pie
223. Yogurt-Gelatin Delight

185—Apple Sorbet   *4 servings*

1   pound McIntosh apples, peeled, cored and sliced
1   cup apple cider
1   lime

1. In a saucepan, combine the apples and cider. Squeeze the lime into the mixture. Cook over a medium heat for 20 minutes, or until the apples are soft.

2. Puree the apple mixture in a blender and then spoon it into a bowl. Place the puree in the freezer for 2 hours.

3. Remove the sorbet from the freezer and break the ice into chunks. Puree the sorbet again until smooth and return it to freezer for 30 minutes. Serve.

186—Applesauce Mousse   *4 servings*

4   apples, cored, peeled and sliced
1½   cups water
1   packet reduced calorie sweetener
1   envelope unflavored gelatin
2   teaspoons grated lemon peel
1   tablespoon lemon juice

1. Place the apples and ½ cup of the water in a saucepan. Cook the apples over a low heat, stirring until they are soft, approximately 10 minutes.

2. Cool the apples, then stir in the sweetener and reserve.

3. In a small saucepan, stir the gelatin into the remaining cup of water. Cook the mixture over a low heat, while stirring, until the gelatin is dissolved, about 2 minutes.

4. Remove the mixture from the heat and add the lemon peel and lemon juice.

5. Pour the gelatin-lemon mixture into the apples, whisking until the ingredients are combined thoroughly and have a creamy look.

6. Spoon the apple mixture into a serving dish and refrigerate for 3 hours or until thoroughly cooled and set before serving.

187—Baked Bananas

4 servings

2   large bananas
½   teaspoon cornstarch
2   tablespoons orange juice
2   teaspoons reduced calorie margarine, melted
1   teaspoon white sugar
1   teaspoon brown sugar
2   tablespoons shredded coconut

1. Preheat the oven to 350 degrees.

2. Peel the bananas and cut into 1-inch pieces. Place them on a nonstick baking sheet.

3. In a small bowl, mix the cornstarch and orange juice and stir until thoroughly blended. Add the margarine and white sugar, and mix thoroughly.

4. Spoon the sauce over the bananas, then sprinkle them with the brown sugar and coconut.

5. Bake the bananas for 15 minutes, until they are soft. Serve warm.

188—Baked Fruit Cup

4 servings

1   medium size orange
1   medium size apple
1   cup grape halves
½   cup orange juice
¼   teaspoon curry powder, optional
4   teaspoons flaked coconut

1. Cut each orange in half crosswise and remove sections with a sharp knife, leaving a shell. Reserve the shell. Place the orange sections in a bowl.

2. Peel and core the apple and chop it coarsely. Add the apple to orange sections. Add the grapes, orange juice and curry powder and mix well.

3. Spoon the fruits into the orange shells. Sprinkle 1 teaspoon coconut over each shell. Place filled shells in a shallow baking dish. (This may be done ahead of time.)

4. Just before serving, bake orange cups in a preheated, 350 degree oven for 20 minutes and serve slightly warm.

189—Baked Peaches
4 servings

4 ripe, whole peaches, peeled
¼ cup sugar
    Zest and juice of 1 lemon
¼ teaspoon mace
    Pinch allspice
¾ cup port wine, or dry red or white wine

1. Preheat the oven to 350 degrees.

2. Place the peaches in a baking dish and reserve.

3. In a saucepan, combine the sugar, lemon juice, zest, mace, allspice and wine. Over a high heat, bring the mixture to a boil, stirring to dissolve the sugar, and cook for 2 minutes.

4. Pour the wine mixture over the peaches and bake, covered, for 20 minutes, basting the peaches occasionally with the juice.

5. Chill peaches for at least 2 hours. Serve with pan juices.

190—Banana Flambé
4 servings

1 teaspoon reduced calorie margarine
4 ripe bananas, peeled
1 tablespoon lemon juice
1 tablespoon sugar
2 tablespoons Grand Marnier

1. Preheat the oven to 450 degrees. Spread the margarine on the bottom of a pie plate.

2. Place the bananas on the plate and sprinkle them with the lemon juice and sugar.

3. Bake the bananas for 20 minutes, or until they are lightly browned.

4. Heat the Grand Marnier. When ready to serve the bananas, place them on a serving dish. Drizzle each with the Grand Marnier and light them at the table.

191—Blueberry Cloud

4 servings

1	cup blueberries
2	teaspoons water
1	tablespoon honey
1	teaspoon lemon juice
1	teaspoon arrowroot, mixed with 1 tablespoon orange juice
½	cup reduced calorie dessert topping
¼	cup blueberries for garnish

1. In a saucepan, combine the blueberries, water, honey and lemon juice. Bring the liquid to a boil over a medium heat and cook for 1 minute.

2. While the blueberry mixture is boiling, stir in the dissolved arrowroot and cook for 1 minute, stirring constantly.

3. Remove the blueberry mixture from the heat and allow to cool to a moderate heat. Pour it into a blender. Puree the mixture, then pass it through a fine sieve.

4. Pour the puree into a bowl and refrigerate until it has cooled completely, about 1½ hours.

5. Just before serving, gently fold ¼ cup of the dessert topping into the blueberry mixture. Spoon the mousse into 4 chilled dessert bowls, top each with a tablespoon of dessert topping and a blueberry or two. Serve at once.

192—Brite Ice

4 servings

8	large ripe plums, pitted, peeled and sliced
1	cup water
1	teaspoon lemon juice
¼	cup sugar
½	cup dry champagne
	Mint leaves

1. In a saucepan, combine the plums, water, lemon juice and sugar. Bring the liquid to a boil over a medium-high heat, reduce the heat and simmer, covered, until the plums are very soft, about 20 minutes. Stir often.

2. In a blender or food processor, puree the plums. Spoon the puree into a bowl and stir in the champagne. Freeze the puree for 2 hours.

3. Remove the puree from the freezer, break up the ice and puree until smooth. Return the mixture to the freezer for 30 minutes.

4. Spoon the ice into dessert dishes, garnish with mint leaves and serve.

193—Carrot Cake

1 8-inch cake, serves 8

1	cup all purpose flour
1	teaspoon baking soda
1	teaspoon baking powder
1½	teaspoons ground cinnamon
⅓	teaspoon salt
⅔	cup vegetable oil
1	cup sugar
1	teaspoon vanilla
2	eggs
¼	cup chopped walnuts
1½	cups grated carrots

1. Preheat the oven to 325 degrees.

2. Sift together the flour, baking soda, baking powder, cinnamon and salt. Reserve.

3. In a large bowl, combine the oil, sugar, vanilla and eggs and beat until the mixture is thoroughly combined. Gradually add the egg mixture to the flour mixture, mixing until thoroughly combined.

4. Add walnuts and carrots to the batter, and stir well.

5. Spoon the batter into an 8-inch, nonstick baking pan and bake for 35–45 minutes, until the cake is done. Cool in the pan for 10 minutes before cutting.

194—Cherry Festival

4 servings

1   envelope reduced calorie cherry gelatin
1   cup boiling water
1   cup cold water
1   cup frozen pitted red cherries
1   cup red grape juice, without sugar
    Mint leaves

1. In a bowl, combine the cherry gelatin and boiling water and stir to dissolve the gelatin. Add the cold water and stir again.

2. Cover the bowl and refrigerate the gelatin for 30 minutes, or until it just begins to set.

3. In a blender, puree the cherries, grape juice and cherry gelatin mixture. Spoon the mixture into 4 dessert glasses and chill until set. Garnish with mint leaves and serve.

195—Citrus Delight

4 servings

½   cup sliced pineapple
1   cup fresh orange juice
¼   cup lemon juice
¼   teaspoon ground cinnamon
1   cantaloupe, thinly sliced
2   oranges, peeled and sliced
1   grapefruit, peeled and sliced

1. In a blender, combine the pineapple, orange juice, lemon juice and cinnamon. Puree until smooth. Spoon the puree into a bowl and freeze until the mixture is set, about 1 hour.

2. Remove the bowl from the freezer. Break up the ice into large chunks with a fork, place the chunks in a blender and puree until smooth, but not melted.

3. Toss together the cantaloupe, orange and grapefruit slices and divide into 4 dessert bowls. Top with the pineapple puree and serve.

196—Cocoa Angel Food Cake

1 8-inch cake, serves 8

⅓   cup cocoa
⅓   cup water
1   teaspoon vanilla extract
5   egg whites
    Pinch of salt
⅓   cup sugar
⅓   cup cake flour
1   teaspoon baking powder

1. Preheat the oven to 300 degrees.

2. In a saucepan, combine the cocoa and water and cook, stirring, over a low heat until the mixture is thick and just comes to a boil, about 3 minutes.

3. Remove the cocoa mixture from the heat and stir in the vanilla. Reserve.

4. Beat the egg whites with a pinch of salt until stiff peaks form. Add the sugar, one tablespoon at a time, and continue beating until the egg whites are glossy. Fold cocoa mixture gradually into the egg white.

5. Sift together the flour and baking powder. Fold the dry ingredients gradually into the egg whites until just mixed.

6. Pour the batter into an 8-inch round tube pan and bake for 25–30 minutes until a cake tester comes out clean. Invert the pan immediately and let the cake cool before serving.

197—Flamed Strawberries

4 servings

1   teaspoon honey
1   teaspoon reduced calorie margarine
1   teaspoon Grand Marnier
1   teaspoon water
1   teaspoon brandy
2   cups strawberries, stems removed and halved

1. In a saucepan, combine the honey, margarine, Grand Marnier and water. Bring the mixture to a boil over a high heat. Then, reduce the heat, add the brandy and flame.

2. After the flame goes out, spoon the liquid over the strawberries and serve immediately.

198—Fluffy Puffs

4 servings

⅔   cup nonfat powdered milk
3   tablespoons granulated sugar
5   egg whites
2   teaspoons vanilla extract
½   teaspoon cream of tartar
1   teaspoon ground cinnamon

1. Preheat the oven to 275 degrees.

2. In a bowl, sift together the powdered milk and sugar. Reserve.

3. In another bowl, beat the egg whites until soft peaks form. Add the vanilla and cream of tartar and continue beating until stiff peaks form.

4. Gently fold the milk-sugar mixture into the egg whites.

5. Using a tablespoon, drop the mixture, in individual spoonfuls, onto a nonstick cookie sheet. There will be about 16 puffs.

6. Bake for 35–40 minutes, until the puffs are lightly browned.

7. Sprinkle the puffs with cinnamon and allow them to cool before serving.

199—Frozen Nectarine Yogurt

4 servings

5   small nectarines, peeled, pitted and sliced
1   cup low fat yogurt
2   packets artificial sweetener, to taste

1. In a blender or food processor, puree the fruit and yogurt until smooth, about 3 minutes. Add the sweetener, to taste.

2. Spoon the yogurt into a dessert mold and place in freezer for 30 minutes.

200—Frozen Orange Yogurt

4 servings

½   cup orange juice
¼   cup lemon juice
2   teaspoons unflavored gelatin
1   tablespoon grated orange rind
1   cup low fat yogurt
3   egg whites, at room temperature
3   tablespoons sugar

1. In a bowl, combine the fruit juices. Pour ¼ cup of the juice into a saucepan. Sprinkle the gelatin over the juice and let it stand for 10 minutes.

2. In the bowl, combine the remaining juice, orange rind and yogurt and mix until smooth. Stir the gelatin into the yogurt mixture and reserve.

3. In another bowl, beat the egg whites, gradually adding the sugar, until the mixture is glossy and peaks form.

4. Gently fold ⅓ of the egg white mixture into the yogurt mixture until thoroughly blended. Fold in the remaining egg whites.

5. Pour the mixture into a freezer tray and freeze for 30–40 minutes, until set. Remove the mixture from the freezer, puree just until smooth and refrigerate for 30 minutes. Serve in individual dessert bowls.

201—Frozen Whipped Berries

4 servings

2   cups raspberry puree
1   pint strawberries, hulled and pureed
2   tablespoons sugar
3   egg whites

1. In a bowl, mix the raspberry and strawberry purees and freeze the mixture for 45 minutes.

2. Remove the frozen puree, chop it up with a fork, then puree in a blender with 1 tablespoon of sugar. Reserve.

3. In a bowl, beat the egg whites, gradually adding the remaining sugar.

4. Pour the berry mixture into a bowl. Gently fold the egg whites into the berry mixture. Freeze the mixture for 30 minutes.

5. When ready to serve the dessert, remove it from the freezer and puree just until smooth, about 30 seconds.

202—Glazed Apple Rings

4 servings

4   Granny Smith, McIntosh or other semi-tart apples
1   tablespoon reduced calorie margarine
1   cup apple cider
¼   teaspoon ground ginger
½   teaspoon ground cinnamon
2   teaspoons brown sugar
1   tablespoon lemon juice

1. Core and peel the apples and cut into half-inch rings.

2. In a saucepan, heat the margarine over medium heat and sauté the apples until lightly browned, approximately 1½ minutes a side.

3. Combine the remaining ingredients in a bowl, mix thoroughly and pour over apple slices.

4. Cover the saucepan and cook to glaze the apples, approximately 10 minutes.

203—Grapefruit Mold

4 servings

1   tablespoon plus ¾ teaspoon unflavored gelatin
½   cup sugar
1   cup boiling water
¾   cup grapefruit juice
¼   cup orange juice
2   tablespoons lemon juice

1. In a bowl, mix the gelatin and sugar.

2. Pour the boiling water over the gelatin mixture, stirring constantly until the gelatin is dissolved. Stir in the remaining ingredients.

3. Pour the mixture into a small mold and chill until firm, about 2 hours.

204—Lemon Baked Apples

4 servings

4   baking apples, cored
2   tablespoons lemon juice
1   teaspoon brown sugar
½   teaspoon grated nutmeg
1   teaspoon grated lemon rind
¼   teaspoon ground cinnamon
1   cup water

1. Preheat the oven to 400 degrees.

2. Place the apples in a nonstick baking pan.

3. Combine the lemon juice, brown sugar, nutmeg, lemon rind and cinnamon. Mix thoroughly and spoon the mixture into the apples. Pour the water into the pan.

4. Bake the apples for 30–40 minutes, until they are tender. Serve with the pan juices.

205—Lemon Chiffon Mousse

4 servings

1   package unflavored gelatin
2   packets artificial sweetener
2   egg yolks
¾   cup water
¼   cup lemon juice
1   teaspoon grated lemon peel
4   egg whites

1. To a bowl, mix the gelatin and sweetener. Add the egg yolks, water, and lemon juice. Beat the gelatin mixture and let it stand for 2 minutes.

2. Pour the mixture into a saucepan and cook, while stirring over a low heat, for 2 minutes, until the mixture begins to thicken.

3. Return the mixture to the bowl. Stir in the lemon peel and refrigerate the mousse for 30 minutes.

4. Beat egg whites until stiff peaks form. Gently fold the gelatin mixture into the egg whites, scrape the mixture into a serving bowl, and chill for 30 minutes before serving.

206—Lemon Soufflé

4 servings

1   envelope unflavored gelatin
¼   cup lemon juice
¼   cup water
2   egg yolks
2   tablespoons sugar
1   cup skim milk
3   egg whites
½   cup reduced calorie dessert topping
      Lemon slices and shredded lemon peel for garnish

1. In a small saucepan, sprinkle the unflavored gelatin in lemon juice and water. Heat the mixture over a low heat just until the gelatin dissolves, about 1 minute, then remove the pan from the heat.

2. In a small bowl, beat the egg yolks until they turn pale yellow, about 2 minutes. Gradually add the sugar, while beating, until the mixture thickens and turns lemon-colored. Slowly beat in the hot gelatin mixture, then the milk. Cool the mixture until it is partially set, about 10 minutes.

3. Beat the egg whites just until stiff peaks form.

4. Fold ¼ cup of the dessert topping into the gelatin mixture. Gently fold the new gelatin mixture into the egg whites. Pour the gelatin mixture into a 3-cup soufflé dish. Refrigerate at least 1 hour, or until set. Cover with remainder of the dessert topping. Garnish with shredded lemon peel and lemon slices, and serve.

207—Melon Rings with Strawberries

4 servings

1   ripe cantaloupe, cut into 4 1-inch rings, seeded and peeled
1   cup strawberries, hulled and sliced
1   tablespoon Grand Marnier
      Mint sprigs

1. Place one melon ring on each plate.

2. Spoon ¼ cup of the strawberries in the center of each ring. Drizzle Grand Marnier over the strawberries, garnish with mint sprigs and serve.

208—Orange Custard

4 servings

2   tablespoons cornstarch
4   tablespoons sugar
2   cups skim milk
3   egg yolks, beaten
1½   teaspoons orange extract
1   teaspoon finely grated orange rind
1   orange or tangerine, peeled and separated into segments

1. Combine cornstarch and sugar in the top of a double boiler. Cook over low heat and add the milk slowly, stirring constantly.

2. Add the egg yolks and continue cooking while stirring until the mixture is thick, about 15 minutes.

3. Remove the pan from the heat and stir in the orange extract and orange rind.

4. Spoon the mixture into custard cups or dessert dishes, garnish with orange segments and serve.

209—Orange Rhubarb Parfait

4 servings

1   pound rhubard, thickly sliced
1   cup orange juice
2   teaspoons freshly grated orange peel
4   packets artificial sweetener

1. In a saucepan, combine the rhubarb, orange juice, orange peel and sweetener. Cook the mixture over a low heat for 30–40 minutes, stirring occasionally, until the mixture is thick and the rhubarb is very soft.

2. Serve warm or cold.

210—Orange Sorbet   *4 servings*

2   cups orange juice
2   cups water
2   tablespoons grated orange rind
1   packet artificial sweetener
     Mint sprigs

1. Combine the orange juice, sweetener, water and orange rind in a bowl and place in the freezer until the mixture is frozen, about 1 hour.

2. Remove the bowl from the freezer and break up the orange ice into large chunks with a fork. Place the chunks in a food processor or blender, and puree until smooth, but not melted.

3. Spoon the puree into the bowl and return to the freezer for 30 minutes. Divide into 4 champagne glasses, garnish with mint sprigs and serve.

211—Peach Ambrosia   *4 servings*

2   cups low fat yogurt
¼   cup instant nonfat dry milk
1   cup peach slices
2   teaspoons honey
¼   teaspoon allspice
6   ice cubes

1. Place all the ingredients in a blender and puree until smooth.

2. Spoon the mixture into dessert dishes and refrigerate for 30 minutes before serving.

212—Peach Shortcake   *10 servings*

1   tablespoon reduced calorie margarine
1¾   cups all purpose flour
2½   teaspoons baking powder
¼   cup sugar
½   teaspoon salt
½   cup solid vegetable shortening, such as Crisco
¾   cup skim milk
1   tablespoon flour for dusting board

Filling

1½   cups water
½   cup sugar
8   ripe medium size peaches, peeled and sliced
⅛   teaspoon cloves
1   cup reduced calorie dessert topping

1. Preheat the oven to 425 degrees. Grease a baking sheet with the margarine.

2. In a bowl, sift together the flour, baking powder, sugar and salt. Cut in the shortening with a fork until the mixture is crumbly.

3. Stir in ⅔ cup of the milk. Add the remaining milk, 1 tablespoon at a time, until a soft dough is formed.

4. Turn the dough onto a lightly floured board and knead it lightly until smooth and elastic. Roll the dough out into a ½-inch thick slab and cut it into 10 3-inch rounds. Place the dough on a baking sheet.

5. Bake the dough for 20 minutes, or until the tops of the shortcake rounds are light gold and the sides are firm. Remove the shortcakes to a rack and cool.

6. In a saucepan, combine the water and sugar and cook over a low heat until the sugar dissolves.

7. Add the peaches and cloves to the water-sugar syrup, bring the liquid to a simmer and poach the peaches until they are soft, about 10 minutes.

8. Split the shortcakes horizontally and arrange the bottom halves on dessert plates. Spoon peaches onto the shortcakes with a slotted spoon. Brush the peaches with syrup to moisten. Spoon dessert topping over the peaches, top with the remaining shortcake halves and serve.

213—Pears and Ginger

4 servings

2   cups water
½   cup sugar
2   cinnamon sticks
1   tablespoon diced gingerroot
      Zest and juice of 1 lemon
4   firm ripe pears, peeled, cored and quartered

1. In a large saucepan, combine the water, sugar, cinnamon sticks, ginger, lemon zest and juice. Over a high heat, bring the liquid to a boil and cook for 10 minutes.

2. Reduce the heat to low, add the pears to the syrup and simmer uncovered for 20 minutes, or until the pears are tender. Remove the pan from the heat and allow the pears to cool in the syrup.

3. With a slotted spoon, remove the pears to a serving dish. Pour the syrup over the pears and chill for 1 hour before serving.

214—Pears in Red Wine

4 servings

4   firm ripe pears
1   cup dry red wine
¼   cup sugar
¼   cup creme de cassis
2   tablespoons fresh lemon juice
4   strips orange rind
½   teaspoon vanilla extract
1   whole clove, optional

1. Peel and carefully core the pears from the bottom, leaving the stems intact.

2. Choose a pan large enough to hold the pears on their sides in a single layer. Add the wine, sugar, creme de cassis, lemon juice, orange rind, vanilla and clove to the pan and cook over a moderate heat until the sugar dissolves, about 5 minutes.

3. Gently place the pears in the wine mixture, turning to coat them. Bring the liquid to a boil, then cover the pan, reduce the heat and simmer gently for 30 minutes, turning the pears after 15 minutes.

4. Lift the pears from the pan and stand them in a shallow serving dish. Pour the wine mixture over the pears and set them aside to cool completely, basting often with the liquid.

5. Cover the pears and refrigerate overnight. Baste again with the liquid just before serving.

215—Persimmon Pudding   *4 servings*

½   teaspoon reduced calorie margarine
¾   cup ripe persimmon pulp, mashed
1   egg, beaten
1   cup low fat milk
1½   tablespoons reduced calorie margarine, melted
½   cup all purpose flour
½   teaspoon baking soda
⅓   cup sugar
½   teaspoon ground cinnamon
¼   teaspoon ginger

1. Preheat the oven to 325 degrees. Grease a shallow baking pan with the teaspoon of margarine.

2. In a mixing bowl, combine the persimmon, eggs, milk and melted margarine. Stir until all the ingredients are thoroughly combined. Reserve.

3. Sift together the flour, baking soda, sugar, cinnamon and ginger. Add the dry ingredients to the persimmon mixture and beat until the batter is well mixed.

4. Spoon the batter into the prepared pan and bake for 45–50 minutes, or until the pudding is set.

5. Remove the pudding from the oven and let it cool for 1 hour. Cut into squares and serve.

216—Pineapple-Lemon Dessert-in-a-Glass   *4 servings*

1   cup crushed pineapple, fresh or juice packed
1   cup low fat lemon yogurt
½   cup skim milk
1   cup ice cubes
     Fresh mint

1. In a blender, puree the pineapple, yogurt and milk. Add the ice cubes, one at a time, blending until smooth after each addition.

2. Pour the mixture into 4 glasses and chill for 30 minutes before serving. Garnish with fresh mint and serve.

217—Rice Pudding   *4 servings*

2   cups low fat milk
¼   cup long grain rice
2   tablespoons sugar
1   egg
¼   teaspoon nutmeg
     Pinch allspice
½   teaspoon vanilla extract

1. In large saucepan, heat the milk, rice and sugar over a medium heat until the mixture comes to a boil. Reduce the heat and simmer for about 30 minutes.

2. Beat the eggs in a small bowl. Stir in 1 cup of the hot rice mixture. Then, pour the egg-rice mixture back into the remaining rice. Cook, stirring over a low heat for 5 minutes.

3. Remove the pudding from the heat, blend in the nutmeg, allspice and vanilla. Refrigerate for 2 hours, or until the pudding is set.

218—Steamed Apples with Honey   *4 servings*

4   Rome or Winesap apples
1   tablespoon lemon juice
2   tablespoons honey
1   teaspoon nutmeg
1   teaspoon grated lemon rind
⅛   teaspoon cinnamon
1   cup water

1. Preheat the oven to 325 degrees.

2. Cut the tops off the apples ½-inch from the top. Then, core the apples and remove the seeds. Line a baking pan with foil and lay the apples in the pan.

3. In a bowl, whisk together the lemon juice, honey, nutmeg, lemon rind and cinnamon until the mixture is well blended. Drizzle the sauce over the tops of the apples.

4. Pour the water into the bottom of the pan, cover the apples with aluminum foil and bake for 40–50 minutes, until the apples are tender.

5. Remove the apples and let cool for 10–15 minutes before serving, or chill and serve cold.

219—Strawberry Chiffon Pie   *1 8-inch pie, 6 servings*

1	cup enriched white flour
½	teaspoon salt
5	tablespoons shortening
3–4	tablespoons ice water
1	pint strawberries
1	envelope unflavored gelatin
¾	cup water
2	egg whites
¼	cup sugar
1	cup reduced calorie dessert topping

1. Preheat the oven to 450 degrees.

2. In a bowl, stir together the flour and salt. Using a pastry fork, or food processor, cut in the shortening until it is just blended and the dough resembles coarse cornmeal.

3. Sprinkle 2 tablespoons of the ice water over the dough and mix quickly. Repeat with 1–2 more tablespoons water until the flour is moistened. Using your hands, form the dough into a ball.

4. On a lightly floured board, roll out the dough and lay it carefully into an 8-inch pie plate. Trim and flute the edges. Prick the bottom several times with a fork and bake the shell for 10–12 minutes, until the edges just begin to brown. Remove the shell and cool completely before filling.

5. Cut the stems off the strawberries. Reserve 3 to 5 to use as garnish. Then crush enough of the remaining berries so that you have 1½ cups. Reserve.

6. In a small saucepan, sprinkle the gelatin over the water. Heat the mixture over a low heat, and cook, stirring, until the gelatin dissolves. Let the gelatin cool for 20 minutes, then stir in the crushed strawberries. Let the strawberry mixture chill until it begins to set, about 45 minutes.

7. Beat the egg whites until stiff peaks form. Gradually beat in the sugar, one tablespoon at a time. Gently fold the egg whites into the gelatin. Then fold in the dessert topping until just mixed.

8. Pour the filling into the pastry shell and chill for several hours, until the pie is set. Garnish with the reserved strawberries and serve.

220—Tangerine Whip
4 servings

1   6-ounce can tangerine juice concentrate, undiluted
2   cups buttermilk

1. In a blender, mix the tangerine concentrate and half the buttermilk and blend at a high speed for 30 seconds, or until smooth.

2. Add the remaining buttermilk and blend at a low speed until smooth.

3. Pour the mixture into 4 dessert cups, cover and freeze for 3 hours, or until the mixture is firm. Remove from the freezer 20 minutes before serving, so that it softens slightly.

221—Tangerine Sorbet
4 servings

1   cup tangerine juice, freshly squeezed, if possible
1   teaspoon lemon juice
1   cup water
1   tablespoon grated tangerine rind
2   teaspoons artificial sweetener, or to taste
    Mint sprigs

1. Combine the tangerine juice, lemon juice, water and tangerine rind in a bowl and freeze for 1 hour. Remove the bowl from the freezer and break the sorbet into large chunks with a fork.

2. Using a food processor or blender, puree the chunks until the sorbet is smooth and creamy. Add artificial sweetener to taste. Spoon the mixture into a bowl and freeze for at least 30 minutes.

3. Divide into chilled wineglasses, garnish with mint and serve.

222—Tofu Lemon Pie
1 8-inch pie, serves 6

1	cup enriched white flour
½	teaspoon salt
5	tablespoons shortening
3–4	tablespoons ice water
2	cups water
2	teaspoons artificial sweetener
⅓	cup cornstarch
¾	pound silken tofu, crumbled
½	cup lemon juice
2	teaspoons grated lemon rind
¼	teaspoon grated nutmeg

1. Preheat the oven to 450 degrees.

2. In a bowl, stir together the flour and salt. Using a pastry fork, or food processor, cut in the shortening until it is just blended and the dough resembles coarse cornmeal.

3. Sprinkle 2 tablespoons of the ice water over the dough and mix quickly. Repeat with 1–2 more tablespoons water until the flour is moistened. Using your hands, form the dough into a ball.

4. On a lightly floured board, roll out the dough and lay it carefully into an 8-inch pie plate. Trim and flute the edges. Prick the bottom several times with a fork and bake the shell for 10–12 minutes, until the edges just begin to brown. Remove the shell and cool completely before filling.

5. Mix together the 2 cups of water, sweetener and cornstarch in a saucepan. Cook, stirring, over a medium heat until the mixture is smooth and thick, about 10 minutes.

6. Add the tofu, lemon juice, lemon rind and nutmeg to the saucepan and cook until the mixture is very hot but not boiling, about 3 minutes.

7. Pour the filling into the pie shell and chill for 2 hours, or more, before serving.

223—Yogurt-Gelatin Delight

4 servings

2 packages fruit flavored, reduced calorie gelatin
2 cups boiling water
2 cups low fat yogurt, the same flavor as the gelatin

1. In a bowl, whisk the gelatin into the boiling water, stirring well until the gelatin is completely dissolved. Chill the mixture until it just begins to set.

2. Fold the yogurt into the gelatin, stirring to combine thoroughly. Return the mixture to the refrigerator and chill for at least 1 hour before serving.

BEVERAGES

224—Apple Cider Spritzer

2 servings

    crushed ice
1   cup apple cider
½   cup carbonated water
2   cinnamon sticks

    1. Put crushed ice into two glasses. Pour half a cup of apple cider into each glass.

    2. Add ¼ cup carbonated water to each glass and stir with cinnamon sticks.

225—Carrot Juice

2 servings

½   cup fresh, or canned, carrot juice, chilled
½   cup unsweetened pineapple juice, chilled
1   tablespoon fresh unstrained lemon juice, chilled
1   teaspoon finely chopped fresh mint, or ¼ teaspoon dried
1   cup crushed ice
¼   cup water

    1. In a blender, puree all the ingredients until the mixture is thoroughly blended.

    2. Strain the juice, divide it between 2 glasses and serve immediately.

226—Carrot Lime Drink

2 servings

    Crushed ice
1   cup carrot juice
1   cup lime flavored carbonated water
2   lemon slices

    1. Fill two glasses with crushed ice. Divide the carrot juice into the glasses.

    2. Stir ½ cup carbonated water into each glass. Garnish with a lemon slice and serve.

227—Cherry Sling

2 servings

½   cup fresh or frozen pitted dark sweet cherries
2   tablespoons fresh lemon juice
    Crushed ice
1   cup carbonated water

1. In a blender, puree the cherries and lemon juice.
2. Fill 2 glasses with crushed ice. Pour the cherry mixture over the ice, stir in the carbonated water and serve.

228—Chocolate Soda

2 servings

2   teaspoons chocolate extract
2   drops mint extract
½   cup skim milk
    Crushed ice
8   ounces carbonated water

1. Combine the chocolate extract, mint and skim milk and mix well.
2. Fill two glasses with crushed ice. Pour the chocolate mixture into the glasses, add the carbonated water, stir and serve.

229—Cucumber Mint Frappe

2 servings

1½   cucumbers, peeled and seeded
2   teaspoons honey
6–8 large fresh mint leaves
     Crushed ice

1. Cut the cucumber into chunks and puree with the honey and 4–6 of the mint leaves in a blender, or food processor.
2. Add the ice to the frappe and continue to puree until the mixture is smooth. Pour the frappe into chilled goblets, garnish with the remaining mint leaves and serve.

230—Frosty Spiced Tea

2 servings

½   cup cool water
1   cinnamon stick
¼   teaspoon grated nutmeg
    Pinch ground cloves
2   cups boiling water
2   tea bags
1   packet artificial sweetener

1. Combine the cool water with the cinnamon, nutmeg and cloves in a saucepan. Bring the water to a boil over a high heat, lower the heat and allow the liquid to simmer for 10 minutes. Remove from heat.

2. Pour the spiced water and the boiling water into a pitcher. Add the tea bags and sweetener and steep for 15 minutes.

3. Remove the tea bags and discard. Stir the tea well and refrigerate until cool. Serve over ice.

231—Gingerade

2 servings

1   ounce fresh ginger, peeled and finely chopped
1   packet artificial sweetener
2   cups water
1   whole clove
½   cup carbonated water

1. In a pitcher, combine the ginger, sweetener, water and cloves and refrigerate for 8 hours or overnight.

2. Strain the liquid and pour into two tall glasses. Add some ice and top with the carbonated water.

232—Grape Spritzer

2 servings

1   cup unsweetened grape juice
    Crushed ice
½   cup carbonated water

1. Fill two glasses with crushed ice and pour in the grape juice.

2. Add the carbonated water, stir just to blend and serve.

233—Grapefruit Sling

2 servings

½ cup grapefruit juice
¼ cup apricot nectar
½ cup pineapple juice
   Crushed ice
   Carbonated water

1. In a blender, combine the grapefruit juice, apricot nectar and pineapple juice and blend thoroughly.
2. Fill two glasses with crushed ice and fill with the juice mixture. Top with carbonated water and serve.

234—Grapefruit Spritzer

2 servings

   Crushed ice
1 cup grapefruit juice
½ cup carbonated water
   Mint leaves

1. Fill 2 glasses with crushed ice and pour in the grapefruit juice.
2. Top the juice with the carbonated water, garnish with leaves and serve.

235—Hot, Spiced Apple Cider

2 servings

2 cups apple cider
⅛ teaspoon ground cloves
⅛ teaspoon ground cardamon
2 cinnamon sticks

1. Heat the cider over a medium heat, but do not boil. Add the cloves and cardamon, stir, and simmer for 10 minutes.
2. Pour the cider into 2 mugs, or cups, and serve with the cinnamon sticks.

236—Iced Espresso

Crushed ice
1 cup cold espresso coffee
Artificial sweetener, to taste
Cinnamon sticks

1. Fill two glasses with crushed ice.

2. Pour the espresso into the glasses sweeten to taste, and garnish with cinnamon sticks.

237—Lemonade

2 large lemons
10 mint leaves
½ cup boiling water
1½ cups cold water
2 packets artificial sweetener
2 sprigs mint

1. Squeeze the juice from the lemons, strain, and pour it into a pitcher. Add the mint leaves and the boiling water to the pitcher.

2. Let the mixture steep for 10 minutes. Then remove the mint leaves.

3. Pour the cold water into the pitcher and stir in the sweetener.

4. Refrigerate the lemonade until cold, garnish with the mint sprigs and serve over ice.

238—Lime Cooler

Crushed ice
2 tablespoons fresh lime juice
2 cups carbonated water
2 lime peels

1. Fill two glasses with crushed ice.

2. Pour the lime juice into each glass, then fill with carbonated water. Stir, garnish with a lime peel and serve.

239—Mint Iced Tea

2 servings

2   tea bags
1   teaspoon chopped fresh mint, or ¼ teaspoon dried
2   cups boiling water
    Artificial sweetener, to taste
2   lemon slices

1. In a pitcher, mix the tea bags and mint with the boiling water. Let the tea steep for 5 minutes. Then, remove the tea bags and chill the tea until cool.

2. Pour the tea into two large glasses. Sweeten to taste, and garnish with lemon slices.

240—Mint Lemonade

2 servings

5   mint leaves
½   cup boiling water
½   cup freshly strained lemon juice
    Ice cubes
    Raspberry flavored carbonated water

1. Let the mint leaves steep in the boiling water for 5 minutes, then strain and add the lemon juice. Refrigerate for 1 hour.

2. Pour the mint mixture into two glasses over ice cubes. Top with raspberry flavored carbonated water and serve.

241—Orange Spritzer

2 servings

    Crushed ice
1   cup fresh orange juice
    Carbonated water
2   dashes orange bitters
    Orange slices

1. Fill two glasses with crushed ice. Pour half the juice in each glass. Then fill both glasses with carbonated water.

2. Add the bitters, stir, garnish with orange slices and serve.

242—Piña Colada Spritzer

2 servings

½ cup unsweetened pineapple juice
¼ teaspoon coconut extract
¼ teaspoon rum extract
½ cup crushed ice
Carbonated water

1. Combine the pineapple juice, coconut extract and rum extract and mix thoroughly. Pour the mixture over the crushed ice, shake well, then pour into two glasses.
2. Top the piña coladas with carbonated water and serve.

243—Pineapple Mint Spritzer

2 servings

4–6 mint leaves
1 cup unsweetened pineapple juice
½ cup carbonated water
Ice cubes

1. Combine the mint and pineapple juice and mix thoroughly.
2. Add the carbonated water and pour the mixture into two glasses. Add a few ice cubes and serve.

244—Spiced Coffee

2 servings

3 cups water
2 tablespoons instant coffee
2 tablespoons sugar
1 teaspoon unsweetened cocoa
1 teaspoon cinnamon
⅛ teaspoon ground cloves
½ teaspoon vanilla extract

1. In a saucepan, combine all the ingredients, except the vanilla. Bring the liquid to a simmer and cook for 10 minutes.
2. Remove the pan from the heat, stir in the vanilla and serve.

245—Strawberry Spritzer

2 servings

4–6   large strawberries, sliced
1   cup white grape juice
       Crushed ice
1   cup club soda, or seltzer

1. Reserve a few strawberry slices for garnish. In a blender, puree the remaining strawberries until smooth, add the grape juice and puree to blend.

2. Fill 2 glasses with crushed ice. Divide the strawberry mixture between the glasses. Stir in the club soda, garnish with strawberry slices and serve.

246—Tangelo Delight

2 servings

½   cup fresh tangelo juice
2   tablespoons canned crushed unsweetened pineapple
½   cup reduced calorie cranberry juice cocktail
     Ice cubes

1. Place all ingredients, except the ice cubes, in a blender and puree until smooth.

2. Fill 2 glasses with ice cubes, pour in the juice mixture and serve.

247—Tangerine Spritzer

2 servings

4   ice cubes
1   cup tangerine juice
½   cup carbonated water
2   mint sprigs

1. Distribute the ice cubes into two glasses. Add ½ cup of the tangerine juice to each glass.

2. Top each drink with carbonated water and stir quickly, just to mix. Garnish the spritzers with mint sprigs and serve.

248—Tropical Fizz

1   cup unsweetened grapefruit juice
½   cup unsweetened orange juice
¼   cup unsweetened pineapple juice
     Crushed ice
1   cup club soda
     Mint leaves for garnish

1. In a pitcher, mix the fruit juices.

2. Fill 2 glasses with crushed ice and pour in the fruit juice. Stir ½ cup of the carbonated water into each glass, garnish with mint leaves and serve.

249—Watermelon Cooler

2   cups watermelon chunks
½   cup unsweetened grape juice
4–6   mint leaves, chopped
½   cup crushed ice

1. In a blender, puree the watermelon, grape juice and mint until smooth.

2. Place the ice in 2 large glasses. Pour the watermelon mixture over the ice and serve.

BIBLIOGRAPHY

1. Ackerman, G. E.; MacDonald, P. C.; Gudelsky, G.; Mendelson, C. R.; and Simpson, E. R. 1981. Potentiation of epinephrine-induced lipolysis by catechol estrogens and their methoxy derivatives. *Endocrinology*, vol. 109, no. 6 (Dec.), pp. 2084–2088.

2. Adlercreutz, H.; Fotsis, T.; Bannwart, C.; Hämäläinen, E.; Bloigu, S.; and Ollus, A. 1986. Urinary estrogen profile determination in young Finnish vegetarian and omnivorous women. *Journal of Steroid Biochemistry*, vol. 24, no. 1 (Jan.), pp. 289–296.

3. Adlercreutz, H.; Höckerstedt, K.; Bannwart, C.; Bloigu, S.; Hämäläinen, E.; Fotsis, T.; and Ollus, A. 1987. Effect of dietary components, including lignans and phytoestrogens, on enterohepatic circulation and liver metabolism of estrogens and on sex hormone binding globulin (SHBG). *Journal of Steroid Biochemistry*, vol. 27, no. 4–6, pp. 1135–1144.

4. Agricultural Research Service, Consumer and Food Economics Research Division. 1970 revision. The nutritive value of foods. *Home and Garden Bulletin No. 72.* Washington, D.C.: U.S. Department of Agriculture.

5. Alvares, A. P.; Anderson, K. E.; Conney, A. H.; and Kappas, A. 1976. Interactions between nutritional factors and drug biotransformations in man. *Proceedings of the National Academy of Sciences, U.S.A.*, vol. 73, no. 7 (July), pp. 2501–2504.

6. Anderson, K. E.; Kappas, A.; Conney, A. H.; Bradlow, H. L.; and Fishman, J. 1984. Influence of dietary protein and carbohydrate on the principal oxidative biotransformations of estradiol in normal subjects. *Journal of Clinical Endocrinology and Metabolism*, vol. 59, no. 1 (July), pp. 103–107.

7. Ball, P.; Gelbke, H. P.; and Knuppen, R. 1975. Excretion of 2-hydroxyestrone during the menstrual cycle. *Journal of Clinical Endocrinology and Metabolism*, vol. 40, no. 3 (Mar.), pp. 406–408.

8. Barris, M. C.; Dawson, W. W.; and Theiss, C. L. 1980. Visual sensitivity of women during the menstrual cycle. *Documenta Ophthalmologica*, vol. 49, no. 2 (Oct. 15), pp. 293–301.

9. Biskind, M. S. 1943. Nutritional deficiency in the etiology of menorrhagia, metrorrhagia, cystic mastitis and premenstrual tension; treatment with vitamin B complex. *Journal of Clinical Endocrinology and Metabolism*, vol. 3, no. 4 (Apr.), pp. 227–234.

10. Bonsnes, R. W. 1947. Plasma amino acid and amino nitrogen concentration during normal pregnancy, labor, and early puerperium. *Journal of Biological Chemistry*, vol. 168, no. 1 (Apr.), pp. 345–350.

11. Bourget, C.; Femino, A.; Franz, C.; and Longcope, C. 1988. Estrogen and androgen dynamics in the cynomolgus monkey. *Endocrinology*, vol. 122, no. 1 (Jan.), pp. 202–206.

393

12. Bruce, L. A., and Behsudi, F. M. 1979. Progesterone effects on three regional gastrointestinal tissues. *Life Sciences,* vol. 25, no. 9 (Aug. 27), pp. 729–734.

13. Castro, L. de P. 1967. Reflux esophagitis as the cause of heartburn in pregnancy. *American Journal of Obstetrics and Gynecology,* vol. 98, no. 1 (May 1), pp. 1–10.

14. Cohen, I.; Sherwin, B.; and Fleming, A. 1987. Food cravings, mood, and the menstrual cycle. *Hormones and Behavior,* vol. 21, pp.457–470.

15. Conlay, L. A., and Zeisel, S. H. 1982. Neurotransmitter precursors and brain function. *Neurosurgery,* vol. 10, no. 4 (Apr.), pp. 524–529.

16. Dalvit, S. 1981. The effect of the menstrual cycle on patterns of food intake. *The American Journal of Clinical Nutrition,* vol. 34, pp. 1811–1815.

17. Diamond, M.; Diamond, A. L.; and Mast, M. 1972. Visual sensitivity and sexual arousal levels during the menstrual cycle. *Journal of Nervous and Mental Disease,* vol. 155, no. 3 (Sept.), pp. 170–176.

18. Doty, R. L.; Snyder, P. J.; Huggins, G. R.; and Lowry, L. D. 1981. Endocrine, cardiovascular, and psychological correlates of olfactory sensitivity changes during the human menstrual cycle. *Journal of Comparative and Physiological Psychology,* vol. 95, no. 1 (Feb.), pp. 45–60.

19. Feldman, E. B., ed. 1983. *Nutrition and Heart Disease.* New York: Churchill Livingstone.

20. Fishman, J.; Boyar, R. M.; and Hellman, L. 1975. Influence of body weight on estradiol metabolism in young women. *Journal of Clinical Endocrinology and Metabolism,* vol. 41, no. 5 (Nov.), pp. 989–991.

21. Fishman, J., and Martucci, C. 1980. Biological properties of 16 alpha-hydroxyestrone: implications in estrogen physiology and pathophysiology. *Journal of Clinical Endocrinology and Metabolism,* vol. 51, no. 3 (Sept.), pp. 611–615.

22. Frank, R. T. 1931. Hormonal causes of premenstrual tension. *Archives of Neurology and Psychiatry,* vol. 26, no. 5 (Nov.), pp. 1053–1057.

23. Goldin, B. R.; Adlercreutz, H.; Dwyer, J. T.; Swenson, L.; Warram, J. H.; and Gorbach, S. L. 1981. Effect of diet on excretion of estrogens in pre- and postmenopausal women. *Cancer Research,* vol. 41, no. 9, pt. 2 (Sept.), pp. 3771–3773.

24. Goldin, B. R.; Adlercreutz, H.; Gorbach, S. L.; Warram, J. H.; Dwyer, J. T.; Swenson, L; and Woods, M. N. 1982. Estrogen excretion patterns and plasma levels in vegetarian and omnivorous women. *New England Journal of Medicine,* vol. 307, no. 25 (Dec. 16), pp. 1542–1547.

25. Goldin, B. R.; Adlercreutz, H.; Gorbach, S. L.; Woods, M. N.; Dwyer, J. T.; Conlon, T.; Bohn, E.; and Gershoff, S. N. 1986. Relationship between estrogen levels and diets of Caucasian American and Oriental immigrant women. *American Journal of Clinical Nutrition,* vol. 44, no. 6 (Dec.), pp. 945–953.

26. Goldin, B. R., and Gorbach, S. L. 1988. Effect of diet on the plasma levels, metabolism, and excretion of estrogens. *American Journal of Clinical Nutrition,* vol. 48, no. 3 suppl. (Sept.), pp. 787–790.

27. Henkin, R. I. 1974. Sensory changes during the menstrual cycle. In *Biorhythms and Human Reproduction,* ed. by Ferin, M.; Halberg, F.; Richart, R. M.; and Vande Wiele, R.; pp. 277–285. New York: John Wiley and Sons.

28. Hervey, E., and Hervey, G. R. 1967. Effects of progesterone on body weight and composition in the rat. *Journal of Endocrinology,* vol. 37, no. 4 (Apr.), pp. 361–384.

29. Hullin, R. P. 1976. Metabolism of indole amines in depression. *Postgraduate Medical Journal,* vol. 52, suppl. 3, pp. 18–24.

30. Hytten, F. E., and Leitch, I. 1971. *The Physiology of Human Pregnancy,* 2nd ed. Oxford: Blackwell Scientific Publications.

31. Jellinck, P. H.; Krey, L.; Davis, P. G.; Kamel, F.; Luine, V.; Parsons, B.; Roy, E. J.; and McEwen, B. S. 1981. Central and peripheral action of estradiol and catecholestrogens administered at low concentration by constant infusion. *Endocrinology*, vol. 108, no. 5 (May), pp. 1848–1854.

32. Jones, B. and Jones, M. K. 1976. Alcohol effects in women during the menstrual cycle. *Annals of the New York Academy of Sciences*, vol. 273, pp. 576–587.

33. Jurkowski, J. E. H.; Jones, N. L.; Toews, C. J.; and Sutton, J. R. 1981. Effects of menstrual cycle on blood lactate, O_2 delivery, and performance during exercise. *Journal of Applied Physiology: Respiratory, Environmental and Exercise Physiology*, vol. 51, no. 6 (Dec.), pp. 1493–1499.

34. Jurkowski, J. E.; Jones, N. L.; Walker, W. C.; Younglai, E. V.; and Sutton, J. R. 1978. Ovarian hormonal responses to exercise. *Journal of Applied Physiology: Respiratory, Environmental and Exercise Physiology*, vol. 44, no. 1 (Jan.), pp. 109–114.

35. Kappas, A.; Anderson, K. E.; Conney, A. H.; Pantuck, E. J.; Fishman, J.; and Bradlow, H. L. 1983. Nutrition-endocrine interactions: induction of reciprocal changes in the delta 4-5 alpha-reduction of testosterone and the cytochrome P-450-dependent oxidation of estradiol by dietary macronutrients in man. *Proceedings of the National Academy of Sciences, U.S.A.*, vol. 80, no. 24 (Dec.), pp. 7646–7649.

36. Kendall, K. E., and Schnurr, P. P. 1987. Effects of vitamin B_6 supplementation on premenstrual symptoms. *Obstetrics and Gynecology*, vol. 70, no. 2 (Aug.), pp. 145–149.

37. Landau, R. L.; Bergenstal, D. M.; Lugibihl, K.; Dimick, D. F.; and Rashid, E. 1957. Relationship of estrogen and of pituitary hormones to the metabolic effects of progesterone. *Journal of Clinical Endocrinology and Metabolism*, vol. 17, no. 2 (Feb.), pp. 177–185.

38. Landau, R. L.; Bergenstal, D. M.; Lugibihl, K.; and Kascht, M. E. 1955. Metabolic effects of progesterone in man. *Journal of Clinical Endocrinology and Metabolism*, vol. 15, no. 10 (Oct.), pp. 1194–1215.

39. Landau, R. L.; Lugibihl, K.; Bergenstal, D. M.; and Dimick, D. F. 1957. Metabolic effects of progesterone in man: dose response relationships. *Journal of Laboratory and Clinical Medicine*, vol. 50, no. 4 (Oct.), pp. 613 620.

40. Landau, R. L., and Lugibihl, K. 1961. Effect of dietary protein on the catabolic influence of progesterone. *Journal of Clinical Endocrinology and Metabolism*, vol. 21, no. 11 (Nov.), pp. 1345–1354.

41. Landau, R. L., and Lugibihl, K. 1967. Effects of progesterone on the concentration of plasma amino acids in man. *Metabolism: Clinical and Experimental*, vol. 16, no. 12 (Dec.), pp. 1114–1122.

42. Mair, R. G.; Bouffard, J. A.; Engen, T.; and Morton, T. H. 1978. Olfactory sensitivity during the menstrual cycle. *Sensory Processes*, vol. 2, no. 2 (June), pp. 90–98.

43. Mellinkoff, S. M.; Frankland, M.; Boyle, D.; and Griepel, M. 1956. Relationship between serum amino acids concentrations and fluctuations in appetite. *Journal of Applied Physiology*, vol. 8, pp. 535–538.

44. Minton, J. P.; Foecking, M. K.; Webster, D. J.; and Matthews, R. H. 1979. Caffeine, cyclic necleotides and breast disease. *Surgery*, vol. 86, pp. 105–109.

45. Musey, P. I.; Collins, D. C.; Bradlow, H. L.; Gould, K. G.; and Preedy, J. R. K. 1987. Effect of diet on oxidation of 17 beta-estradiol in vivo. *Journal of Clinical Endocrinology and Metabolism*, vol. 65, no. 4 (Oct.), pp. 792–795.

46. Public Health Service. 1988. *Surgeon General's Report on Nutrition and Health*, pub. no. 88. Washington, D.C.: U.S. Department of Health and Human Services.

47. Root, W. 1980. *Food: An Authoritative and Visual History and Dictionary of the Foods of the World*. New York: Simon and Schuster.

48. Schneider, J.; Bradlow, H. L.; Strain, G.; Levin, J.; Anderson, K.; and Fishman, J. 1983. Effects of obesity on estradiol metabolism: decreased formation of nonuterotropic metabolites. *Journal of Clinical Endocrinology and Metabolism*, vol. 56, no. 5 (May), pp. 973–978.

49. Seelig, M. S. 1980. *Magnesium Deficiency in the Pathogenesis of Disease*. New York: Plenum Medical Book Company.

50. Segal, K. R., and Pi-Sunyer, F. X. 1989. Exercise and obesity. *Medical Clinics of North America*, vol. 73, pp. 217–236.

51. Shoupe, D.; Montz, F. J.; and Lobo, R. A. 1985. Effects of estrogen and progestin on endogenous opioid activity in oophorectomized women. *Journal of Clinical Endocrinology and Metabolism*, vol. 60, no. 1 (Jan.), pp. 178–183.

52. Siiteri, P. K. 1982. Review of studies on estrogen biosynthesis in the human. *Cancer Research*, vol. 42, suppl. to no. 8 (Aug.), pp. 3269s–3273s.

53. Sommerville, I. F., and Marrian, G. F. 1950. Urinary excretion of pregnanediol in human subjects following the administration of progesterone and of pregnane-3alpha:20alpha-diol (Version 2). *Biochemical Journal*, vol. 46, no. 3 (Mar.), pp. 290–296.

54. Steingrimsdottir, L.; Brasel, J.; and Greenwood, M.R.C. 1980. Hormonal modulation of adipose tissue lipoprotein lipase may alter food intake in rats. *American Journal of Physiology*, vol. 239, *(Endrocrinol. Metab.)*, pp. E162–E167.

55. United Fresh Fruit and Vegetable Association. 1970–present. *Fruit and Vegetable Facts and Pointers*. (Reports covering 80 commodities.) Alexandria, Va.

56. Valette, A.; Mercier, J.; Benoit, V.; Meignen, J. M.; and Boyer, J. 1987. Nutritional dependence of the effect of estrogen on fat cell lipoprotein lipase. *Journal of Steroid Biochemistry*, vol. 28, no. 4 (Oct.), pp. 445–447.

57. Wade, G. N.; Gray, J. M.; and Bartness, T. J. 1985. Gonadal influences on adiposity. *International Journal of Obesity*, vol. 9, suppl. 1, pp. 83–92.

58. Wald, A.; Van Thiel, D. H.; Hoechstetter, L.; Gavaler, J. S.; Egler, K. M.; Verm, R.; Scott, L.; and Lester, R. 1981. Gastrointestinal transit: the effect of the menstrual cycle. *Gastroenterology*, vol. 80, no. 6 (June), pp. 1497–1500.

59. Webb, P. 1986. 24-hour energy expenditure and the menstrual cycle. *American Journal of Clinical Nutrition*, vol. 44, no. 5 (Nov.), pp. 614–619.

60. Winton, A. L., and Winton, K. B. 1932–1939. *The Structure and Composition of Foods*, vols. I–IV. New York: John Wiley and Sons.

61. Wong, S., and Tong, J. E. 1974. Menstrual cycle and contraceptive hormonal effects on temporal discrimination. *Perceptual and Motor Skills*, vol. 39, no. 1 (Aug.), pp. 103–108.

62. Wood, C.; Larsen, L.; and Williams, R. 1979. Menstrual characteristics of 2,343 women attending the Shepherd Foundation. *Australian and New Zealand Journal of Obstetrics and Gynaecology*, vol. 19, no. 2 (May), pp. 107–110.

63. Zumoff, B. 1982. Relationship of obesity to blood estrogens. *Cancer Research*, vol. 42, suppl. to no. 8 (Aug.), pp. 3289s–3294s.

Day of the Month	Day of the Cycle	Cycle Phase	Food Group	Weight	PMS Sympton	Food Craving	Exercise
	1	Menstrual	FORBIDDEN FOODS				
	2						
	3						
	4						
	5						
	6						
	7						
	8						
	1	Postmenstrual	FABULOUS FRUITS AND VEGETABLES				
	2						
	3						
	4						
	5						
	6						
	7						
	8						
	9						
	10						
	11						
	12						
	13						
	14						
	15						
	16						
	17						
	18						
	19						
	20						
	1	Ovulatory	PASTA PLUS				
	2						
	3						
	4						
	5						
	6						
	1	Premenstrual	PROTEIN POWER				
	2						
	3						
	4						
	5						
	6						
	7						
	8						
	9						
	10						
	11						
	12						
	13						
	14						

Day of the Month	Day of the Cycle	Cycle Phase	Food Group	Weight	PMS Sympton	Food Craving	Exercise
	1	Menstrual	FORBIDDEN FOODS				
	2						
	3						
	4						
	5						
	6						
	7						
	8						
	1	Postmenstrual	FABULOUS FRUITS AND VEGETABLES				
	2						
	3						
	4						
	5						
	6						
	7						
	8						
	9						
	10						
	11						
	12						
	13						
	14						
	15						
	16						
	17						
	18						
	19						
	20						
	1	Ovulatory	PASTA PLUS				
	2						
	3						
	4						
	5						
	6						
	1	Premenstrual	PROTEIN POWER				
	2						
	3						
	4						
	5						
	6						
	7						
	8						
	9						
	10						
	11						
	12						
	13						
	14						

Day of the Month	Day of the Cycle	Cycle Phase	Food Group	Weight	PMS Sympton	Food Craving	Exercise
	1	Menstrual	FORBIDDEN FOODS				
	2						
	3						
	4						
	5						
	6						
	7						
	8						
	1	Postmenstrual	FABULOUS FRUITS AND VEGETABLES				
	2						
	3						
	4						
	5						
	6						
	7						
	8						
	9						
	10						
	11						
	12						
	13						
	14						
	15						
	16						
	17						
	18						
	19						
	20						
	1	Ovulatory	PASTA PLUS				
	2						
	3						
	4						
	5						
	6						
	1	Premenstrual	PROTEIN POWER				
	2						
	3						
	4						
	5						
	6						
	7						
	8						
	9						
	10						
	11						
	12						
	13						
	14						

Day of the Month	Day of the Cycle	Cycle Phase	Food Group	Weight	PMS Sympton	Food Craving	Exercise
	1	Menstrual	FORBIDDEN FOODS				
	2						
	3						
	4						
	5						
	6						
	7						
	8						
	1	Postmenstrual	FABULOUS FRUITS AND VEGETABLES				
	2						
	3						
	4						
	5						
	6						
	7						
	8						
	9						
	10						
	11						
	12						
	13						
	14						
	15						
	16						
	17						
	18						
	19						
	20						
	1	Ovulatory	PASTA PLUS				
	2						
	3						
	4						
	5						
	6						
	1	Premenstrual	PROTEIN POWER				
	2						
	3						
	4						
	5						
	6						
	7						
	8						
	9						
	10						
	11						
	12						
	13						
	14						

Day of the Month	Day of the Cycle	Cycle Phase	Food Group	Weight	PMS Symptom	Food Craving	Exercise
	1	Menstrual	FORBIDDEN FOODS				
	2						
	3						
	4						
	5						
	6						
	7						
	8						
	1	Postmenstrual	FABULOUS FRUITS AND VEGETABLES				
	2						
	3						
	4						
	5						
	6						
	7						
	8						
	9						
	10						
	11						
	12						
	13						
	14						
	15						
	16						
	17						
	18						
	19						
	20						
	1	Ovulatory	PASTA PLUS				
	2						
	3						
	4						
	5						
	6						
	1	Premenstrual	PROTEIN POWER				
	2						
	3						
	4						
	5						
	6						
	7						
	8						
	9						
	10						
	11						
	12						
	13						
	14						

Day of the Month	Day of the Cycle	Cycle Phase	Food Group	Weight	PMS Sympton	Food Craving	Exercise
	1	Menstrual	FORBIDDEN FOODS				
	2						
	3						
	4						
	5						
	6						
	7						
	8						
	1	Postmenstrual	FABULOUS FRUITS AND VEGETABLES				
	2						
	3						
	4						
	5						
	6						
	7						
	8						
	9						
	10						
	11						
	12						
	13						
	14						
	15						
	16						
	17						
	18						
	19						
	20						
	1	Ovulatory	PASTA PLUS				
	2						
	3						
	4						
	5						
	6						
	1	Premenstrual	PROTEIN POWER				
	2						
	3						
	4						
	5						
	6						
	7						
	8						
	9						
	10						
	11						
	12						
	13						
	14						

Day of the Month	Day of the Cycle	Cycle Phase	Food Group	Weight	PMS Sympton	Food Craving	Exercise
	1	Menstrual	FORBIDDEN FOODS				
	2						
	3						
	4						
	5						
	6						
	7						
	8						
	1	Postmenstrual	FABULOUS FRUITS AND VEGETABLES				
	2						
	3						
	4						
	5						
	6						
	7						
	8						
	9						
	10						
	11						
	12						
	13						
	14						
	15						
	16						
	17						
	18						
	19						
	20						
	1	Ovulatory	PASTA PLUS				
	2						
	3						
	4						
	5						
	6						
	1	Premenstrual	PROTEIN POWER				
	2						
	3						
	4						
	5						
	6						
	7						
	8						
	9						
	10						
	11						
	12						
	13						
	14						

Day of the Month	Day of the Cycle	Cycle Phase	Food Group	Weight	PMS Sympton	Food Craving	Exercise
	1	Menstrual	FORBIDDEN FOODS				
	2						
	3						
	4						
	5						
	6						
	7						
	8						
	1	Postmenstrual	FABULOUS FRUITS AND VEGETABLES				
	2						
	3						
	4						
	5						
	6						
	7						
	8						
	9						
	10						
	11						
	12						
	13						
	14						
	15						
	16						
	17						
	18						
	19						
	20						
	1	Ovulatory	PASTA PLUS				
	2						
	3						
	4						
	5						
	6						
	1	Premenstrual	PROTEIN POWER				
	2						
	3						
	4						
	5						
	6						
	7						
	8						
	9						
	10						
	11						
	12						
	13						
	14						

Day of the Month	Day of the Cycle	Cycle Phase	Food Group	Weight	PMS Sympton	Food Craving	Exercise
	1	Menstrual	FORBIDDEN FOODS				
	2						
	3						
	4						
	5						
	6						
	7						
	8						
	1	Postmenstrual	FABULOUS FRUITS AND VEGETABLES				
	2						
	3						
	4						
	5						
	6						
	7						
	8						
	9						
	10						
	11						
	12						
	13						
	14						
	15						
	16						
	17						
	18						
	19						
	20						
	1	Ovulatory	PASTA PLUS				
	2						
	3						
	4						
	5						
	6						
	1	Premenstrual	PROTEIN POWER				
	2						
	3						
	4						
	5						
	6						
	7						
	8						
	9						
	10						
	11						
	12						
	13						
	14						